Geographies of Girlhood

Identities In-Between

Inquiry and Pedagogy Across Diverse Contexts
Kathleen deMarrais, Series Editor

Geographies of Girlhood

Identities In-Between

Edited by

Pamela J. Bettis
Washington State University

Natalie G. Adams
University of Alabama

LAWRENCE ERLBAUM ASSOCIATES, PUBLISHERS
2005   Mahwah, New Jersey   London

Lawrence Erlbaum Associates, Inc., Publishers
10 Industrial Avenue
Mahwah, New Jersey 07430
www.erlbaum.com

Cover design by Jonathan S. Billing

Library of Congress Cataloging-in-Publication Data

Geographies of girlhood : identities in-between / edited by Pamela J. Bettis, Natalie G. Adams.
   p. cm. — (Inquiry and pedagogy across diverse contexts)
   Includes bibliographical references and index.
ISBN 0-8058-4673-5 (cloth : alk. paper)
ISBN 0-8058-4674-3 (pbk. : alk. paper)
1. Girls—United States—Social conditions. 2. Girls—United States—Psychology. 3. Teenage girls—United States. 4. Preteens—United States. 5. Identity (Psychology)—United States. I. Bettis, Pamela, 1955- II. Adams, Natalie Guice, 1962- III. Series.
HQ777.G46 2004
305.235'5—dc22   2004053289
                                                          CIP

Books published by Lawrence Erlbaum Associates are printed on acid-free paper, and their bindings are chosen for strength and durability.

Printed in the United States of America
10 9 8 7 6 5 4 3 2 1

We dedicate this book to our fabulous girlfriends.

Contents

Preface

Geographies of Girlhood: Identities In-between is written for those who are curious about how and where adolescent girls live their day-to-day lives. It explores how they come to understand themselves as female in this culture, particularly during a time when they are learning what it means to be a woman, and their identities are in between that of child and adult, girl and woman. The authors in this edited collection take seriously what girls have to say about themselves and the places and discursive spaces that they inhabit daily. Instead of focusing on girls in classrooms, the purpose of this book is to explore adolescent female identity in a myriad of kid-defined spaces from bedrooms to school hallways to the Internet to discourses of cheerleading, race, sexuality, and ablebodiness. These are the geographies of girlhood, the important sites of identity construction for girls and young women, and we situate this collection of studies within the fledgling field of Girls Studies.

Because *Geographies of Girlhood* is about the various spaces in which girls construct who they are, we thought it appropriate to organize the text in a geographical manner. Thus, we divided the 14 chapters into three parts, Before School, At School, and After School, based on the physical location of the girls in these studies. Hopefully, this organizational structure will not inhibit the reader from seeing the interconnections of the studies, all of which are drawn from data obtained through various forms of qualitative inquiry, nested in rich theoretical discussions, and use the concept of liminality to theorize the in-between spaces of schools that are central to how adolescent girls construct a sense of self. We asked the authors to open up the spaces, both physical and/or discursive, in which adolescent girls/young women performed their identity work. We believe that the chapters in this book will illuminate for readers the myriad ways in which girls figure out who they are as females in this culture and from their perspective. Such a collection will challenge teachers, pre-service teachers, and those interested in gender studies to take seriously the everyday concerns of adolescent girls and rethink how normative femininity, as a highly contested construct, is resisted, appropriated, and assumed in different ways by different girls.

We call Part I, "Before School." Every day, millions of children and adolescents walk out the doors of their homes and board the big yellow bus for the trip to school. The two chapters that comprise this short part disrupt most of our taken-for-granted understandings of this seemingly mundane act. In "Barbies, Bases, and Beer: The Role of the Home in Junior High School Girls' Identity Work," Don Merten challenges the assumption that home, as a place for adolescent identity development, diminishes in importance as girls grow up. Merten counters that the home is a space that provides both continuity to girls' past identity work (i.e., the Barbie collection in her bedroom) and the opportunity to engage in new and more adult-like activities (i.e., sexual and alcohol experimentation). Laura Jewett takes the reader for a provocative ride with the Backseat Bad-Asses as they harangue fellow passengers and pedestrians, dish out advice and gossip, and occupy the seats of power in the back of a school bus. In "Power Beads, Body Glitter, and Backseat Bad-Asses: Girls, Power, and Position on the School Bus," Jewett explores the important identity work in which adolescent girls engage on the school bus, a liminal space between the private home and the public school and a space that is also neglected in the research literature.

We entitled Part II, "At School," and the bulk of the chapters are located here, within the school setting, but not necessarily in the usual classroom spaces. Arranged sequentially by the age of the study's participants, these chapters find important identity work taking place in bathrooms, on playgrounds, and surrounding beauty pageants. In "Girl Talk: Adolescent Girls' Perceptions of Leadership," Dawn Shinew and Debi Thomas Jones asked 5th-grade girls, "What does it mean to be a good leader?" The authors describe how these young girls enacted and understood leadership in ways very different from the patriarchal perspective found in much of the leadership literature. Pam Bettis, Debra Jordan, and Diane Montgomery were intrigued with how girls in groups construct collective female identities. In "Girls in Groups: The Preps and the Sex Mob Try Out For Womanhood," they explored how two 7th-grade peer groups, the Preps and the Sex Mob, enacted and embodied very different versions of femininity, each with particular privileges and costs. Rosary Lalik and Kim Oliver used a perennial Southern school ritual, the Beauty Walk, as a space in which to construct a transformative curricular project. "'The Beauty Walk' as Social Space for Messages About the Female Body: Toward Transformative Collaboration" describes how 8th grade girls make sense of the social construction of beauty through a critical analysis of the Beauty Walk, an annual beauty pageant. In "Fighters and Cheerleaders: Disrupting the Discourse of 'Girl Power' in the New Millennium," Natalie Adams challenges the assumptions of ideal femininity that undergird "Girl Power," the popular-culture term and movement. When comparing the discursive practices of girl fighters and cheerleaders, Adams demonstrates that although Girl Power literature positions girls in supposedly more liberatory spaces, it is still driven by dominant conceptions of ideal femininity.

Laura Fingerson takes the reader into the intimate and not-so-intimate conversations and interactions of adolescent girls surrounding menstruation at school in "'Only 4-Minute Passing Periods!' Private and Public Menstrual Identities in School." Although half of the high school student population experiences menstruation, little research has explored how girls actually negotiate this "time of the month" with teachers, other girls, and boys at school. Stacey Elsasser's study is situated in the classrooms and everyday interactions among students and teachers in a Christian school; however, her participants struggle with the in-between place of being both an Evangelical Christian and a 20th century female. Elsasser's chapter, "In the World But Not of It: Gendered Religious Socialization at a Christian School," attempts to unravel these identity complexities. Sandra Spickard Prettyman's study takes the reader into the daily school lives of pregnant teens inhabiting an alternative high school. In "'We Ain't No Dogs': Teenage Mothers Re(Define) Themselves," Prettyman highlights the girls' attempts to disrupt the dominant and troubling discourse of teenage motherhood along with their own internal struggles of who is considered a "good" mother.

Part III, "After School," includes several studies in which adult women reflect on their identity work as adolescents as well as studies in which the female participants are on the cusp of adulthood yet still engaged in important identity work. Cerri Banks asked African American women who attended predominantly White public schools what growing up was like in "Black Girls/White Spaces: Managing Identity through Memories of Schooling." In this chapter, female African American graduate students recount stories in which their race, gender, and class intersected and sometimes collided during elementary camp, in high school hallways, and school courtyards. In "Unstraightening the Ideal Girl: Lesbians, High School, and Spaces to Be," John Petrovic and Rebecca Ballard also interviewed adult women about their past identity work as adolescent females. In this case, Petrovic and Ballard wanted to know where high school girls could be lesbians and how they negotiated the space of ideal girlhood, one that is assumed by dominant society to be heteronormative. Dolores Liston and Regina Moore-Rahimi describe how the marker of "slut" in high school shaped the life trajectories of girls/women who live in the South, a geographical region known for its Christian conservatism. In their chapter, "Disputation of a Bad Reputation: Adverse Sexual Labels and the Lives of 12 Southern Women," Liston and Moore-Rahimmi challenge the stereotype of a slut and use their participants' varied experiences to demonstrate the multiple ways that "slutty" girls are labeled and marginalized.

The two final chapters both investigate the identity work of women on the cusp of adulthood. Lyn Mikel Brown and Sandy Marie Grande invited a diverse group of undergraduate women attending a predominantly White liberal arts university to join together informally and interrogate gender, race, sexual identity, and class through watching movies together. In "Border Crossing—Border Patrolling: Race, Gender, and the Politics of Sisterhood," Brown and Grande describe the tensions and uneasy communication between White women and women of color and what this means for coalition building among feminists. We end the book with a chapter by Nirmala Ereveles and Kagendo Mutua who listen intently to the words of a 20-year-old girl/woman with Down syndrome, and use her words and the insights of Disability Studies to challenge the current construction of girlhood found in the Girl Power movement. In "'I Am a Woman Now!' Rewriting Cartographies of Girlhood From the Critical Standpoint of Disability," Erevelles and Mutua highlight their participant's assertion that she is a sexual being amid the denials and interruptions of her mother and society at large.

Finally, we present a concluding chapter that imagines what a pedagogy of place and gender might be, a tentative feminist pedagogy of place. Our thinking here was to draw from all of the studies presented and construct a vision of what school life could be if the words of the girls and young women in these pages were taken seriously.

All of these chapters unsettle the easy characterization of girlhood and womanhood. They undo the simplicity of characterizing girls as sluts, lesbians, Preps, disabled, Backseat Bad-Asses, leaders, fighters, and Christians. They take seriously what girls and women say about who they are and where they came to be, and they map the myriad routes that girls travel to their destination of womanhood. Race, class, sexuality, religion, and ability intersect with these routes and at times direct girls to particular journeys. However, as the reader will discover, no route is fixed.

ACKNOWLEDGMENTS

This book project has been a long but mostly fun road trip. We want to thank the many people who sent us on this trip and the many people who ensured that we were heading generally in the right direction and those who provided assistance when we broke down.

First, we thank the adolescent girls whom we taught in Arkansas, Virginia, and Louisiana and to those who participated in our research projects in Ohio, Georgia, Idaho, Louisiana, and Oklahoma. All of you have reminded us that we are adults and often don't get it. You helped us rethink identity, gender, and schooling. We also appreciate the fact that you were so forthright about our clothing and hair styles although we didn't always follow your advice.

Thanks to the contributing authors of this book. They wrote thoughtful and provocative chapters that make this book work and that gave us more insights into the lives of girls and young women. It's a pleasure to have colleagues who are smart and fun.

Thanks to the reviewers of the initial manuscript draft. Their encouragement and critiques strengthened the book.

Thanks to Kathleen de Marrais, the editor of this LEA series, Inquiry and Pedagogy Across Diverse Contexts. Kathleen has always been critical of the lack of pedagogical sensitivity in scholarly texts, and she encouraged us to make this book a more friendly place for the reader and consequently, a more meaningful one.

Finally, thank you Naomi Silverman. Naomi has been an inspiration to both of us for her thoughtful feedback, encouragement for the project, and as important, her joy and fun. How often do you get a cool editor?

Chapter 1

Landscapes of Girlhood

Pamela J. Bettis
Washington State University

Natalie G. Adams
University of Alabama

WHAT WAS MISSING AT LUNCH, IN THE LITERATURE, AND IN THE FEMINIST SHOE CLOSET

This book began as a conversation we had several years ago over lunch about our disappointment with the lack of books that focus on the material realities of adolescent girls in schools. Both of us had been adolescent girls at one point in our lives, obviously. Both us had been middle and high school teachers as well. Furthermore, the two of us had conducted research on and with girls for many years, and we had just completed a year-long ethnography in a Midwestern middle school exploring girls and leadership. What the girls in this middle school made clear to us, which was supported by all of our personal and professional experiences, was their disregard for the formal curriculum of the school in terms of defining themselves. Instead, we observed and listened to the importance associated with peer group dynamics in the cafeteria, cheerleading tryouts, Saturday night mingling at a local dance club, life on the Internet, and fights in the school bathroom. We have taken these girls' comments seriously, and their words provided the initial impetus for this book.

In the early 1990s, research, such as the Association of American University Women's (AAUW) initial report *How Schools Shortchange Girls*

1

(1992) and Sadker and Sadker's (1994) *Failing at Fairness*, documented how girls' academic and social needs were neglected in schools, which led to renewed interest in making schools girl friendly. At about the same time, a plethora of popular-press books, such as Orenstein's *Schoolgirls* (1994) and Pipher's *Reviving Ophelia* (1995), decried the status of girls as victims of a "girl-poisoning culture." Since that time, Girl Power, as the girl empowerment movement was named, has been used by girls and corporate interests to reframe girls as sassy, independent, and assertive (Inness, 1998), and girls around the globe have turned to radical cheerleading, girls' zines, and girl bands to express this newly emerging girl sensibility. Not surprisingly, in the late 1990s and early 21st century, another wave of popular-press books on girls hit the best-seller list and dovetailed with this new girl sensibility, which was definitely not framed as "nice." Instead of positioning girls as victims, this time girls were depicted as mean, backbiting victimizers in Simmons' (2002) *Odd Girl Out* , and Wiseman's (2002) *Queen Bees and Wannabes*. Furthermore, girls' sexuality, a taboo and neglected topic for many years, was explored in both the popular-press literature such as *Fast Girls* (White, 2002) and *Promiscuities* (Wolfe, 1997), as well as the more academic literature, such as *The Secret Lives of Girls* (Lamb, 2001), *Flirting With Danger* (Phillips, 2000), and *Dilemmas of Desire* (Tolman, 2002). All of these books sent parents scurrying to bookstores for help in navigating the tumultuous adolescent years of their daughters. When we mentally surveyed this last decade of girl literature, we again came to the conclusion that there was something missing. As helpful as all of these books were, they did not address the kinds of daily concerns that the girls we taught and the girls we observed and interviewed lived on a daily basis.

Furthermore, we were frustrated with the feminist researchers who took what were "women's issues" and transplanted them onto the lives of girls. For some feminist researchers, all identity discussions must be located in the global economy of shifting gender regimes and must be grounded in concerns for racial, ethnic, and social-class inequities. No doubt, these are important concerns for us as well and they are certainly part of the macro landscape that all girls and women inhabit (Walkerdine, Lucey, & Melody, 2001). But if you listen closely, these global concerns are not found in the everyday talk of teenage girls when they walk through the hallways, chat in the bathrooms, and play sports. Although most adult feminist researchers spend little time contemplating how they can negotiate a tampon change in the 4 minutes allowed for middle and high school classroom changes, this concern, among the many others raised in this book, is much more salient to the daily lives of adolescent girls than any concern about the impact of a postindustrial economic shift. Along the same lines, most adult feminists have dismissed the activity of cheerleading, yet whether or not one will make the squad is still a pressing question for thousands of adolescent girls (Adams & Bettis, 2003a).

We use the last two examples, tampon changing and cheerleading, both topics discussed in this book, to frame the tensions that, some have argued, exist between feminists in Women's Studies and those feminists studying girls and girl culture. Nash (2001) speculated that Women's Studies scholars see their mission as one of addressing the "serious political and economic barriers to women's equity" whereas Girls' Studies scholars, who often draw from mass and popular culture in their research, are perceived as engaging in less-weighty feminist scholarship. And we all know what being a lightweight implies for women. Nash has also speculated that these tensions may emanate from the differences between Second and Third Wave Feminists, the former constructed as "sensible shoes" scholars and the latter as ones wearing "dancing slippers."

Although we do not support the dualisms and hierarchies inherent in these tensions, we are enamored with the shoe metaphor. We see the authors of this book wearing both kinds of shoes, if one can imagine ... a sort of fashionable yet sturdy (i.e., chunky) platform. In this book, the contributors had to wear dancing slippers in order to keep up with girls and young women as they traversed the landscape of femininity on the Internet, in fashion, with friends, and in watching movies. By themselves, sensible shoes would not have been able to keep the pace. Thus, we situate this book in the emerging field of Girls' Studies with the sensible-shoe mission of helping teachers and administrators construct more healthy and vibrant ways of life for adolescent girls/women. But to be able to do that, adult feminist scholars must know what the day-to-day habits of life are for adolescent girls. And if these daily habits include talk of who is nice, who is not, and how to change a tampon, then that talk and focus must be taken seriously, explored, played with, explained, and theorized. That is what this book attempts to do.

The contributing authors of this book describe girls/women and their understandings of their lives in a variety of discursive and physical landscapes. In this book, girls consider what to wear in the Beauty Walk, what to do when they are labeled slut, how to decorate bedrooms, and how to control the backseat of the bus. These are the kinds of daily material concerns that frame the analysis and theorizing found in this book. From these daily material concerns, the authors attempt to provoke new possibilities for understanding girls and their transition to womanhood, how they are produced and how they produce themselves (Davies, 1989, 1993, 2000; Jones, 1993; Walkerdine, 1990, 1993). Although the authors note the "disadvantages" with which girls are faced, particularly those whose social class, race, ethnicity, mental ability, and sexual orientation diverge from the dominant culture, they do not simplify these lives and present them as oppressed, nor do they valorize them. The girls' understandings of where they are, who they are, and who they can become, are all central in this text, and those under-standings are joyful, disturbing, edgy, and typically complex, just like the lives we all lead as adults.

WHO AM I? WHERE AM I?
AND THE IMPORTANCE OF THE LOCAL

In much of the research literature, identity has been conceptualized as an-swering the question, "Who am I?" Typically, a critical lens has focused identity issues on race, ethnicity, social class, gender, and sexual orienta-tion. Although these layers of identity are salient in this book, we would like to encompass an undeveloped question, "Where am I?" (Cuba & Hammond, 1993; Hall, Coffey, & Williamson, 1999; J. B. Jackson, 1994). Although scholarship on globalization and its ramifications on the eco-nomic, social, and political lives of people around the world continues to grow, "for many people in the world, everyday life continues to take place in a restricted locale" (McDowell, 1999, p. 3). In this book, we explore how a variety of local contexts and discursive practices, both in between the for-mal design of schooling as well as outside its purview, influence how girls construct their identities (Bettis, 2001). "Emergent identities require space of their own in which to assert themselves, and are also grounded in (if not tied to) the specificities of particular locations" (Hall et al., 1999, p. 505). The "emergent identities" of the girls with whom we talked asserted themselves in a variety of spaces, particularly those that they controlled. Who they were also shifted according to the spaces they inhabited and how they used these spaces. We see the concept of place as illuminating various facets of the identity work of the girls that we highlight in the following chapters.

The concept of place has been conceptualized differently in recent years (McDowell, 1999) and provides those of us who are interested in identity a new and useful conceptual tool. In the past, geographers de-fined place as a set of coordinates on a map that fixed and defined a per-son's spatial location. "Geographers now argue that places are contested, fluid and uncertain. It is socio-spatial practices that define places and these practices result in overlapping and intersecting places with multiple and changing boundaries, constituted and maintained by social relations of power and exclusion" (McDowell, 1999, p. 4). The chapters that follow mirror this claim in a myriad of ways. For example, riding the bus to and from school is certainly a fixed place and practice in the minds of most parents of school-age children. However, for many children and adoles-cents, the bus is a nebulous place where the social hierarchy that defines children's status during the school day dissipates, and new identities are mapped in the transitional time and space between home and school that the bus provides.

Focusing on specific places and the discursive practices associated with these places mandates that we note that often a particular place can be read as one of exclusion(s) and inclusion(s) (Sibley, 1995). "Places are made through power relations which construct the rules which define the boundaries. These boundaries are both social and spatial—they define who belongs to a place and who may be excluded, as well as the location or site of the experience" (McDowell, 1999, p. 4). We believe that the landscape of schooling exemplifies this claim. For example, we observed two cheerleading preparation classes held in a gymnasium for a semester and learned early on that the identity work of becoming a cheerleader was not limited to the cheer exercises performed in class every day in that particular gymnasium. Trying out for cheerleading was, more fundamentally, a celebrated route for trying out for womanhood in that the discourse of cheerleading illuminated characteristics of the ideal female in this society. That discourse had powerful implications for girls, particularly for those who were not White and middle class, in their ability to envision themselves in the space of cheerleading. Thus, although the physical place of the gym during fifth and sixth periods identified girls as aspiring to be cheerleaders, the dominant discourse of cheerleading that constructed a specific type of girl as cheerleader, and that we found circulating in the girls' talk and understandings of cheerleading, created another space, one of power, privilege, and inclusion, for who could be a cheerleader.

Another facet of place is that it operates at the intersection of both global and local processes, and these processes include social, economic, political, and technological shifts and understandings (Massey, 1994). In one of the following chapters, adolescent lesbians use the virtual space of the Internet to connect with other lesbians and explore a space in which they are safe from the homophobia often found in their schools.

We are using the preceding discussion and examples to illustrate how we are framing our understanding of place and its relationship to identity. We agree with Weis and Fine (2000) that "a sustained look at the ways in which youth develop political and social identities, investments, and relations, both within and outside school contexts, is noticeably absent from the literatures on education and on adolescence" (p. xi). Furthermore, they note Maxine Greene's focus on the "vibrancy of the 'in-between' " of adolescent lives. It is the in-between spaces and places found within and outside the formal domain of schools that we believe to be central to how girls make sense of themselves. We want to nest our discussion of girl's identity at the juncture of place and this "in-between" vibrancy. These theoretical interests deposited us at the conceptual door of liminality.

LIMINALITY AND GIRLHOOD

Liminality, a term coined by the anthropologist Victor Turner (1967) to describe the "betwixt and between" place that adolescents in traditional societies inhabited when undergoing rites of passage, is a construct that we have found helpful. Although aware of its history and conceptual short-comings (Crapanzano, 1992; Weber, 1995), we still believe that the construct can be of use in making sense of the complexities, simplicities, and contradictions of girls' lives. We believe that liminality, as an umbrella construct, opens up different ways to think about these in-between spaces and places of female adolescent identity, the focus of this book.

Turner was referring to the time when pubescents were neither adults nor children, but in some in-between and nebulous social place whose rules were unclear and status uncertain. The liminal period was an "inter-structural stage" in which individuals or groups gave up one social state but had yet to enter the new prescribed social state and adopt its accompanying responsibilities and perspectives. As Turner (1967) noted, "This coinci-dence of opposite processes and notions in a single representation charac-terizes the peculiar unity of the liminal: that which is neither this nor that, but both" (p. 99). This contradictory space and understanding made sense to us as we surveyed our own work and that of colleagues and students who were exploring how girls made sense of growing up. It also spoke to the con-tradictory social landscape that girls inhabit. Protected by statutory rape laws, rendered childlike and/or hypersexualized in media, and expected to be strong, assertive, and yet nice, the lives of girls today exemplify the concept of liminality.

We found that Turner (1977) revisited his initial understanding of liminality. Along with another anthropologist, Colin Turnbull (1990), Turner berated himself for not initially understanding the transformative possibilities of the liminal period, one in which the social conventions and hierarchies are shed. During these rites of passage, then, persons can try on new ways of being and identity, even if only temporarily. Both Turner and Turnbull also highlighted how a playfulness was engendered during the liminal time. Thus, we see the liminal spaces of being an adolescent and of being female as offering possibilities, uncertainties, play, and performance. That is what drives the hope embedded in this book, that new spaces for girls can be created in which they more fully explore all of who they can be-come. We see the following chapters as contributing to an ongoing effort by thoughtful teachers and researchers everywhere: "The more fertile a school in terms of opportunities, role models, and recognition for a wide range of female behaviors and achievement, the more apt girls are to flourish" (Research for Action, Inc., 1996, p. 9).

In this book, we are using the concept of liminality both as originally designated by Turner but also adapting it to a different social and economic context, and broadening its application. First, although we recognize the limitations of describing the adolescent period as a liminal state, we think that naming it as such is still helpful in theorizing this period of time. Second, we are using the term to describe the indeterminate space of femininity, as rules for what constitutes the "ideal girl" shift. Third, we draw from Sibley's (1995) geographical understanding of liminal spaces in thinking about where children and adolescents construct their worlds and consider how girls' bodies play an important role in that thinking. Finally, we situate all of this discussion within a liminal economic and social context, one in transition from industrialism to postindustrialism, modernism to postmodernism and exhibiting characteristics of both (Bettis, 1996; Zukin, 1991).

Adolescence as a Liminal Space

Adolescence, as a period of time distinct from childhood and adulthood, has been the subject of much research and theorizing. Its unquestioned existence, developmental traits, and characteristics are deemed a necessary part of most teacher education programs, and this is typically what preservice teachers and graduate students are offered to understand the lives of adolescents. Much of this type of literature emanates from the work of turn-of-the-century psychologist G. Stanley Hall, whose pioneering work, *Adolescence: Its Psychology and Its Relations to Physiology, Anthropology, Sociology, Sex, Crime, Religion, and Education*, framed the concept for generations to come.

Typically, adolescence is constructed as a time period of life situated between childhood and adulthood. Its onset in the past has been set at 12 or 13 years of age, and its demise was thought to occur when adolescents leave home to start lives of their own making, usually at 18. During this time period, adolescents exhibit particular characteristics such as: increased physical growth with a focus on secondary sexual attributes; a desire to rebel against the mores of the adult world and to exert more independence; a desire to associate more closely with peers; a need for self-expression as seen through consumer choices of clothing and music; and a time to explore one's sexuality (de Marrais & LeCompte, 1999; George & Alexander, 1993).

Although fixed in the culture at large, the concept of adolescence is not necessarily fixed in the academic community. Several scholars have questioned the very nature of the adolescent period, arguing that the concept is a social construction and more of a reflection of the time period in which it was conceived rather than a "natural" phenomenon of life (Lesko, 1996; Walkerdine, 1990). Their argument points to the turbulence of the turn of the century when American society was in transition from an agricultural economy to an industrial economy, from a predominantly rural lifestyle to an urban lifestyle, and from a time when children and adolescents were seen as cheap labor to a time when they were required to attend not only elementary schooling but also secondary. Furthermore, during this same era, another wave of immigrants, primarily people from southern and eastern Europe, increased the fervor for the inculcation of American (i.e., White, Protestant, middle-class, and masculine) values in all youth through formal schooling and extracurricular activities such as athletic games (Spring, 1990). Thus, in some ways, the concept of adolescence cohered with a changing political, economic, and social context.

Another critique of the concept of adolescence has been its conceptualization through research conducted primarily on boys and not girls. As Dyhouse (1981) noted in her research on working-class females in Britain in the late nineteenth and early 20th century, adolescence was a contrived developmental stage that had very little meaning for their everyday lives. "Girls were much less likely than their brothers to have been allowed a period of legitimate freedom, however transitory, removed from adult surveillance and unencumbered by responsibility for domestic chores" (p. 119). Along these same lines, Hudson (1984) claimed that adolescence itself was a masculine construct as evident in the images on which the concept has been based—the Hamlet figure, the sower of wild oats, the lovesick Romeo, and the black-jacketed "rebel without a cause."

With feminist and poststructuralist critiques, the concept of adolescence is in somewhat of a liminal state itself, between being fixed and "scientific" and being deconstructed and found lifeless. Moreover, some of the fundamental characteristics of the concept as rooted in the biological realm are in flux. With the average age of the onset of menarche dropping, and that age variable by race and ethnicity, the markers of entrance into adolescence for girls shift. Furthermore, the end of adolescence is being questioned as well if financial independence is still used as an end marker. With larger numbers of adolescents attending some form of postsecondary education, that financial dependence has lengthened with some groups. The Society for Adolescent Medicine, which is a physicians' organization, sets the adolescent time period as 10–24 years of age on its Web site.

Recognizing adolescence's historical construction and the changing nature of its characteristics, we still believe that the concept can be useful in thinking about the lives of girls during this time period. Obviously there are physical and hormonal changes taking place that have a powerful impact on how girls think about themselves, their bodies, and their move toward womanhood. Clearly, society has mixed perceptions of this group, from its seeking to protect the group from inappropriate adult behaviors, for example through the institutionalization of statutory rape laws and juvenile courts, to its fear of this group as seen in night curfews for adolescents that have been enacted in recent years. In this book, we want to use the concept but unfix it from its essentialist and developmentalist perspective. In addition, we wish to use it as a vehicle to unfix femininity from its essentialist and developmentalist framings.

Femininity as a Liminal Space

Because we want to honor the concrete realities of girls' lives, we must speak to the problems of traditional approaches in theorizing girlhood, especially approaches found in developmental psychology and socialization theories. Just as the concept of adolescence was constructed during a time period when the daily lives of this age group were in transition along with the economic, social, and political life of the nation (Lesko, 1996), so too has the theorizing of girlhood reflected the historical time in which it is embedded. There is a distinguished tradition of developmental psychologists, like the aforementioned G. Stanley Hall, who have posited stages of normative development that inevitably placed girls outside the acceptable normal behavior. Additionally, socialization theories maintained that females learn cultural scripts that determine normative female behavior through direct reinforcement and by modeling processes. However, these theories are inadequate because they begin with the presumption that the girl child is a psychosocial being who is made social rather than as a "being located within history, produced in and through the circumstances, fictions, and fantasies which tell us what femininity is" (Walkerdine, 1993, p. 14).

From this perspective, femininity itself becomes a highly contested construct that is resisted, appropriated, and assumed in different ways by different girls. In this book we follow the approach of Walkerdine and others who assert that scholars studying girlhood need to understand that girlhood is a construction made and remade through the material realities and discursive practices of the society. As many scholars of girlhood have documented (Adams, 1999; Budgeon, 1998; Inness, 1998; McRobbie, 1993; Mitchell, 1995; Nelson & Vallone, 1994; Walkerdine, 1993), ideal girlhood is constantly being rewritten.

In recent work, feminist scholars like McRobbie (1993) and Budgeon (1998) have argued that new subject positions are being made available to girls that provide a counterdiscourse to the girl as passive victim. As mentioned earlier, this latter perspective was seen in such popular-press books as *Reviving Ophelia*. New markers of ideal girlhood, such as participation in sports, self-assertiveness, and self-confidence, have begun to emerge whereas passivity, quietness, and acquiescence no longer represent the primary markers for signifying normative girlhood. Girls today are being taught that self-determination, individualism, self-efficacy, independence, sexual subjectivity, and assertiveness are all desirable traits of the new ideal girl. The Girl Power movement, emerging in the mid-1990s, signaled a shift in thinking about girlhood that accentuates girls' strengths, talents, and accomplishments rather than their victimization (Adams, 2001; Adams & Bettis, 2003b).

However, the shifting landscape of ideal girlhood still mandates an adherence to certain nonnegotiable markers of ideal femininity. One such marker is that of attractiveness. As one of the girls in Lemish's (1998) study stated: "A girl could be anyone—as long as she was pretty" (p. 155). Another marker is that of heterosexuality. Normative femininity continues to be defined against the expectation that normal women eventually marry and have children (Inness, 1998). Douglas (1997) described the tenuous landscape of contemporary girlhood in this way: "Girls today are being urged, simultaneously, to be independent, assertive, and achievement oriented, yet also demure, attractive, soft-spoken, fifteen pounds underweight, and deferential to men" (p. 21).

Thus, contemporary meanings of ideal girlhood have changed to accommodate shifting expectations about normative femininity and the role of women in the 21st century. Normative femininity is in a liminal state with the old markers of normative girlhood such as prettiness alongside the new markers of assertiveness and independence.

What we wish to highlight in this book is that it is not just these discursive practices that construct adolescent female identity but also the different material landscapes that girls inhabit and the various social practices created by the girls associated with these landscapes. Race, ethnicity, social class, and sexual orientation are filtered through these different spaces; although certainly powerful markers of identity, we maintain that they are fluid in their manifestations depending on the context, the space a girl inhabits. The power and privileges of certain groups sometimes become unsettled in different contexts, and girls have the opportunity to write new scripts for who they are and who they want to be. Social practices and the positions one can assume within these social practices take on different meanings in different places. Because "girls are productions and producers of themselves and their times" (Kenway, Willis, Blackmore, & Rennie, 1994, p. 201), we see this book as offering a way to consider the fluidity of identity amidst a shifting discursive and material landscape. And part of that material landscape is the institutional space of school.

Liminal Spaces and Bodies

One of the most powerful lessons that children learn in schools is to control and regulate their bodies (Foucault, 1979; P. Jackson, 1968; Nespor, 1997). The result of such regulatory practices in our society is the production of "docile" bodies. Bartky (1990) describes how these regulatory practices function in school:

> The student, then, is enclosed within a classroom and assigned to a desk he cannot leave; his ranking in the class can be read off the position of his desk in the serially ordered and segmented space of the classroom itself.... The student must sit upright, feet on the floor, head erect; he may not slouch or fidget; his animate body is brought into a fixed correlation with the inanimate desk. (p. 64)

The classroom desk is perhaps the most obvious and concrete way in which children are regulated in the use of their bodies while at school. Another means of regulation is the lack of children- and adolescent-controlled spaces in which kids may use their bodies in performance, in play, and in any way they desire. In elementary schools, playgrounds are typically considered kid spaces yet even this space is supervised, and the time allowed there limited. Middle schools and high schools offer fewer places that are adolescent controlled so that typically kids create moving arenas of ownership where they can play and be in control. Thus, hallways, bathrooms, lunchrooms, and even classrooms at times, all of which have utilitarian purposes, can become kid spaces in which they can exert their power at least temporarily. "Kids value settings for the possibilities they allow for bodily play and performance." (Nespor, 1997, p. 119). We believe that the girls who participated in our middle school ethnography hungered for these kinds of settings and continually sought them out.

These liminal spaces are transitory in that who controls them is always shifting. Hallways allow the school's inhabitants to move through the institution, but they also serve as a space for kids to banter among each other and to let their bodies exert their independence, away from the gaze of adults and the constraints of desks. Likewise, cafeterias allow for choices of food and with whom to congregate. As peer groups come to play a more important role in defining identities in schools, particular places such as alcoves, the backseats of the bus, stairwells, and particular tables in the cafeteria are marked as belonging to particular groups, which are themselves somewhat in flux.

Liminal spaces are inhabited by bodies, and as Bordo (1989), Haug (1987), and Brumberg (1997) argue, bodies are sexually specific; thus, the regulatory practices controlling female bodies differ from those that control male bodies. Adolescence is a particularly significant time for girls as it signals the time in which girls must make sense of the contradictory messages they receive about their bodies. On the one hand, popular culture glorifies and commodifies the adolescent female body as the ideal sexualized body; on the other hand, the adolescent female body suddenly becomes suspect in the institutional spheres of the school, church, and family as a tainted body in need of control.

One of the primary ways in which the school operates to define what is considered appropriate behavior is through the "micropractices of regulation" (Foucault, 1980). Institutional regulation often starts with regulating bodies and thus encourages an erasure of self. After all, it is our bodies that prove that we are real; our bodies take up space—they signify that we do exist—that we are somebody. Women have been continuously defined by their bodies, and because adolescence marks girls' initiation into womanhood, adolescent girls have difficulty separating their "selves" from their bodies.

In school, the bodies of girls are regulated by the "micropractices" of schooling that either control or dismiss their sexuality and femininity. The ways are often subtle (e.g., a gentle reprimand from a well-meaning teacher regarding "inappropriate" dress), yet they remind girls that female sexuality must be contained. For girls who fail to meet the culturally sanctioned ways of being an adolescent girl today (e.g., girls who are overweight; girls who wear clothes considered too tight or revealing), the consequences are severe—from being positioned as the sexually promiscuous skank or ignored as the fat girl not worthy of attention.

Some scholars see liminal spaces as ambiguous and therefore dangerous, especially for those who are already marginalized (Sibley, 1995). We are aware that ill-defined and unsupervised spaces in public schools carry the danger of sexual harassment and bullying, which have very real consequences for girls' minds and bodies (Merten, 1997; Shakeshaft et al., 1997). At the same time, these liminal spaces offer room in which to move and to become somebody of your own making. We harken back to Turner's and Turnbull's later characterization of the liminal time period as one in which adolescent girls can try on various identities and facets of what it means to be a girl in the 21st century.

WHY THIS BOOK MATTERS?

In his study of the meaning and practices of meanness among middle school girls, Merten (1997) observed that meanness occurred in places in which teachers were not present such as school hallways and the cafeteria and over the phone. His study, along with numerous others (Adler & Adler, 1998; Eckert, 1989; Eder, 1995; Evans & Eder, 1993; MacLeod, 1995; Nespor, 1997; Weis & Fine, 2000; Wexler, 1992), demonstrated the importance of these in-between places for the identity work of adolescents. Beauty contests, hallways, bathrooms, movies, extracurricular activities, bus rides, and the backseats of cars all provide important contexts for the production of selves and futures. Part of Merten's point was that teachers were oblivious to the activities of the peer groups that wielded such power on various girls. Merten's implied critique is that adults, including faculty, administrators, and parents, knew very little about the worlds that adolescent girls construct on their own.

We are certainly not advocating the increased "intervention" or "regulation" by school personnel or other adults in their relationships with girls. There is certainly enough of that type of thinking. However, we are advocating the taking seriously of these in-between places, what is said there and what happens there. We are advocating that adults learn about the day-to-day lives of children and adolescents in a way that the following chapters no longer surprise, that peer groups and bus rides and bathrooms all matter to adolescent girls.

Adults often talk about schooling as the site of children's and adolescents' jobs, that just as adults work every day, so do children but their job is that of achieving well at school. What gets missed with this easy characterization is all of the different types of "work" that takes place at schools, particularly that of identity, and where that work takes place. In this book, we examine girls in schools but we do not look at girls in classrooms. Others have done that effectively and have demonstrated gender bias and gender stereotyping (AAUW, 1992, 1998; Sadker & Sadker, 1994). Furthermore, we do not focus solely on girls' identities as raced, classed, and gendered adolescents. Although these markers of identity are infused throughout the following chapters, they are not necessarily the focus of this book. Others have maintained that critical focus effectively and demonstrated the power of class and race/ethnicity in shaping the futures of adolescent girls (Walkderdine, Lucey, & Melody, 2001; Weis & Fine, 2000). Rather, the authors of this book take up the examination of girls in schools by going outside the formal classroom and curriculum to the spaces in schools in which girls have more say about who they are becoming. We want readers to "see" the material realities, bodily movement, and discursive practices of girls in all of their complexities and in all of their places. We also believe that if the worlds of adolescent girls are understood differently, different policies and school practices may be created, ones that celebrate the diverse ways that girls achieve their identities. And perhaps adults will see that the "real" work of schools is not that found in the pages of school texts and the marks of the standardized test scores only but as a network of social spaces and places in which girls configure their identities and become women.

REFERENCES

Adams, N. (1999). Fighting to be somebody: The discursive practices of adolescent girls' fighting. *Educational Studies, 30*(2), 115–139.

Adams, N. (2001, April). *Girl power: The discursive practices of female fighters and female cheerleaders.* Paper presented at the annual meeting of the American Educational Research Association, Seattle, WA.

Adams, N., & Bettis, P. J. (2003a). *Cheerleader! An American icon*. New York: Palgrave/Macmillan.

Adams, N., & Bettis, P. J. (2003b). Commanding the room in short skirts: Cheering as the embodiment of ideal girlhood. *Gender & Society, 17*(1), 73–91.

Adler, P., & Adler, P. (1998). *Peer power: Preadolescent culture and identity*. New Brunswick, NJ: Rutgers University Press.

American Association of University Women. (1992). *The AAUW Report: How schools shortchange girls*. Washington, DC: American Association of University Women Educational Foundation.

American Association of University Women. (1998). *Gender gaps: Where schools still fail our children*. Washington, DC: American Association of University Women Educational Foundation.

Bartky, S. (1990). *Femininity and domination*. New York: Routledge.

Bettis, P. J. (1996). Urban students, liminality, and the postindustrial context. *Sociology of Education, 69*(2), 105–125.

Bettis, P. J. (2001, April). *Introduction to symposium: Geographies of girlhood: Identity in-between*. Paper presented at the annual meeting of the American Education Research Association, Seattle, WA.

Bordo, S. (1989). *Unbearable weight: Feminism, Western culture, and the body*. Berkeley: University of California Press.

Brumberg, J. (1997). *The body project: An intimate history of American girls*. New York: Random House.

Budgeon, S. (1998). "I'll tell you what I really, really want": Girl power and self-identity in Britain. In S. Inness (Ed.), *Millennium girls: Today's girls around the world* (pp. 115–143). Lanham, MD: Rowman & Littlefield.

Crapanzano, V. (1992). *Hermes' dilemma and Hamlet's desire: On the epistemology of interpretation*. Cambridge, MA: Harvard University Press.

Cuba, L., & Hammon, D. (1993). A place to call home. Identification with dwelling, community, and region. *The Sociological Quarterly, 34*, 111–131.

Davies, B. (1989). *Frogs and snails and feminist tales*. Sydney, Australia: Allen & Unwin.

Davies, B. (1993). *Shards of glass: Children reading and writing beyond gendered identity*. Cresskill, NJ: Hampton Press.

Davies, B. (2000). *A body of writing 1990–1999*. New York: AltaMira Press.

de Marrais, K. B., & LeCompte, M. (1999). *The way schools work: A sociological analysis of education* (3rd ed.). White Plains, NY: Longman.

Douglas, S. (1997). Girls n' spice: All things nice? *The Nation, 25*, 21–24.

Dyhouse, C. (1981). *Girls growing up in late Victorian and Edwardian England*. London: Routledge.

Eckert, P. (1989). *Jocks and burnouts: Social categories and identity in the high school*. New York: Teachers Colley Press.

Eder, D. (1995). *School talk: Gender and adolescent culture*. New Brunswick, NJ: Rutgers University Press.

Evans, C., & Eder, D. (1993). "No exit": Processes of social isolation in the middle school. *Journal of Contemporary Ethnography, 22*(2), 139–170.

Foucault, M. (1979). *Discipline and punish*. New York: Vintage Books.

Foucault, M. (1980). *Power, knowledge: Selected interviews and other writings, 1972–1977*. Sussex, England: Harvester Press.

George, P., & Alexander, W. (1993). *The exemplary middle school*. Fort Worth, TX: Harcourt Brace Jovanovich College.

Hall, T., Coffey, A., & Williamson, H. (1999). Self, space, and place: Youth identities and citizenship. *British Journal of Sociology of Education, 20*(4), 501–514.

Haug, F. (1987). *Female sexualization*. London. Verso.

Hudson, B. (1984). Femininity and adolescence. In A. McRobbie & M. Nava (Eds.), *Gender and generation* (pp. 31–53). London: Macmillan.

Inness, S. (1998). *Millennium girls: Today's girls around the world*. Lanham, MD: Rowman & Littlefield.

Jackson, J. B. (1994). *A sense of place, a sense of time*. New Haven, CT: Yale University Press.

Jackson, P. (1968). *Life in classrooms*. New York: Holt, Rinehart & Winston.

Jones, A. (1993). Becoming a "girl": Post-structuralist suggestions for educational research. *Gender & Education, 5*(2), 157–167.

Kenway, J., Willis, S., Blackmore, J., & Rennie, L. (1994). Making "hope practical" rather than "despair convincing": Feminist post-structuralism, gender reform and educational change. *British Journal of Sociology of Education, 15*(2), 187–210.

Lamb, S. (2001). *The secret lives of girls: What good girls really do—sex, play, aggression and their guilt*. New York: The Free Press.

Lemish, D. (1998). Spice Girls talk: A case study in the development of gendered identity. In S. Inness (Ed.), *Millennium girls: Today's girls around the world* (pp. 145–167). Lanham, MD: Rowman & Littlefield.

Lesko, N. (1996). Denaturalizing adolescence: The politics of contemporary representations. *Youth & Society, 28*(2), 139–161.

MacLeod, J. (1995). *Ain't no makin' it: Aspirations and attainment in a low-income neighborhood*. Boulder, CO: Westview Press.

Massey, D. (1994). *Space, place, and gender*. Minneapolis: University of Minnesota Press.

McDowell, L. (1999). *Gender, identity, and place: Understanding feminist geographies*. Minneapolis: University of Minnesota Press.

McRobbie, A. (1993). Shut up and dance: Youth culture and changing modes of femininity. *Cultural Studies, 7*, 406–426.

Merten, D. (1997). The meaning of meanness: Popularity, competition, and conflict among junior high school girls. *Sociology of Education, 70*, 175–191.

Mitchell, S. (1995). *The new girl: Girls' culture in England 1880–1915*. New York: Columbia University Press.

Nash, I. (2001, December 21). Girls' Studies and Women's Studies. WMST listserv. Retrieved March 17, 2004, from http://research.umbc.edu/~korenman/wmst/girlstudies.html

Nelson, C., & Vallone, L. (1994). *The girl's own: Cultural histories of the Anglo-American girl, 1830–1915*. Athens: University of Georgia Press.

Nespor, J. (1997). *Tangled up in school: Politics, space, bodies, and signs in the educational process*. Mahwah, NJ: Lawrence Erlbaum Associates.

Orenstein, P. (1994). *Schoolgirls: Young women, self-esteem, and the confidence gap*. New York: Doubleday.

Phillips, L. M. (2000). *Flirting with danger: Young women's reflections on sexuality and domination*. New York: New York University Press.

Pipher, M. (1995). *Reviving Ophelia: Saving the selves of adolescent girls*. New York: Ballantine.

Research for Action, Inc. (1996). *Girls in the middle: Working to succeed in school*. Washington, DC: American Association of University Women Educational Foundation.

Sadker, M., & Sadker, D. (1994). *Failing at fairness: How America's schools cheat girls*. New York: Scribner's.

Shakeshaft, C., Mandel, L., Johnson, Y., Sawyer, J., Hergenrother, M. A., & Barber, E. (1997). Boys call me cow. *Educational Leadership, 55*(2), 22–25.

Sibley, D. (1995). *Geographies of exclusion*. New York: Routledge.

Simmons, R. (2002). *Odd girl out: The hidden culture of aggression*. New York: Harcourt.

Spring, J. (1990). *The American school 1642–1990* (2nd ed.). White Plains, NY: Longman.

Tolman, D. L. (2002). *Dilemmas of desire: Teenage girls talk about sexuality*. Cambridge, MA: Harvard University Press.

Turnbull, C. (1990). Liminality: A synthesis of subjective and objective experience. In R. Schechner & W. Appel (Eds.), *By means of performance: Intercultural studies of theatre and ritual* (pp. 50–81). New York: Cambridge University Press.

Turner, V. (1967). *The forest of symbols*. Ithaca, NY: Cornell University Press.

Turner, V. (1977). Variations on a theme of liminality. In S. F. Moore & B. G. Myerhoff (Eds.), *Secular ritual* (pp. 36–52). Amsterdam: Van Gorcum.

Walkerdine, V. (1990). *Schoolgirl fictions*. London: Verso.

Walkerdine, V. (1993). Girlhood through the looking glass. In M. de Ras & M. Lunenberg (Eds.), *Girls, girlhood, and girls' studies in transition* (pp. 9–25). Amsterdam: Het Spinhuis.

Walkerdine, V., Lucey, H., & Melody, J. (2001). *Growing up girl: Psychosocial explorations of gender and class*. New York: New York University Press.

Weber, D. (1995). From limen to border: A meditation on the legacy of Victor Turner for American Cultural Studies. *American Quarterly, 47*(3), 525–536.

Weis, L., & Fine, M. (2000). *Construction sites: Excavating race, class, and gender among urban youth*. New York: Teachers College Press.

Wexler, P. (1992). *Becoming somebody: Towards a social psychology of school*. Washington, DC: Falmer Press.

White, E. (2002). *Fast girls: Teenage tribes and the myth of the slut*. New York: Scribner's.

Wiseman, R. (2002). *Queen bees and wannabes*. Westminster, MD: Three Rivers Press.

Wolfe, N. (1997). *Promiscuities: The secret struggle for womanhood*. New York: Fawcett Columbine.

Zukin, S. (1991). *Landscapes of power: From Detroit to Disney World*. Berkeley: University of California Press.

Part ❙

BEFORE SCHOOL

Barbies, Bases, and Beer: The Role of Home in Junior High School Girls' Identity Work

Don E. Merten
Ball State University

Home is where we start. In literature and myth, home is the point of departure for our heroes (Hollander, 1993). For girls growing up in suburban America, their movement through different parts of the house often serves to mark their developmental progress. At some point, certain cabinets have to be "child-proofed," because a girl's mobility and curiosity exceed her knowledge and judgment. Later, child-proofing devices will be removed and that too is a sign of development. As a girl ventures out into the yard, then into the neighborhood, and then into grade school, she utilizes and moves through increasingly expansive spaces that take her farther and farther from home. An important correlate of increased maturity, therefore, is increased mobility in space. Entry into junior high is one more important step in this movement into the world and away from home. It is not surprising, however, that the literature on early-adolescent girls largely focuses on school and extracurricular activities. In part this is because middle-class girls talk "almost exclusively about trials and tribulations of their school lives and very little about home lives" (Brown, 1998, p. 27). In the geography of early-adolescent girls, a great deal is assumed about the role of home but little is reported.

The relative neglect of home in the social-science literature is consistent with the assumption that as girls make the transition to junior high, they will shift their focus from home and family to school and peers. School is the place where peer contact is most sustained and most intense. Moreover, as girls work out who they are, they are expected to do so vis-à-vis their peers—that identity work usually taking place during interactions in school. Accompanying the transition to junior high is movement away from childhood where girls were dependent on adults and compliant to adult directives. This aspect of the transition is underwritten and encouraged by parents and teachers as they emphasize the need for girls to be more self-motivated, self-reliant, and generally more autonomous—but in *responsible* ways. All of this is part of what Bellah, Madsen, Sullivan, Swidler, and Tipton (1985) refer to as "leaving home" and part of the processes of "individuation" according to psychologists. Thus in the cultural imagination of mainstream parents and their daughters, home is expected to diminish in significance as peer group influence increases. Yet this linear construal of developmental and spatial movement obscures an important point: the liminal status of junior high girls. That is, these girls are no longer children and are not yet teenagers. Moreover, their liminal status both motivates their actions and infuses those actions with meanings grounded in girls' interstitial developmental and educational location.

Stepping back for a moment to consider the larger role and meaning of home, we find that "there is no word so loaded as 'home' in the Romance languages and English" (Hollander, 1993, p. 38). Home is a benchmark in the geography of our life world and in the West, home is ideally a place of security and privacy—a place where one can be "oneself," feel protected, and accepted (Allan & Crow, 1989; Lasch, 1977). This is, in part, why violations of the home as a sanctuary, for example, child and spousal abuse that occur at home, seem especially vile; such actions violate the meaning of home as well as the meaning of family. Such actions remind us, however, that home is not always a haven from the larger world, but a microcosm of the larger society (McDowell, 1999). Like the social order, home is a cultural construct insofar as it is more than the physical structure we label a house (Rykwert, 1993).

Houses are not necessarily homes but become homes through the accretion of experiences while in them and the meanings appropriated (Werner, Altman, & Oxley, 1985) from those experiences. Often this transformation of house to home is accomplished through the enactment of rituals. Saile (1985) points out, "Through such rituals not only is the physical environment transformed but so too are the human participants" (p. 87). We as humans try to make houses into homes by making them extensions of ourselves—the home helps constitute our identity and vice versa. Even as we move from house to house, we create *continuity* by retaining those objects and arrangements with which we identified in our previous home. It is because of these sorts of interconnections that people and their environment constitute "an integral and inseparable unit" (Werner et al., 1985, p. 2). It is also why we learn something important about acquaintances when we first visit their homes. As Hall, Coffey, and Williamson (1999) note, "emergent identities require space of their own in which to assert themselves, and are also grounded in (if not tied to), the specificities of particular locations" (p. 505). Yet Massey (1994) notes that in this relationship between place and identity, the notion of *place* "has remained relatively unexamined" compared to the notion of identity (p. 167).

The conceptualization of identity has been approached from many perspectives but is commonly thought to consist of multiple parts, for example, "I" and "me" (Mead, 1968). Such dualistic frameworks have a girl treating herself as both subject and object, with multiple "me's" that are created in different settings. How the various parts of identity are held together to give us an "illusion of wholeness" (Ewing, 1990) becomes an increasingly pressing issue as the multiplicity of selves gains attention. A productive approach to this issue focuses on the narrative structure of our lives (McAdams, 1997), insofar as narrative pulls together the multiplicity of identities through the stories we tell about ourselves and others. Different stories told about oneself in different places reveal the representations of self associated with those different places. Holland, Lachicotte, Skinner, and Cain (1998) suggest, however, that we also establish who we are by the meaning we bestow on what we do—that our practices help forge our identities.

This chapter explores the role home played in girls' identity work by examining their narratives about the practices they engaged in at home. Home was not just a place in which girls negotiated and expressed changes in their identity, but it was also a salient symbolic location in the cultural geography within which girls operated. The question asked here is whether home is as unimportant for the identity work of early-adolescent girls as its lack of attention by scholars would suggest. That is, does home decrease in importance as girls expand their geographic range? Or does home remain an important place and symbol as girls negotiate their liminal status? In order to address this question, we need to briefly describe the community context and the junior high that the girls attended. Then excerpts from girls' narratives about home are provided. The chapter closes with a discussion of how what girls had to say about home and what they did there contributes to our understanding of home in the geography of girls' identity work.

The data on which this chapter is based came in many forms. Some of it was from casual conversations we had with girls or conversations we overheard in classrooms, hallways, and elsewhere. The bulk of the data, however, was gathered through multiple open-ended interviews we conducted with girls during the 2 years they were in junior high—from when they entered seventh grade until they graduated from eighth grade. These interviews sought to elicit girls' accounts of their everyday experiences and how they made sense of those experiences. Through these interviews, girls shared with us the everyday triumphs and tragedies in academics, peer relationships, and family life. Girls' concerns were often framed in terms of the tension between continuity and change—who they had been and who they were becoming. In 2 years, we had 326 interviews with 85 girls. The interview sample included girls from different status categories (e.g., preppies), neighborhoods, and levels of academic, social, and activity success. The interviews, conducted by two female ethnographers, were tape-recorded and took place in a small room at school set aside for this purpose. A third ethnographer interviewed parents.

COMMUNITY, SCHOOL, AND TRANSITION

In many ways, this community was typical of small towns that have become caught in metropolitan expansion as the rural spaces between towns were filled by new housing developments. The community became an affluent Chicago suburb because of its newly built expensive subdivisions. It was a place that reflected success and that was designed to perpetuate that success by creating an opportunity-rich environment for children. The social-reproduction effort started with outstanding school facilities and was supplemented by a broad range of extracurricular activities. For example, each year before school started, parents and incoming seventh graders were invited to an Activities Showcase where sponsors of 17 distinct extracurricular activities (more if one counted duplicates, i.e., seventh- and eighth-grade girls basketball) told about their activity. The number of activities available in junior high represented a significant increase over the number in grade school. The vast majority of parents we interviewed had grown up elsewhere and had moved here for career-related reasons. For the most part, these parents were individuals who already had experienced the sacrifices that prepared the way for success. To many parents, geographic mobility had been the precursor to economic and social mobility. Thus they encouraged their children to take advantage of available opportunities and were concerned if their daughters did not. One mother lamented: "She's good as far as attitude at home is concerned but I can't seem to get her to participate in things at school or to enlarge her circle of friends—to round her out more." This expansionist agenda was articulated and supported by many parents.

Parents and teachers viewed the transition to junior high as a major leap forward in the educational/developmental process. Teachers expected students to work more independently and generally to do more for themselves. Organizationally students were divided into sections (homerooms) and generally moved with section mates from classroom to classroom and from teacher to teacher. Parents also expected their daughters to expand their spatial and social horizons as they became friends with peers who had come from other grade schools to attend the junior high, which contained approximately 300 seventh graders and about the same number of eighth graders. Drawing students from six grade schools meant there were six students who had enjoyed being the smartest, prettiest, most popular, and so on, in the schools from which they came. This increased the competition not only to be the best, but even to be noticed. Moreover, the terms of the competition were changed by the presence in junior high of a strong adolescent ethos, that is, the evaluative and aesthetic elements that gave adolescence, as a cultural construct, its feeling tone (Geertz, 1973). This ethos that dominated junior high centered on popularity, sociability, male–female relationships, and an exuberant spontaneity that challenged adult constraints—on being cool. This expression of adolescentness was imposed by students on their peers.

Girls in this community were encouraged not only to take advantage of opportunities but to excel in them. They participated in soccer, baseball, gymnastics, swimming, skating, dancing, singing, and did so very competitively. The seriousness with which they sought to acquire and develop skills was a testament to the value they placed on achievement. The same seriousness characterized teachers' attitudes. Marcia, who was academically successful, nevertheless, objected to excluding fun from the classroom:

> I think we should be able to have parties like Valentine's Day parties or Halloween parties, but teachers won't let us have any. They think we are too old for that; that we are too mature to do something that is childish. I don't think I'm too mature. The teachers think that we should just stick with our studies. This isn't play time anymore.

Marcia was also quite aware of her parents' high expectations for her future. Her comments, when asked how soon she could be involved with boys, were illuminating: "After college. After I start a good career—a lawyer. That's what she [mother] thinks. That's not what I think. She like plans my whole life out for me. 'Once you have gotten accepted in Harvard, you can become a lawyer, and then you can marry a millionaire.' " Even when daughters recognized their parents' expectations, they did not always agree. Marcia's mother's plan, it is worth noting, indexed both geographic and economic mobility. Thus entering junior high was an important step in leaving home and becoming the self-reliant person a girl needed to be in order to be successful. Even as this scenario seemed to diminish the role of home and family, parents frequently expressed satisfaction that their children were "finally getting away from us," as one parent put it.

GIRLS AND HOME

The trajectory of change in junior high was not as uniformly "forward" as what its linear imagery suggested. It was strongly marked by the tensions between continuity and change that related to the interstitial position of junior high, that is, as an institution between grade school and high school. The transition had not created the instantaneous transformation that many parents and girls expected, and therefore continuity remained a pervasive part of the present during this liminal period. Some girls did their best to obliterate any signs of the past, others tenaciously tried to preserve the past, and still others sought to negotiate a balance between change and continuity. Despite some obvious continuities with their previous educational experiences, the anticipated character of junior high was one of change. Home, by comparison, had more perceived continuities but was also expected to change as less time was spent there and more time was spent away participating in extracurricular activities. Home was, therefore, not expected to remain the place it once had been, nor did it turn out to be the place that most girls and their parents assumed it would be. It became a site where the tensions between continuity and change were played out in dramatic fashion and where these tensions were negotiated in different ways by individual girls.

HOME AND PRACTICES OF CONTINUITY

Many girls found the new organizational structure and increased academic expectations of junior high perceptibly different from elementary school. Initially these changes were great enough that many girls experienced themselves as different—even older. Accepting the teen ethos seemed unnecessary for making the transition. These girls wanted to control change by emphasizing continuity where they could. Home turned out to be more congenial than school to enact practices of continuity. What girls did with their rooms at home was a reflection of how they saw themselves or how they wanted to be seen. Some girls made subtle changes to their room that signified the emergent and provisional nature of the changes they were undertaking. For example, Rachael took down her posters of kittens and puppies and replaced them with rock star posters. She, however, did not dispose of the kitten and puppy posters but rather hung them in her closet. The exchange was one of emphasis and thus maintained a simultaneous connection with childhood and with adolescence in her room.

Some girls, however, attempted to negate their childhood past by removing all signs of it from their rooms. Donna tells what she felt like when she visited her friend Jennifer and saw the changes Jennifer had made to her room after entering junior high:

> I felt kind of strange being in a room like that 'cause I'm used to having my teddy bears. Like I have a pink room and all my pink stuff. I go to Jennifer's room and everything is white. Her walls are white and she doesn't have any stuffed animals or anything. I just felt kind of uncomfortable sitting there. There is a picture of a little girl; that is the only thing that I have seen that she has kept.

For girls like Donna, the completeness of the change to Jennifer's room was shocking. Donna felt uncomfortable because the Barbie pink of her room was very distant from the stark white of Jennifer's room. Donna went on to describe the contrast and the implications for her sense of self:

> I have so many teddy bears. I got another one for Christmas. I still sleep with one and I still arrange them all different ways. I made little clothes for them and stuff. Jennifer seems to want to grow up so much that she is trying to forget everything in the past. She has put her stuffed animals away. She doesn't want to hold on to something. She wants to grow up real fast.

For girls, the issue of continuity and change between childhood and adolescence was very sensitive and the dramatic contrast represented by Jennifer's room raised questions about the appropriateness of Donna's own room. Given this contrast, if Jennifer wanted to "grow up real fast," did that suggest that Donna was failing to grow up? Whereas Jennifer tried to negate the past by getting rid of everything, Donna seemed to be preserving the past by keeping her stuffed animals.

Despite pressure to change that accompanied the transition to junior high, some girls managed to continue the activities that they had previously enjoyed. It was unwise, however, to talk about these practices at school—where the standards of adolescentness were sometimes viciously enforced (Merten, 1994, 1996). To engage in patterns of play that were continuous with grade school suggested that girls did not subscribe to the adolescent ethos. Such girls were often the objects of ridicule. Nevertheless some girls continued these patterns by inviting their friends to their house where they could play without their school peers being aware of it. Carla described what happened when she was at her friend April's house:

> Like with April, I'll play a board game with her. I would never play a board game with Brenda. Brenda is more active—she's not the board game type. We go over to April's house and play Monopoly or something. More little kids' stuff, I guess. I could play Barbies with April because she still has all of her Barbies. Don't tell her I told you. They are all in the bottom of her closet. We just got those out one night as a matter of fact and we watched cartoons. Things I'd never have done with Brenda.

Whereas Carla was reluctant to play board games, much less Barbies, with her more "active" friend Brenda, she still felt comfortable doing so with

April. Yet she also made it clear that both April and she knew that doing so was now inappropriate "little kid stuff." After all, even April kept her Barbies in the bottom of her closet, and Carla was sure that April would not want the interviewer to know she still played Barbies.

Other girls, even highly successful ones, also considered home a place where they could get away from the popularity pressures at school. Cheryl was very popular, and at school she associated with her popular cheerleader friends. However, before and after school she spent time with her neighborhood friend Lisa, who was not nearly as popular as Cheryl. At school, although she was friendly to Lisa, Cheryl did not spend time with her and explained their relationship in these terms: "She's always there. She just got to know the friends at school a couple days ago. Well, Lisa knew them in fourth grade but they didn't like her. After fourth grade, she went to a different school. But she is my best friend since fourth grade." Cheryl went on to say why she would not give up her friendship with Lisa just because her popular school friends did not like Lisa: " 'Cause Lisa is better than even they are. She treats me better. Not that they treat me bad, but Lisa is always there when I need to talk to her. She is always understanding. She always knows what to say. She is never off with someone else when I need to talk to her. She is nicer." Although it was unusual for a girl as popular as Cheryl to keep a best friend who was not also popular, she seemed comfortable operating under a different set of principles at home and at school. Popularity was the primary concern in school but not at home. Cheryl made it clear that she was not the kind of girl who judged all relationships through the lens of popularity, and she used home to make this identity statement.

HOME AND PRACTICES OF DISCONTINUITY

Although going to junior high opened the door to major changes, it did not automatically produce changes at home commensurate with the adolescent ethos that dominated school. Therefore, some girls sought to enact adolescent scenarios at home and to thereby change who they were in that setting. That is, girls used their rooms to enact practices that symbolized discontinuity. Home was a place that girls went to smoke, drink, and become sexually involved. In this respect home, or someone else's house, became a place where girls could go to engage in and conceal actions of which adults disapproved. The willingness to violate adult expectations by engaging in such prohibited actions signaled that a girl was no longer a compliant child and was instead becoming more independent. Also girls demonstrated independence by leaving their homes and going elsewhere without parental approval.

It was not unexpected for girls to retreat to their rooms in order to be away from their family. In fact, some parents consider such retreats a normal part of their daughter's development. Other parents were less willing, however, to accept their daughter's withdrawal from family life. Carol had previously accepted her parents' protectiveness, but since entering junior high she began to resist it. She described an incident that occurred when her mother came into her room. Her mother said: "You act like you don't even need us anymore. Like you're just here and not even a part of the family." Carol replied, "Why do I have to have your consent whenever I want to do something? I hate that. I want to live on my own. I can't wait until I go to college. I want to go out of state. I want to get away." Getting away from home was both an immediate desire and a long-term goal for symbolizing her independence—the greater the distance, the greater the independence. Getting away was framed also as simply getting out of the house and away from parental supervision. Carol continued: "Most of the time now I've been going to Dawn's house to get out of my house, 'cause I don't like my parents giving me lectures. So I call up Dawn and go, "I just want to get out my house' and she goes, 'OK, come over.' " For Carol, getting out of the house meant she was more autonomous and contributed to a sense of herself as less dependent on her parents.

Getting out of the house was definitely the adolescent-like thing to do. Going to friends' houses whose parents were not home was viewed by many girls as especially desirable. As Morgan noted about her friend Cynthia: "Cynthia is lucky because her parents work and like she can have people over when her parents aren't home. Her parents don't mind that. If I had people over when my parents weren't home, my parents would kill me." Of course Morgan was not talking about just any "people," but was specifically referring to boys. She knew that her parents would not give her permission to be at a boy's house, much less be there when his parents were not home. Therefore Morgan and her friends resorted to deceiving their parents about where they were going: "We will say we're going to track practice because our parents don't want us going over to boys' houses without the parents being home. I can't tell my mom because she will go like, 'I don't want you to go over to a boy's house.' So I'll say, 'I'm going to track'." Again, it is important to note that Morgan was not referring to just any assortment of boys and girls getting together, but this was about couples getting together. If her boyfriend could not be there, she said she would not go either. Houses provided privacy in boy/girl relationships and the latter were paramount in the imagery of teenhood.

Having peers over to one's house or going to their's also provided opportunities for actions adults found problematic. Grace told of drinking at a friend's house:

Well, I was over at Jenny's Monday, me and Rayann and Jenny all got bombed. Then we went back to Cindy's. She said, "I'm going to ask if you guys can spend the night and then we can drink." So me and Heather go, "OK." So we spent the night. Cindy had two six packs of beer and we each had four. I didn't feel anything and we started drinking some wine. I started swaying back and forth and Heather started giggling. When I got drunk, it was funny. We were trying to say stuff. We made up a dance and we were all trying to do it but we were drunk and couldn't do it.

Heather became so drunk that she took a shower with her clothes on to try to regain sobriety. Stories about going to each other's houses to drink, smoke, and meet boys commonly circulated among girls.

At school girls could go along with peer narratives about drinking, smoking, and sex, which signaled a commitment to teenness without actually having done anything. Yet to go home with girls who engaged in these practices or to invite them over to one's house, risked having to participate in these prohibited activities. By going along with such talk at school, if a girl later refused to do anything, she was viewed as phony. Therefore, girls had to be very careful about whom they invited over or to whose house they went. Even Christy who did not pretend to drink told of her difficulty dealing with a friend's drinking and smoking: "Darian goes to parties with her cousins and her cousins are older and so she's never around younger people; that's why she's growing up too fast. She smokes pot and all this other stuff and I don't like it. She drinks beer." Christy went on to say why she did not want to attend a party at Darian's house:

> Because I know that her older friends smoke pot and I don't do that, I'll ask her what she is going to do at the party. She says, "Well, you can come and you don't have to do that [smoke] if you don't want to." I just stay away. I don't want to grow up too fast. I just want to take my time.

Although Darian suggested that Christy did not have to drink beer or smoke marijuana if she did not want to, Christy knew that she would feel odd if she refused. Yet if she drank beer or smoked marijuana, it would push her beyond where she wanted to be.

It is not just relatively quiet girls like Christy who were concerned about growing up too fast. Megan, who was involved with boys, was also concerned. She described how her friend Sue had invited her boyfriend home and had gone to "third base" with him. Girls used the baseball metaphor to characterize how far they had gone with a boy. That is, first base was "kissing," second base was "up the shirt," and so on. When Megan was asked if she were prepared to go to third base with her boyfriend if he came over, she replied: "I probably wouldn't let him. I mean if I'm going to third in seventh grade. How far will I go in eighth? In my freshman year? When I'm a senior, who knows?" Megan recognized the inherently progressive nature of sexual involvement. She herself had gone to second base and was comfortable with that, but noted the constant tension between not doing enough sexually and doing too much. She added: "Well if I never kissed a boy before [her friends would say], 'Oh wow, you are so inexperienced, you're in seventh grade and you have never kissed a boy before!' But if you go to third, that is too far for seventh grade." The question that girls struggled with and tried to negotiate among themselves was, how far was far enough and what was too far given where they located themselves in growing up. Girls did not want to be accused of being either "babies" or "sluts" (Tannenbaum, 1999; White, 2002). Home was often the setting where these questions had to be answered.

DISCUSSION

Even though the transition forced girls to rethink who they were, they did not respond to this challenge in a uniform manner. Though girls chose different practices by which to express their identities, none of these practices was highly unusual, even when they violated adult expectations. Home was the site of much of this identity work, but more than that it was also an important symbol in that work. Because the meanings girls bestowed upon home varied, the relationship between home and identity was also variable *and* complex. Thus despite the relative neglect of home in the literature on junior high girls, it remained a significant place for identity work. Therefore, it is necessary to consider in greater detail the role of home in girls' geography. In particular, what can we learn from what girls said about what they did at home and who they were when there? Knowing how girls used home in formulating their identities should also tell us what they were becoming—not simply what they were told to become.

The foregoing narratives make it clear that neither home nor school can be considered isolated sites of identity work; that is, each place influenced how girls thought about themselves in the *other* setting. Even when there was behavioral continuity at home, for example, playing Barbies, it no longer had the same meaning due to the dominance of the adolescent ethos at school. This dialectic between home and school existed whether girls were playing Barbies or drinking beer. In fact separating proscribed practices that were highly identity-relevant from everyday life infused both the practices and the homes in which they occurred with meanings that reflected the liminal status of these girls. In addition, we need to keep in mind that these two sites were located in the geography of White suburban America. Given what has been written about girls in suburbia (Kenny, 2000), one has to wonder whether the injunction to become more independent was meant to be realized. Girls seemed willing to resist secretly both adult expectations (e.g., by being with boys when adults were absent) and the adolescent ethos (e.g., by doing "kid stuff"). Yet it was unclear whether such concealed practices reflected positive self-determination or whether concealing actions signaled something problematic, for example, that girls were afraid to be themselves.

The practices girls enacted to symbolize independence at home were often concealed from critical adult and peer audiences. That is, engaging in adolescent practices at home, for example, drinking beer, allowed girls to sever the association between home and childhood by negating their "little kid" identity at home. Even though it seemed like common sense for junior high girls to conceal their drinking from adults, why did they do so? The obvious answer is that girls would get in trouble because they were violating adult rules. Just as important, they were also violating gender expectations by doing something that could lead to loss of control. That is, junior high girls drinking beer violated a sense of gender appropriateness and therefore raised questions about their ability to enact acceptable images of femininity. Parenthetically, boys were not allowed to drink beer either, but drinking for them did not violate expectations with regard to masculinity—it actually confirmed such expectations. Yet it was not just adolescent practices that were concealed at home but also practices that symbolized childhood continuity. For example, even though April played with her Barbies, she kept the practice secret and hid her Barbies in the bottom of her closet. She was unwilling to resist *openly* the adolescent ethos, even by having her Barbies visible in her room. By keeping secret what they did at home, girls remained silent about practices that related to important parts of their identity they could not enact publicly.

The identity work that occurred at home involved practices that were, by virtue of being concealed, rendered deviant. Although these practices may also have been a form of resistance, they were largely without social impact. By concealing these "deviant" practices, girls inadvertently validated the publicly acceptable practices they opposed. That girls' identity work at home would proceed in relative silence is not unexpected. This silence is commonplace when women and girls confront a patriarchal world (Brown, 1998). Secrecy thereby helped reproduce a lifestyle that was grounded in practices and assumptions that could not be talked about openly, for example, the desire to be special or the privileged lives they enjoyed as suburban girls. Marcia was keenly aware of the career and social success that her parents expected of her. She was told to avoid serious involvement with boys until she had attained her law degree and was ready to marry a millionaire—even though it was acceptable to "play" at being involved. Marcia neither followed this directive nor openly rejected it; she secretly had boyfriends with whom she went to "second base." Her parents would have been upset to learn this; yet to expect her to be both popular and uninvolved with boys was unrealistic. Neither parents nor their daughters seemed inclined to deal openly with such fundamental issues. Girls, in general, assumed that they did not have the power to undertake their identity work in public. Instead they enacted unacceptable facets of their identities at home where they could be concealed with relative ease. That is, girls were learning the lesson that most women understand: If they cannot control their lives, they have to control themselves.

Finally, it is important to recognize the tacit cultural framework that gave meaning to the geography of girlhood described here. The assumed connection between growing up and leaving home was underwritten by the spatialization (Shields, 1991) of development. The extent of a girl's developmental progress was gauged by how far she had gone—literally and figuratively. For example, as girls moved through the educational system, their progress was marked hierarchically by being promoted to the next "higher" grade and horizontally by moving to schools increasingly distant from home. More important, the pace and progress of many facets of growing up were evaluated by how fast and how far girls had moved. Nowhere was this clearer than in the baseball metaphor, which spatialized a girl's sexuality. If a girl did not "do anything" intimate with boys, she simply stayed at home (plate) and was labeled "inexperienced" or a "baby." Only purposive action took a girl to first base and beyond. Of course, touching all bases and returning to home (plate) also symbolized "going all the way": having sex. Therefore, home in the baseball metaphor represented both continuity (nonsexual) and change (sexual). Moreover, the spatialization of sexuality led girls to question themselves as to whether they were "going far enough" or "going too far." The latter was invariably linked to "growing up too fast." That home was the implied starting point *and* ending point in this image of spatialized development made home important in fundamental ways that seldom were recognized or fully appreciated. Finally, this both/and character of home in girls' lives resonated strongly with girls' liminal status and the important symbolic role that home played in dealing with their "betwixt and between" identity.

CONCLUSION

Entering junior high did not diminish the importance of home as many parents and their daughters assumed it would. Rather it remained an important site of identity work in which the tension between continuity and change was addressed. In some instances home served as a refuge from the demands of adolescentness at school, but in other instances it was the place where key practices associated with adolescence were enacted. Because home generally symbolized continuity, this association had to be negated by girls who wanted to see themselves as adolescent-like. They "left home" as the symbol of childhood by engaging in adolescent practices that helped forge a new identity—even when those practices actually took place in the same home in which they had lived for years. To conceal practices that are important to one's identity is not unheard of, but doing so often creates an identity that is fundamentally flawed. This concealment relates to the larger pattern described by Taylor, Gilligan, and Sullivan, (1995), whereby a girl finds it necessary to go underground "with her feelings and knowledge" (p. 26) in order to protect herself. Rather than openly resist the expectations girls opposed, they disassociated themselves from important aspects of their lives. The girls here had already begun to take for granted that such concealment was necessary, even when it felt uncomfortable. What girls did at home did not simply make them more or less adolescent, but also led them toward being persons who concealed, in order to control, important aspects of their lives. This was something girls shared whether—favoring Barbies or beer.

DISCUSSION QUESTIONS

1. Does the idea that junior high school is a liminal institution fit with the cultural construction of development as spatialized?

2. Can we speak of the geographies of other age grades in American society, for example, the geography of old age? If so, what are some of the key metaphors that locate people in this geography? If not, why not?

3. How does the spatialization of development shape the way Americans talk about and experience their own development and the development of others?

REFERENCES

Allan, G., & Crow, G. (1989). *Home and family: Creating the domestic sphere*. New York: Macmillan.

Bellah, R. N., Madsen, R., Sullivan, W., Swidler, A., & Tipton, S. (1985). *Habits of the heart: Individualism and commitment in American life*. Berkeley: University of California Press.

Brown, L. M. (1998). *Raising their voices: The politics of girls' anger*. Cambridge, MA: Harvard University Press.

Ewing, K. (1990). The illusion of wholeness: "Culture," "self," and the experience of inconsistency. *Ethos, 18*, 251–278.

Geertz, C. (1973). *The interpretation of cultures*. New York: Basic Books.

Hall, T., Coffey, A., & Williamson, H. (1999). Self, space, and place: Youth identities and citizenship. *British Journal of Education, 20*, 501–513.

Holland, D., Lachicotte, W., Skinner, D., & Cain, C. (1998). *Identity and agency in cultural worlds*. Cambridge, MA: Harvard University Press.

Hollander, J. (1993). It all depends. In A. Mack (Ed.), *Home: A place in the world* (pp. 27–45). New York: New York University Press.

Kenny, L. D. (2000). *Daughters of suburbia: Growing up White, middle class, and female*. New Brunswick, NJ: Rutgers University Press.

Lasch, C. (1977). *Haven in a heartless world: The family besieged.* New York: Basic Books.

Massey, D. (1994). *Space, place, and gender.* Minneapolis: University of Minnesota Press.

McAdams, D. (1997). The case for unity in the (post)modern self. In R. Ashmore & L. Jussim (Eds.), *Self and identity: Fundamental issues* (pp. 48–73). New York: Oxford University Press.

McDowell, L. (1999). *Gender, identity, and place: Understanding feminist geographies.* Minneapolis: University of Minnesota Press.

Mead, G. H. (1968). *The self in social interaction.* New York: Wiley.

Merten, D. E. (1994). The cultural context of aggression: The transition to junior high school. *Anthropology & Education Quarterly, 25,* 29–43.

Merten, D. E. (1996). Visibility and vulnerability: Responses to rejection by nonaggressive junior high school boys. *Journal of Early Adolescence, 16,* 5–26.

Rykwert, J. (1993). House and home. In A. Mack (Ed.), *Home: A place in the world* (pp. 47–58). New York: New York University Press.

Saile, D. G. (1985). The ritual establishment of home. In I. Altman & C. M. Werner (Eds.), *Home environments* (pp. 87–111). New York: Plenum Press.

Shields, R. (1991). *Places on the margin: Alternative geographies of modernity.* New York: Routledge.

Taylor, J. M., Gilligan, C., & Sullivan, A. M. (1995). *Between voice and silence: Women and girls, race and relationship.* Cambridge, MA: Harvard University Press.

Tanenbaum, L. (1999). *Slut!: Growing up female with a bad reputation.* New York: Seven Stories Press.

Werner, C. M., Altman, I., & Oxley, D. (1985). Temporal aspects of homes: A transactional perspective. In I. Altman & C. M. Werner (Eds.), *Home environments* (pp.1–31). New York: Plenum Press.

White, E. (2002). *Fast girls: Teenage tribes and the myth of the slut.* New York: Scribner's.

Chapter 3

Power Beads, Body Glitter, and Backseat Bad-Asses: Girls, Power, and Position on the School Bus

Laura Jewett
Louisiana State University

> *Putting the Excellence in education starts on the steps of that big yellow school bus.*
>
> —DeBruyn (1985, p. 1)

Each day, 22.5 million children make the round trip journey between school and home via the familiar yellow school bus ("School Bus Safety," 2000). Though often considered a "component part of going to school" (Fox, 1996, p. 25), or referred to as an "extension of the classroom" (DeBruyn, 1985), very little scholarly attention has been paid to the actual experiences of this daily rite of passage. Obscured perhaps by the "patina of the mundane," knowledge regarding the lived experience of the school bus amounts to a near vacant lot (G. Fine & Sandstrom, 1988, p. 76). Similarly, according to Inness (1998), *serious* research that focuses on the lives of girls—particularly girls who are also marginalized by race, ethnicity, class, and sexual orientation—is nearly as scant. As Inness writes regarding girls: "They are still second-class citizens doubly marginalized by their age and gender, and their lives are rarely taken seriously or are disregarded entirely" (p. 1).

This chapter focuses on girls, power, and position on the school bus. Specifically, it focuses on a particular group of girls (self-described as "backseat bad-asses") and how they influence and, arguably, enforce the spatial and social boundaries in the particular and particularly complex social milieu of Bus No. 21. Drawing on data from a yearlong ethnographic study of school bus culture, this chapter examines un/common conceptualizations of gender in a mobile culture on the outskirts of education proper. But watch your step: The school bus is a risky liminal space where the public and private worlds of girls intersect, and disparate constructions of gender merge and sometimes crash.

FIELDWORK

Sitting next to a 9-year-old girl self-pseudonymed Unique (my most consistent insider informant), I tried to explain field notes: "The field is the place where you're studying, so the bus is the field and field notes are notes about what happens on the bus." Although she had read fleetingly many of my entries, and taken notes of her own in extemporaneously constructed folded paper notebooks, Unique had a difficult time getting past the literality of the "field" part. "The bus can *not* be a field. It's inside, like a car, it moves," she insisted. Pointing out the window, Unique continued, "There's your field." During my time in "the field"—the perpetual points of departure and overlapping intersections that constitute school bus culture—I gathered data by riding Bus No. 21 three days per week throughout one school year. I analyzed documents ranging from official district business from the bus barn to wadded-up homework on the bus. I looked at training materials, flyers, memos, and countless other categories of paper scraps. Additionally, I was privy to several months of "conducts" (records containing descriptions and recommendations concerning episodes of passenger misconduct). This study, however, is primarily driven by participant observation. Moving around the bus and sitting with a variety of passengers, I took extensive on-the-spot field notes that I later expanded into more detailed accounts. Additionally, in the course of my travels among various seats, I conducted very informal interviews asking passengers identical questions such as: "What was the funnest time you ever had on the bus?" or "Why do you always sit here?"

Though I was a participant-observer—talking with and moving among my subjects—I remained what Adler and Adler (1998) describe as a "peripheral-member-researcher," in that I established myself as a "sort-of" member of Bus No. 21 culture. Passengers knew me, not by my name, but by my function as a researcher. Even Unique—with whom I sat for at least a minute or two on every ride except one—called me the "bus lady." My role was, in a sense, well defined. All the riders on No. 21 knew I was doing research on the bus—or more specifically that I was a student from "the university" writing a "report" on what it's like for kids on their bus. But the notion of research and its ultimate end product, however, meant very different things to different passengers, drivers, and transportation officials. Even after I had ridden for several months, Libby, a redheaded third grader asked: "Haven't you passed the bus driver test yet?" Other passengers conflated the role of researcher with that of newspaper reporter and probably still remain convinced, despite repeated explanations to the contrary, that some day Bus No. 21 will make the paper.

There is no question that my presence frequently overtly interrupted or altered "normal" activity. My pursuit of data was no secret; no flies on these moving walls (Van Maanen, 1988). As later discussed in more detail, passengers usually switched seats at least three times per ride. During the course of a 2-hour route, I switched seats upwards of seven times per route as well. Passengers would often move in response, sometimes to facilitate, but more often to dodge documentation. Many days, participant observation on No. 21 resembled a not-so-subtle game of elaborately mapped chase.

CONTEXT

This study took place in a town, smack dab in the middle of America, called Cimarron. The Cimarron Public School District enrolls approximately 5,200 students in five elementary schools, one middle school, one junior high, and one high school (Davis, 1998). Roughly half those students use school transportation. "The Cimarron Public Schools Transportation Department," reads the district's 1997–1998 annual report, "is a necessary part of a sound educational system" (Davis, 1998, p. 4).

Walk through the office door of Cimarron's transportation director and the first thing you see is a wall-size district map dotted with numbered red pins, connected by a flummoxing network of intersecting and overlapping lines. Though it is nearly incomprehensible to the uninitiated, this route map gives what Michelle Poole, transportation director, describes as a "big-picture view" of how school transportation is configured in the Cimarron school district. Look closely, and you can even see a squiggly line representing the route of No. 21. From this view, the trajectories of school bus routes seem to map a "planned and readable" and spatially defined culture (de Certeau, 1984, p. 93). The experience of riding the bus, however, reminds us that the spaces of culture are anything but one-dimensional. As the bus runs its route, seemingly static categories of setting (social and spatial) overlap, intersect, and interpenetrate: They move.

On my first ride on each school bus, I asked several passengers individually: "Where does this bus go?" This is a complicated question, since only the passengers at the very last stop have a complete picture of where the bus travels. Influenced by temporal as well as spatial constraints, the geographical perspective of the rest of the riders is inherently partial. No. 21 went to four different schools: an elementary school, a middle school, a junior high, and a high school. Its 15 other stops fell along a route linking several, mostly White middle-class subdivisions, a historically African American, working-class neighborhood, and a public housing complex (Southern Woods) situated on the edge of Cimarron's city limit.

Passengers described this route in different ways. As Nespor (1997) explains them, spatial regimes are "externally imposed in one instance, partially self-designed in the other" (p. 94). Thus, whereas African American Herkeesha talked about No. 21's route in terms of the "hood," Nathan, her White bus mate, positioned it cardinally as "south of town." Another White male rider whispered to me that No. 21 was "the Black bitch bus." Tara, a Latina junior high girl, mapped the route for me along relational lines: "Oh, we start at Atlantis', then Vicki's house, and Andrea's. Oh yeah, there's Dave our old driver's house." Todd, a White junior high boy, decked head-to-toe in Nike swooshes, told me in regard to queries about the bus route: "We're all ghetto here." As any transportation director's route map indicates, school bus routes serve to regulate the flow of bodies to and from school. These routes, however, also travel a social landscape as a "spatial regime" that constructs and is constructed by the lived experience of school bus passengers as well.

The population of Bus No. 21 was composed of roughly 32 sixth-through 11th-grade students, kindergarten through 5th-grade students, and three different drivers. Passengers ranged in age from 5 to 18 years old. There were roughly equal numbers of males and females, though girls rode more consistently. I say roughly, because school bus populations are not static. Riders come and go for a variety of reasons: a change in schools, a move, piano lessons, renegotiated custody agreements, court-ordered mandates, slumber parties, and the countless other realities that constitute young lives.

The core group of the 25 most frequent passengers contained about 50% White and 50% non-White passengers. Fifty percent of the non-White category was African American. Most of No. 21's riders came from lower-middle-class or working-class homes. No. 21 had a reputation among drivers, riders of other buses, and No. 21's riders themselves as a "bad bus." In school bus parlance, riders consider bus No. 21 to be composed of the "bad kids from the hood" as opposed to the "preps" on other buses. Furthermore, eight different No. 21 passengers on five different occasions remarked in reference to my research: "You picked the worst bus." Probing questions about the meaning of *worst* elicited only giggles, silence, or shrugs.

BETWIXT AND BETWEEN

"The landscape of childhood," asserts Thorne (1994) in her extensive study of playground culture, "includes three major sites—families, neighborhoods, and schools. Each of these worlds contains different people, patterns of time and space and arrangements of gender" (p. 29). I would add race/ethnicity and social class to these arrangements as well. The school bus is a space in which various trajectories of this landscape converge—though not always harmoniously.

According to Nespor (2000), "Spaces are outcomes of complex activities" (p. 25). In his book describing youth landscapes, Childress (2000) demonstrates how the social and spatial construction of schools relies on the complex activity of separation. Referring to the practice of locating schools on the edge of towns/cities, Childress writes: "The school building and grounds are both the evidence of adult desire for separation from children and teenagers and the means of separating them" (p. 219). Via the streets, the school bus crosses this border daily (Huffman, 1999; Martin, 1999). Traveling the contested territory in between and among adult and child spheres, the bus can be seen as a vehicle of liminality that violates the sort of separation described by Childress.

The recurrent notion of the school bus as this visible and somewhat uncontrollable link between school and community occurs frequently in school transportation journals (Bushweller, 1997; Huffman, 1999; Thomas, 1984). As Bushweller writes: "Your yellow school buses, after all, are likely to be the only image of the public schools that many people in your community see morning and afternoon, every day" (p. 37). Likewise, the ride to and from school offers opportunities of spatial and social mobility to its riders, who Nespor (2000) describes as "increasingly immobilized in urban landscapes" (p. 26). In addition to giving students a chance to cruise communities, seeing where and how classmates live, school bus culture as defined by its gender integration, cross-age relations, utilization of space, and peer pedagogy ventures "off-road" from the social and spatial parameters that constitute school life—particularly in relation to the lives of girls.

In his study on the time/distance constraints of school transportation, Fox (1996) rather dramatically describes the school bus as an "unnatural social group situation": "The typical school bus will carry students from 5 to 17. This forces children into a very unnatural social group situation and parents worry about the development of children in such situations, with specific concerns over the use of drugs, violence, and psycho-social maladjustment that may develop" (p. 27). Instead of using the term *unnatural* to describe school bus culture, I prefer *uneasy*, in reference to the uneasiness generated by the indeterminacy of liminality.

The school bus is a space/time of many minglings. Private and public geographies—mediated by salient landscapes of power, themselves saturated with fusing arrangements of race, social class, gender, and age—converge in the mobile transitional space/time of school bus culture. Holman and Harmon (1992) describes a similar space/time in his definition of liminality: "The state of being on a threshold in space or time; a place where many social meanings congregate" (p. 266). In his explorations of rites of passage, Turner (1967) characterizes liminality similarly as a social zone situated betwixt and between powerful systems of meaning "which is neither this nor that, but both" (p. 99). According to Sibley (1995): "For the individual or group socialized into believing that the separation of categories is necessary or desirable, the liminal zone is a source of anxiety" (p. 33). Fox (1996) expresses this sort of anxiety when he describes the bus as an "unnatural social setting" (p. 27).

Bus mates share a risky temporal/spatial relationship that differs from that of classmates. On the school bus, secret alcoves of private geographies run the risk of becoming discovered. Bus mates, unlike classmates, know where you live and in many cases with whom. Throughout my fieldwork, the homes, cars, laundry, parents, siblings, and even the dogs of various riders came under public scrutiny. I watched a middle school girl flinch as her disabled 8-year-old brother tried unsuccessfully to win favor with his peers through incessant boasting. Along with everyone else on the bus, I watched a grandmother mouth "I love you" and blow a kiss to her teenage grandson as he boarded. The humiliation of a junior high girl was palpable as passengers received a panoramic view of her obese mother hanging clothes on a line strung across the front porch of their trailer. Matters like pariah siblings or social class—which to some extent can be successfully rerouted in classrooms—emerge "en route" in ways less easily detoured.

Contrary to the rigid age stratification of schools, bus time also offers students the opportunity to play "up" and "down" across age and gender. For example, Randy, a lanky high school girl, split her bus time between backseat peers and a group of elementary boys near the front. When he wasn't flashing *Pokemon* cards with other fourth graders, one boy with whom I sometimes sat could be found painting his nails with a group of middle school "backseat wannabe" girls. T.J., a charismatic African American kindergartner on No. 21, was wildly popular among backseat girls. They bounced him on their knee, gave him treats, praised his schoolwork, and often yelled good-bye as he disembarked.

I also witnessed episodes of bullying both up and down. I listened as a tiny, freckled, first-grade girl asked (with extreme scrappiness) the fifth-grade boy behind her: "Do you really want me to beat the crap out of you?" Dismissed in my field notes as pig tailed bravado, the incident took on more importance one day later when the little girl did indeed punch the fifth grader in the eye and made him cry. Harkening to the risks involved in merging public and private knowledge, passengers routinely made threats such as, "Don't be messin' with me, I know where you live," to younger, older, and peer boys and girls. Unlike school, No. 21 presented children with opportunities to build relationships—albeit not always positive— across age and gender differences in a mobile environment, free of institutionally imposed age stratification, relatively unmediated by direct adult interference, and defined exclusively by neither school nor home.

POWER POSITIONS

I boarded the bus with an open mind, but I had notions. Interested in seat choice and how this related to the social organization of the bus, I naively assumed that seat choice was singular, made by each rider once per trip. Instead, I found a culture on the move. The school bus, much like Thorne's (1994) findings in an elementary classroom, is a place where "seating and movement are subjects of continual negotiation" (p. 136). Students switch seats at least three times per route. Each time the bus stopped to pick up or deposit a rider, or even paused at a stoplight, at least one rider moved to another seat. Some jockeyed for "better" seats, grabbing the preferred backseats when they became open, or moved away from social pariahs and closer to "cool" kids. However, seats on the school bus are—like culture—not simply up for grabs. Separated by three empty rows of seats, White kids (except for Tina) sat in the front, whereas African American riders (along with other non-White passengers: Hispanic, Latino, Native American, and East Indian children) sat in the back. But on every bus from which I gathered data, African American and other racial/ethnic minority passengers tended to sit in the back third of the bus. By the middle of the year, seating patterns on No. 21 became more integrated, though other sorts of segregation remained. The back section was unequivocally considered teenager territory. Although younger riders sometimes sat there briefly, the social category "backseater" belonged exclusively to teenagers—but not to all teens equally. More girls than boys sat in the back third. African Americans and Hispanic passengers more often than not sat in the back third and/or occupied the very back seat. Mobility is no simple matter.

Social configurations of gender on the school bus also proved to be varied and complex. Unlike Thorne's (1994) findings concerning gender segregation and playgrounds, and Nespor's (1997) observations in school lunchrooms, boys and girls somewhat voluntarily shared space on the bus. In her study, Thorne found that, "On the playground, an area where adults exert minimal control and kids are relatively free to choose their own activities and companions, there is extensive separation by gender" (p. 44). On the school bus (which also is a primarily kid-mediated space that offers riders choice of companions), self-segregation by gender was less prevalent. Broad definitions of space such as front, middle, and back were not divided according to gender. Despite the fact that elementary school riders often boarded the bus in two separate, teacher-supervised lines (one for girls and the other for boys), no section of any bus was labeled girls or boys only, and boys and girls often sat together.

As Foucault (1986) writes: "Space is fundamental in any exercise of power" (p. 252). Subtle and not-so-subtle configurations of race/ethnicity, social class, gender, and age restrict movement, set spatial parameters, and push social boundaries on the bus. However, in the following discussion of how such configurations relate to seating, it is important to consider the mobile context. Situated in time as well as space, the geography of school bus culture quite literally changes shape at every stop.

In positioning seating patterns within the social landscape of school bus culture, I find Thorne's (1994) discussion of social marginalization and the geography of school lines to be a useful foil. At school, particularly elementary school, getting from here to there (lunchroom, playground, etc.) involves lining up (Jackson, 1968; Thorne, 1994). The process of getting to and from school involves similar linear positionings. Passengers queue up to board and unload the bus in a fairly single-file fashion. Furthermore, the actual seating pattern of the bus can be seen as organized into two parallel vertical lines. Thorne's analysis of the process of lining up contrasts the front positions with those in back: "The front of the line is a desired and contested zone. As a reward, the teachers often let a specific child—the 'line leader' or 'goodest one,' as a kindergartner explained— go first …. The back of the line is sometimes defined as the least desired space, even a place of punishment" (p. 41). This distinction is in some ways reversed on the school bus. Although all space on the bus is contested to some degree, the back of the bus is undeniably the most coveted seating space. The front of the bus is far less desirable. Most passengers (myself included) were careful to avoid it.

Passengers who did choose to sit in the front seat did so for complex reasons that intertwined notions of safety, danger, gender, and race. An East Indian middle schooler told me she sat near the front because: "In the backseat they have bad habits." Mel, a White fifth-grade boy, warned me away from the backseat: "Stay up here, back there's cussin' all the time and worse stuff." When I asked Atlantis, a mixed-race junior high girl, about the backseaters, she responded: "Oooh, they're girl perves." The words of these frontseaters construct the back section as a position of unspecified risk. Whereas passengers like Pria, Mel, and Atlantis sit near the front to spatially separate themselves from the "perverted" social influence of backseaters, others sit in the front for physical protection. Second grader Roger avoids the back for this reason: "Not safe—high school, they hit hard." When asked why she never sat in the backseat, fourth grader Unique expresses a similar fear: "My sister and her friends will beat the crap out of me if I go back there." One morning, sitting uncharacteristically up front, former backseaters Jody and Tammy (both in junior high) revealed that they relocated because: "The sexual harassment is bad. Oh yeah, in back it's bad." Considerations of safety—physical and otherwise—position the front section near the driver in opposition to the risky social practices and errant physicality of the mostly African American, adolescent female-mediated backseat.

Yet, the seats farthest in the back of the bus still held great allure for most riders. Passengers scrambled to sit in them, with students typically marginalized at school leading the group (Adler & Adler, 1998; de Marrais & LeCompte, 1999; Fordham, 1993; Thorne, 1994). The back third of the bus generally filled up first, in both the morning and afternoon routes. The seat farthest in the rear was the first pick for nearly all passengers. This behavior runs counter to Thorne's observations about the back section of school lines: "Although generally a devalued space, the back of the line has its uses. During the process of lining up, socially marginal kids often wait to join the line near the end, thereby avoiding the pushing and maneuvering at the front" (p. 41). In contrast to Thorne's analysis, riders push and maneuver themselves in all sorts of ways to position themselves in the very back of the school bus. For several weeks, an enterprising junior high student named Vicki bartered her way to the back by trading band fund-raiser candy. Her brother won his seat scoring cigarettes for youth shelter residents. Other students would let backseaters use their portable CD players or allow them to copy their homework in exchange for the backseat. There was also considerable physical negotiation. Passengers cut in line at the bus stop or pushed their way to the front of the line in order to sit in the rear. You have to board the bus early in order to enjoy backseat privileges, but depending on *who* you are this luxury can be fleeting. Junior high riders who board early were accustomed to relinquishing their hard-won backseats to high school girl backseaters. For example, every afternoon on No. 21, junior high student Eddie surrendered his backseat upon the arrival of his high school-age sister Tonya and her fellow backseat bad-ass, Herkeesha. Such surrender demonstrates how riders put spatial relationships to use in creating and maintaining social boundaries. Further, this seating pattern reflects and reinforces the social hierarchies common to school bus culture, though it represents a slight departure from the social organization typically found in schools, in which African American girls (particularly adolescents) are often marginalized (Adler & Adler, 1998; Adler, Kless, & Adler, 1992; Corsaro, 1997; Thorne, 1994).

Though "back" and "front" are still cogent categories on the bus as well as in school lines, in the mobile, kid-mediated space of the school bus, spatial expressions of marginalization are less linear. On No. 21 as well as on other buses, students such as racial/ethnic minorities, outspoken girls, and adjudicated youth—all of whom are often marginalized in schools—make up the bulk of the backseat population, which enjoys considerable social status within school bus culture (Adler & Adler, 1998; de Marrais & LeCompte, 1999; Fordham, 1993; Thorne, 1994). Unlike the "devalued" rear position in the school lines of which Thorne writes, backseats are hot property in the social geography of the school bus. Although riders sit facing the front, generally it is the back of the bus—defined in opposition to the front seat authority of the driver—that serves as its social center. By positioning themselves in the contested rearward spaces of the bus, passengers on the margins at school move to the center of school bus culture. On No. 21, this central social space was dominated by a group of four "loud," mostly non-White, teenage girls termed by other passengers and themselves "backseat bad-asses" (Fordham, 1993).

BACKSEAT BAD-ASSES

Every bus I rode had a cohesive group of "backseaters." As previously discussed, these are junior high and high school students who sit together in the coveted back section nearly every day for most of each ride, and exhibit the boundary work Adler and Adler (1998) describe as characteristic of cliques:

> Cliques have a hierarchical structure, being dominated by leaders, and are exclusive in nature, so that not all individuals who desire membership are accepted. They function as bodies of power within grades, incorporating the most popular individuals, offering the most exciting social lives, and commanding the most attention. (p. 56)

Both girls and boys occupied the back section of No. 21. However, it was a core group of girls—self-described backseat bad-asses Herkeesha, Sabrina, Tonya, and Tina—that generated and limited the conversations that set and maintained its social and spatial boundaries. All but Tina were African American and lived in the same public housing unit. All but Sabrina, who was in junior high, attended Cimarron High School.

At 18, Herkeesha was the oldest passenger on the bus. She described herself in terms of toughness: "I'm not afraid of anybody. I can kick anybody's ass. The only person I'm scared of is my mother. She can kick my ass. She's done it." Most of the time, Herkeesha looked tough, too. Solidly build and clad in dark colors, Herkeesha smiled only rarely, and did not giggle. Whether clonking a fellow passenger on the head or firing an insult of alarming sharpness directly to this researcher's Achilles' heel, she moved quickly. She moved quicker still in defense of her two younger siblings, who also rode the bus. Her friend Tonya, a 16-year-old high school junior, acted equally tough, though not as convincingly. Tonya was well muscled too, but slower to anger. An avid eye-roller, Tonya described herself as "one laid-back bitch." Although after the announcement of her pregnancy, she often appeared anxious.

Tina, the only White backseat bad-ass, also attended high school. She had lived in the same public housing complex as the other bad-asses, but now—3 years later—lives in an adjacent subdivision. Almost 16 during my research, Tina worked fast food in order to earn money for a car, so she rode the bus only sporadically. The fourth backseat bad-ass was Sabrina, a 14-year-old ninth grader. She also talked about boys: "Too young to be like hangin' with anyone." She says she's "looking around," and look she does. Sabrina is a keen observer and skilled in using her observations wisely to the advantage of the backseaters. She seems to know who is "down" with whom and can gauge—with remarkable accuracy—the mood of the driver. I relied on her observations on multiple occasions. Herkeesha, Tonya, Sabrina, and Tina were the undeniable social center of No. 21. According to Eddie (an African American eighth grader whose older sister is Tonya), "They're like queens or somethin'." And they were. Although these girls functioned as a tight leadership circle, this "clique" differed from those described by Adler and Adler (1998) in several important ways.

Although core-group backseaters commanded the most attention, and to a large degree set social and spatial boundaries on the bus, their popularity was ambiguous. Backseaters were not necessarily popular, and backseat bad-asses were not particularly well liked by other passengers. In fact, most passengers I spoke with used expressions of disgust or fear when referring to backseaters. Terms such as "nasty," "skanky," and "loud bitch" were common descriptors. Riders, however, generally deferred to this exclusive group in seating choice, often gave them treats, and displayed considerable interest in activity they instigated. Yet the all-girl core group of backseaters did not possess or exhibit any of the factors such as high socioeconomic status (SES) and academic performance, appearance, or precocity that Adler et al. (1992) associate with female popularity and leadership.

No. 21's core-group backseaters were not rich or middle class, nor were they considered "pretty" by passengers with whom I spoke. The female entourage—or as Adler and Adler (1998) call them, "wannabes"—who positioned themselves in favorable proximity to the backseat core group, however, were more mixed in terms of social-class affiliation and appearance (p. 81). With elaborately enameled fingernails, multiple strands of gemstone "power bead" bracelets, shimmering eye shadow, and lots of body glitter, the lip-glossed appearance of these "cool followers" stood in contrast to the spartan style of upper-strata backseat girls (Adler & Adler, 1998, p. 81). Remarkably unadorned, core-group backseaters did not adhere to—and in fact separated themselves from—many of the middle-class norms of popular female appearance. They wore, except on rare occasions, no discernible makeup, and their hairstyles demonstrated little fuss.

Like most other riders (male and female), core-group backseaters wore T-shirts, jeans or cargo pants, and tennis shoes on every day that I observed. Unlike other passengers, this core group of backseaters was open about the fact that their clothes came from a local discount store. In fact, they often used the origins of their outfits in rapid-fire verbal play that demarcated conceptions of social-class boundaries, revealing resistance to dominant, generalized conceptions of Gap-obsessed, teenage consumption patterns:

Herkeesha: Yeah, I got these cargoes at Wal-Mart.

Sandra: Yeah, I can tell.

Tonya: Better than all that Hello Kitty crap you buy. I bet when you go to the mall your mother fuckin' spends $200 on Hello Kitty and Abercrombie shit and …

Sabrina: And we're like we do Wal-Mart. So does [points one by one at various male passengers] he, and him, and look at those shoes. Now for fuckin' sure him.
                [Lots of laughter]

Herkeesha: Now, we *are* some poor motherfuckers. But we don't waste all that fuckin' money.

Frequent references to discount shopping and being broke challenge the "glamorous consumption fantasy" whereby youth becomes universally constructed as middle-class brand enslavement (Wulff, 1995, p. 9). Additionally, the unaccessorized appearance of backseat girls resists stereotypical constructions of fashion-crazed femininity (Inness, 1998). When Vicki asked me what my green power bead bracelet "meant" (different "powers" such as romance or intellectual stability are attributed to the type of gemstone beads that make up power bead bracelets), I told her that it was supposed to attract money. The irony was not lost on backseater Sabrina, who commented acerbically: "Looks like you lost in that deal. Spending good money on that power thing."

Backseat bad-asses unraveled conventional notions of female popularity and leadership. Instead of embodying the popularity traits such as high SES, stereotypically pretty appearance, and academic achievement (Adler et al., 1992), backseaters on No. 21 cultivated status through acting tough. Adler et al. discuss toughness as a primarily male attribute involving "displays of physical prowess, athletic skill and belligerence, especially in repartee with peers and adults" (p. 173). The architecture of the school bus severely limits the range of physical displays and makes demonstrations of athletic skill nearly impossible. Consequently, riders conquer school bus space verbally instead of physically. On all buses I rode, backseaters' ability to set social and spatial boundaries was linked to their skill in generating, sustaining, and dominating verbal display and exchange.

Although physical displays such as breath-holding contests were prevalent among particularly younger passengers, tough talk ruled. No. 21's backseat bad-asses entertained, intimidated, and dominated other riders—and sometimes the bus driver—through clever repartee, convincing threats, skillful impersonation, well-timed jokes, venomous insults, and sheer vocal force, which Corsaro (1997) terms "oppositional talk" (p. 146). According to Corsaro, "oppositional talk is playful teasing and confrontational talk that some African American children frequently use to construct social identities, cultivate friendships, and both maintain and transform the social order of their peer cultures" (p. 146). Though I saw children of every race engage in "tough" talk, it was more prevalent in the backseats, and on No. 21 its masters were predominant though not exclusively African American girls. Contrary to studies (see Sadker & Sadker, 1994) that document the silencing of female voices (particularly adolescent female voices) in school, my findings on No. 21 demonstrate the bus to be a discursive space dominated by female voices. Although their oppositional dexterity helped push boundaries of gendered social order by constructing for this group a powerful identity as backseat bad-asses, oppositional talk did not necessarily transform such structures.

For example, take these backseater girls' daily ritual of catcalling out the school bus window to "hot" male college students. Such screaming was against bus rules. As long as there was no swearing, this breach was often tolerated by drivers as harmless fun. Though if the content of the yelling got too "wild," drivers would reprimand: "Settle down, girls." At times, because the driver's hearing was limited by the engine roar, it went unnoticed. Yelling such phrases as, "What's in your jeans, cowboy?" or, "Ooh, I like cowboys. Let me ride your horse," predictably established the all-female, backseat core group as a potent point of attention on No. 21. Though some female passengers were embarrassed by this behavior (particularly Herkeesha's little sister), in general girls enjoyed it and cheered on backseaters. Boys, on the other hand, were not amused. Instead, male passengers expressed indignation in regard to this behavior: "That's disgusting sexual harassment," or, "Yeah, I'd really want to date a girl who yelled at me like that. Loud bitches."

Backseat girls, in employing the discourse of sexual objectification traditionally linked to male privilege, rearranged discursive space on the school bus, regulated male discourse, and disrupted gendered notions of sexual harassment. "Positions of power and powerlessness," writes B. Davies (1993), "are achieved through talk, through social practices and through social and architectural structures" (p. 199). Discursive practices such as the catcalling demonstrate that, although backseat girls make good use of the architectural limitations inherent to school bus space to alter gendered social structures, such alterations do not necessarily represent a wholesale departure from the broader patriarchal landscape of power to which such structures belong.

As their talk reveals, backseat bad-asses did not embody an "egalitarian ethos" often attributed to female solidarity (Thorne, 1994, p. 95). Furthermore, even among themselves, backseat solidarity was slippery. According to riders, members of this powerful and cohesive school bus "clique" did not hang out together at school. Although these four students had ridden the same bus to and from school together for 6 years, they were not, as Tonya put it, "school friends," nor did they often convene socially in their "off time." "Cliques," according to Adler and Adler (1998), "are at their base, friendship circles" (p. 56). As a mobile intersection in social space, the school bus demonstrates that the dense social configurations that compose youth culture are not necessarily static: Boundaries travel, circles change shape, and power coagulates in contradictory ways.

School bus routes and its riders regulate geographical relations and reconfigure the spatial relations of social bodies. New propinquities, situated in space and time, take hold. L. Davies (1984) remarks in this regard: "Children … see proximity, or being with someone, as the first and basic element of friendships" (p. 68). The inherent instability of school bus populations turns proximity plural. The distribution of embarking, disembarking, and seat-switching passengers gives rise to contradictory social mobility.

On the bus, social and spatial relations swirl. No. 21's backseat bad-asses are undeniably "tight." Though it might be thought of as a sphere of temporary coherence, Herkeesha, Tonya, Tina, and Sabrina form a formidable social circle whose bus-time boundaries are maintained spatially, as these backseaters use tough talk to put literal space between themselves and other riders, and to separate themselves from the authority of the driver. However, outside of the bus, the circle does not necessarily hold. Neither does its backseat authority.

MOBILE POWER STRUCTURES AND RESISTANCE IN-TRANSIT

Though this study looks at school bus culture as a fluid transitional space between school and home, as Zukin (1991) writes concerning liminality, "these transitions are not completely fluid situations" (p. 29). By regulating the flow of bodies to and from school sites, school bus routes operate spatially, temporally, and socially as a "technology of power" that reflects and reinforces existing social orders while working simultaneously to produce new ones (Foucault, 1986, p. 252). Such technologies of power engaged in the processes of "regulating the relations of time, bodies, and forces" (Foucault, 1977, p. 157) link the process of school transportation with the broader project of schooling, which employs similar technologies in order to regulate student bodies—particularly female bodies (Inness, 1998; Sadker & Sadker, 1994), and more particularly, girls of color (Dietrich, 1998). Such regulation is inextricably bound to historically, politically, and socially produced constructions of gender. Though school bus culture navigates the "neither" regions betwixt and between school and home and their concomitant, disciplining and normalizing practices, it does not entirely detour the structural realities of the social landscape it travels. Much like Foucault's (1977) Panopticon, the school bus can be seen as "a type of location of bodies in space, of distribution of individuals in relation to one another, of hierarchical organization, of disposition of centres and channels of power" (p. 205). Which bus kids ride—as well as when and where they catch it—situates school bus culture spatially, temporally, and socially. So do seating patterns. Linking the spatial and the social, Massey (1998) writes in reference to the spatial relations of youth culture: "All these relations which construct space, since they are social relations, are always in one way or another imbued with power" (p. 125). Backseat bad-asses used acting tough— their skill at direct verbal conflict—in lieu of collaborative language to reinforce enduringly hierarchical rather than communal backseat boundaries (Thorne, 1994). Yet, acting tough on the school bus means talking tough— in ways that push the boundaries of (resist) normative constructions of adolescent femininity. Backseat bad-asses demonstrate school bus culture to be permeated with power, forming and re-forming itself into mobile power structures and resistance-in-transit.

The tough talk of the predominantly African American, adolescent, fully female, working-class power quadrangle that drove No. 21's backseat scene call background to the foreground, and cause gendered generalizations to swerve. Resisting prevalent "peer culture" approaches to the social lives of girls, research on No. 21 demonstrates the social lives of girls to be "fractured along numerous lines of difference constitutive of overlapping and multiple forms of otherness" (Philo, 1992, p. 201, quoted in Valentine, Skelton, & Chambers, 1998, p. 7). In his later work on liminality, Turner (1977) talks about the transformative power of such fracture. Turner writes about liminoid/liminal phenomena as natural breaks in the sociocultural processes that develop most characteristically along the margins of central political processes. Although, as he adds: Liminal "ideas and images may seep from these peripheries, and cornices into the center" (p. 44). Liminal phenomena, as Turner describes them "are not merely recursive, they are often subversive, representing radical critiques of the central structures" (pp. 44–45). Likewise, positioned betwixt and between school and home, backseat bad-asses—although they function in some ways to reinscribe normative gender constructions—simultaneously embody a radical critique of those constructions. Fractured along numerous lines of differences, backseat bad-asses demonstrate a liminal girl power that is "plural, fragmentary and experimental" (Turner, 1977, p. 44).

The mostly kid-mediated, age-integrated, and female-led culture on the school bus travels "neither" regions. Positioned betwixt and between school and home, the bus is a mobile threshold where multiple social meanings relevant to the lives of passengers overlap and congregate. Such intersections challenge common oppositions between private and public space, curricular and extracurricular time, and safety and danger, while carving out a dense space *in between* from which contemporary educational debate about the lives of girls (particularly though not exclusively adolescent girls) might more profitably position itself. Dominated to a large degree by female adolescent voices, backseat bad-asses demonstrate the school bus to be a space/time of pluralistic power, and a vehicle of contradictory possibility. Such spaces challenge educators to reexamine school spaces in order to "discern what defines, marks, separates and joins this space to surrounding structures and social formations" that might provide more positive and powerful positions for girls and boys (Fine, Weis, Centrie, & Roberts, 2000, p. 133). Situated on a mobile threshold, backseat bad-asses navigate among and between landmark notions of gender, in order to deconstruct and reconstruct (make multiple meanings of) the landscape of their lives. Discussions of gender and schooling might benefit from similar ventures between the boundaries of binary construction and into riskier, liminal zones of reconstruction, where the multiplicities of girls' lives collide.

DISCUSSION QUESTIONS

1. Liminal phenomena, as Turner (1977) describes them, are "not merely recursive, they are often subversive, representing radical critiques of the central structures" (pp. 44–45). In what ways do the backseat bad-asses represent radical critique? What social structures do they critique?

2. This chapter describes the school bus as a "risky liminal zone." In what ways in the school bus risky? It what ways might it actually be "safer" than school? For whom? What could be done to make the bus a "safer" place for boys and girls?

3. This chapter challenges educators to reexamine school spaces in order to "discern what defines, marks, separates and joins this space to surrounding structures and social formations" that might provide more positive and powerful positions for girls and boys (Fine et al., 2000, p. 133). In what ways do the social practices of the school bus merge with those of school? In what ways does school bus culture diverge? How

might the "extracurriculum" of the school bus relate to the formal and hidden curriculum in schools today?

REFERENCES

Adler, P., & Adler, P. (1998). *Peer power: Preadolescent culture and identity*. New Brunswick, NJ: Rutgers University Press.

Adler, P., Kless, S., & Adler, P. (1992). Socialization to gender roles: Popularity among elementary school boys and girls. *Sociology of Education, 65*, 169–187.

Bushweller, K. (1997). 21st century garage. *American School Board Journal, 184*(11), 37–39.

Childress, H. (2000). *Landscapes of betrayal, landscapes of joy: Curtisville in the lives of its teenagers*. Albany: State University of New York Press.

Corsaro, W. (1997). *The sociology of childhood*. Thousand Oaks, CA: Pine Forge Press.

Davies, B. (1993). *Shards of glass: Children reading and writing beyond gendered identities*. Cresskill, NJ: Hampton Press.

Davies, L. (1984). *Pupil power: Deviance and gender in school*. London: Falmer Press.

Davis, C. (1998). *Step by step: Cimarron Public Schools annual report*. Cimarron: Cimarron Public Schools.

de Certeau, M. (1984). *The practice of everyday life*. Berkeley: University of California Press.

de Marrais, K. & LeCompte, M. (1999) *The way schools work: A sociological analysis of education*. New York: Longman.

DeBruyn, R. L. (1985). *About our schools*. Topeka, KS: The Master Teacher.

Dietrich, L. (1998). *Chicana adolescents: Bitches, 'ho's, and schoolgirls*. Wesport, CT: Praeger.

Fine, G., & Sandstrom, K. (1988). *Knowing children: Participant observation with minors*. Newbury Park, CA: Sage.

Fine, M., & Weis, L., Centrie, C., & Roberts, R. (2000). Educating beyond the borders of schooling. *Anthropology & Education Quarterly, 21*(2), 131–151.

Fordham, S. (1993). "Those loud black girls": (Black) women, silence, and gender "passing" in the academy. *Anthropology of Education Quarterly, 24*(1), 3–32.

Foucault, M. (1977). *Discipline and punish*. New York: Vintage Books.

Foucault, M. (1986). Of other spaces. *Diacritics, 16*(1), 22–27.

Fox, M. (1996). Rural school transportation as a daily constraint in students' lives. *Rural Educator, 17*(2), 22–27.

Holman, C. H., & Harmon, W. (1992). *A handbook to literature*. New York: Macmillan.

Huffman, B. (1999). Relating to the general public. *School Transportation News, IX*(12), 6, 17.

Inness, S. (1998). *Millennium girls: Today's girls around the world*. Lanham, MD: Rowman & Littlefield.

Jackson, P. (1968). *Life in classrooms*. Chicago: Holt, Rinehart & Winston.

Martin, M. (1999). Public awareness: It's not going to drive itself. *School Bus Fleet, 45*(4), 55–56.

Massey, D. (1998). The spatial construction of youth cultures. In T. Skelton & G. Valentine (Eds.), *Cool places: Geographies of youth cultures* (pp. 121–129). London: Routledge.

Nespor, J. (1997). *Tangled up in school*. Mahwah, NJ: Lawrence Erlbaum Associates.

Nespor, J. (2000). School field trips and the curriculum of public spheres. *Journal of Curriculum Studies, 23*(1), 25–43.

Sadker, M., & Sadker, D. (1994). *Failing at fairness: How America's schools cheat girls*. New York: Scribner's.

School bus safety: Safe passage for America's children. (2000, April). *School Bus Journal*.

Sibley, D. (1995). *Geographies of exclusion*. London: Routledge.

Thomas, P. (1984). *Driver behavior and motivation*. Paper presented at the annual meeting of the Association of School Business Officials (70th), Atlantic City, NJ.

Thorne, B. (1994). *Gender play: Girls and boys in school*. New Brunswick, NJ: Rutgers University Press.

Turner, V. (1967). *The forest of symbols*. Ithica, NY: Cornell University Press.

Turner, V. (1977). Variations on a theme of liminality. In S. Moore & B. Meyerhoff (Eds.), *Secular ritual* (pp. 36–52). Amsterdam: Vangorcum.

Valentine, G., Skelton, T., & Chambers, D. (1998). Cool places: An introduction to youth and youth cultures. In T. Skelton & G. Valentine (Eds.), *Cool places: Geographies of youth cultures* (pp. 1–32). London: Routledge.

Van Maanen, J. (1988). *Tales of the field. On writing ethnography*. Chicago: University of Chicago Press.

Wulff, H. (1995). Introducing youth culture in its own right: The state of the art and new possibilities. In V. Amit-Yalai & H. Wulff (Eds.), *Youth cultures: A cross-cultural perspective* (pp. 1–18). London: Routledge.

Zukin, S. (1991). *Landscapes of power: From Detroit to Disney World*. Berkeley: University of California Press.

Part II

AT SCHOOL

Chapter 4

Girl Talk: Adolescent Girls'[1] Perceptions of Leadership

Dawn M. Shinew
Deborah Thomas Jones
Washington State University

"What are you guys doing this for?"

"We are looking at how fifth graders identify the qualities of a leader and we're writing a book chapter about what you think about leaders."

"Cool."

In a sociopolitical climate in which the public discourse of power is dominated by military strength and capital interests, we posed a seemingly simple question to more than 140 fifth-grade students in an urban, impoverished school district: "What does it mean to be a good leader?" The girls we surveyed and with whom we spoke were intrigued by our interest in what they had to say, as well as our intention to share their experiences with others. Their responses to the aforementioned question, as well as to que-

---

[1]Like A. Jones (1993), we recognize *girls* as a problematic term in that it has "obscured class and 'race' oppressions and privileges through overlooking their specificity and uneven expression in girls' everyday lives" (p. 157). As Jones suggests we simultaneously use and reject the term, and follow Yates' (1990) lead in working from the questions "Where and how is it helpful to treat girls as a single category? and Where and how is it important to focus on differences among girls?" (cited in A. Jones, 1993, p. 40). For the purpose of this chapter, we have chosen to focus on girls as a single category, while recognizing the limitations of such a class-free, race-free label.

55

ries regarding peers they identified as good leaders and whether or not they perceived themselves as leaders, provided the data for the study presented in this chapter. Participants' words and experiences serve as the basis for narrative vignettes that integrate verbatim quotes, as well as fictional elements in order to provide a rich context for analyzing and generating a new discourse on the meanings of leadership.

Whereas a great deal of research has been done on leadership among adults, not much is known about leadership from the perspective of children (Edwards, 1994). This lack of literature is particularly notable in terms of the ways in which girls construct meanings of leadership and the spaces in which they identify themselves and others as leaders. Open-ended survey responses from this ethnically, racially, and linguistically diverse group offered an interesting challenge to the notion that leadership "describes a relationship occupying a discursive space somewhere beyond persuasion, only slightly short of force" (K. Jones, 1996, p. 75).

The vast majority of the girls who participated in the study focused on informal (unofficial and not elected) leadership roles (Edwards, 1994) and described a "good" leader in feminine terms (Bernard, 1981). They ascribed qualities quite different from the characteristics that frequently dominate definitions of leadership, such as official, knowledgeable, decisive, and compelling (K. Jones, 1996). Data from both the initial surveys and follow-up interviews with 37 girls also challenged previous research in which Morris (1991) found that adolescents ranked compassion, consistency, and flexibility among the lowest in a leadership traits inventory, as well as Crockett, Losoff, and Peterson's (1984) study in which sixth through eighth graders identified personality, dominance, popularity, and physical appearance as key factors in children's perceptions of leaders (K. Jones, 1996).

The disjuncture between the spaces in which these fifth-grade girls construct their identities of (and as) leaders and the landscape upon which masculine definitions of leadership have traditionally been built illuminates a place in which boundaries "define who belongs to a place and who may be excluded" (McDowell, 1999, p. 4). This study challenges these boundaries and creates a more flexible space—one in which the concept of leadership, including how and where it is demonstrated, is contested and re-visioned. We use the constructions of these early-adolescent girls to interrogate the gendered nature in which leadership is often defined, as well as the extent to which their understandings challenge the "mechanics of power" and how or why "one may have a hold over others' bodies, not only so that they may do what one wishes, but so that they may operate as one wishes, with the techniques, the speed, and the efficiency that one determines" (Foucault, 1979, p. 29). As suggested by A. Jones (1993), the uneasy union between "feminist scholarship and poststructuralist thought provides new possibilities for understanding girls' socialization, or the 'production of girls,' in ways which go beyond seeing girls primarily as 'disadvantaged' and socialized within oppressive patriarchal structures" (p. 157, citing Bordo, 1992).

METHODOLOGY

As is the case for all of the chapters in this book, this project is grounded in the field. Teachers and students from two elementary schools in a large, urban, "high-need" school district in the Pacific Northwest agreed to participate in the study. The student population of these schools is culturally and ethnically diverse, with nearly three quarters of the students at or below the poverty level. Given the White, privileged, male hegemony of leadership, we were particularly interested in how girls in this context constructed identities of/as leaders.

Participants were recruited from fifth-grade classrooms. In the initial phase of the study, the fifth-grade teachers distributed a survey in which students were asked to define the qualities of a good leader, identify peers in their classrooms who were good leaders, and explain why. Unlike studies in which children were given leadership traits inventories (see Crockett et al., 1984; Morris, 1991), this survey was open-ended and encouraged students to generate their own language to describe and define leadership. We received 143 responses to the surveys. The survey data were analyzed to identify common themes. In addition, within each class, the girls most frequently "nominated" as a leader by their peers were identified.

Seventy-three follow-up interviews were conducted with the "elected leaders," as well as with participants who had identified these individuals. The interview questions focused on expanding our understanding of their constructions of leaders, exploring their perceptions of themselves as leaders, and identifying contexts in which they believe leadership is demonstrated. Interviews were audiotaped and transcribed verbatim. In addition, the study draws on observational data collected over a 3-year period in which we have been involved in a school–university partnership with these schools. During these years, we have conducted additional research on the ways in which White, middle-class, heterosexual preservice teachers shape and reshape their identities and those of their students as they complete practicum and student teaching experiences with diverse, low-socioeconomic-status students. This research focus resulted in hundreds of hours of observations in classrooms and school contexts.

Data were analyzed using a variation of the constant-comparative method (Strauss & Corbin, 1990). As a framework for all of the data developed, we used a "postmodern constant-comparative method" (Shinew, 2001). Unlike the constant-comparative method of analysis posited by Glaser and Strauss (1967), in which data are broken down into discrete parts and then compared with other "units" of data to create categories, this process involved keeping the data intact and juxtaposing pieces of theoretical literature against the discussion to add other layers to the discourse. This strategy supports Richardson's (1994) rejection of one dimension: "Rather, the central image is the crystal, which combines symmetry and substance with an infinite variety of shapes, substances, transmutations, multi-dimensionalities, and angles of approach" (p. 522). The data, with leadership as the crystal, was not intended to provide a clear (we would argue flat) representation. Instead, the process was intended to portray the extent to which constructions of leadership change based on where and who we are, as well as the moment in which the image is captured.

These data served as the basis for narrative vignettes (Heilman, 1998) or stories (Goodson, 1998). These vignettes are grounded in the data, but also include fictional elements. The vignettes intentionally blur the boundaries between "facts" and "fictions." The integration of verbatim quotes from the data and fictional elements creates a richer understanding of the context of participants' lives. This space between fact and fiction also represents a place in which data can be seen and understood from a variety of interpretations. As Gough (1998) notes, "fact and fiction are much closer, both culturally and linguistically, than ... narrative strategies imply." Likewise, Tierney (1997) suggests, "As we explore the epistemological no-man's land between factual realism and fiction we will enrich our ways to explain the worlds we study, interpret and create" (p. 31). The literature is layered on the vignettes to produce a discursive text. If, as Foucault (1991) suggests, knowledge and power are generated through discourse, the elements of this process need to be clearly illustrated.

Although constructing narrative vignettes or stories from the data is not yet conventional in educational research, Eisner (1993) suggests, "The battle that once ensued to secure a place for qualitative research in education has largely been won.... Now the question turns to just what it is that different forms of representation employed within the context of educational research might help us grasp" (cited in Kvale, 1997, p. 270). Eisner's statement is not about the "mental representation" of cognitive science, but "the process of transforming the contents of consciousness into a public form so that they can be stabilized, inspected, edited, and shared with others" (cited in Kvale, 1997, p. 271).

The two vignettes and discussions included in this chapter are not an exhaustive representation of the issues, or even the data. Instead, they have been selected because of the perspectives they bring and their contribution to understanding leadership in contradictory and, we hope, compelling ways. One vignette describes one of the girls most frequently nominated by her peers as a leader from the perspective of one of her "nominators." Jessica, a pseudonym, was a straightforward, confident 11-year-old. Her teacher was somewhat surprised that she had been identified as a "leader" by so many of her peers because she was not an out-standing student. Instead, however, the girls who described Jessica as a leader focused on the extent to which Jessica made sure "people were treated fairly" and her role in negotiating the complicated social circles of the class. Her slight build concealed the power of her personality and the respect she commanded from others.

The second vignette portrays Britney, a girl who identified herself as a leader, though none of her peers had recognized her as such. At 12, she was physically more mature and heavier than many of her peers. Britney took great care to ensure that her clothes, hair, and the small amount of makeup her mother allowed her to wear, were perfect. Britney was described by her teacher as a "quiet" student who could easily go unnoticed by both the adults and students in the classroom.

Both girls lived in the neighborhood surrounding their schools. The streets are lined with small houses and a few multifamily dwellings. Although many of the houses are dilapidated and in need of repair, every fifth or sixth house is neatly kept with a nice garden. The neighborhood, one of the poorest in the district, has been in transition for the past 10 years and has seen an increase in drug and gang activity. The school population also represents one of the most transient in the state, with many families moving in an out of the district throughout students' lives. Students' lives in these schools are what one of the principals once described as "harder than most adults would ever be able to bear." As researchers, we were particularly interested in how girls in this context identify themselves and others as leaders.

LEADERSHIP AS COMPASSION

The screen door slammed behind Jessica as she ran out of the house. "Jessica, I told you a million times not the slam that door!" Her grandmother's words floated out into the small, green front yard but were barely audible by the time they reached Jessica and Aisha on the sidewalk. A school bus passed and drowned the last echo of the reprimand. Aisha smiled at her companion who was still chewing the banana that she'd shoved in her mouth as she exited the house.

Aisha felt grateful that Jessica walked with her to school. As a new student in the school, Aisha felt overwhelmed by what seemed to be a strange and hostile environment. Her teacher, an experienced veteran with nearly 30 years of experience in the classroom, ran a pretty tight ship. In their fifth-grade classroom, Mrs. Gabriel made sure students knew what was expected. On her first day, Aisha felt Mrs. Gabriel's firm, but gentle, hand on her shoulder as the teacher's soft, reassuring voice said, "I know it's hard to be the new student, Aisha. But in no time, I'm sure you'll make lots of new friends." Aisha wanted to believe her, but felt much less confident when she left the security of the classroom, and Mrs. Gabriel's knowing eyes.

Aisha met Jessica on that first day. At recess, several girls gathered around Aisha and started asking her questions. When Aisha mentioned the name of her previous school, one of the girls responded, "I've heard about that school. Only 'ho's go to that school." Aisha felt her face getting hot. She turned her eyes downward and wished she could disappear. The silence that seemed to beg for her response felt oppressive, especially because no words found their way through her throat.

Suddenly, a soft, but confident, voice broke in, "You don't know nothin', Monika. You haven't even heard of that school before." The small circle that had gathered around Aisha and Monika parted as Jessica continued. "Come on," she said to Aisha, "let's go jump rope."

"Ah, Jessica, I was just teasin' her," Monika retorted, slightly hurt. Aisha fell in at Jessica's side. "Don't mind Monika," Jessica explained as they made their way across the blacktopped playground. "She just like to get on new girls. Don't worry. I got your back if she gives you a bad time."

Since that first day, Aisha noticed that, though Jessica was not the prettiest or most popular girl in the class, she seemed to be accepted and liked by nearly everyone. More than once in the past couple of weeks, Aisha had seen Jessica defend other students, help them in class, include others in play, and scold classmates for teasing or bullying. Jessica was assertive but not bossy. She often used the language modeled by Mrs. Gabriel. As the girls approached the redbrick elementary school, they passed a group of fourth graders. "You gonna be late if you don't get a move on," admonished Jessica.

"Yeah? Who put you in charge?" replied the smallest of the girls, sticking out her tongue? "I did." And you are lucky that she is, thought Aisha.

A great deal has been written about "meanness," cliques, and competition among girls (Adler, 1995; Eder, 1990; Hughes, 1988; Merten, 1997). Although this study focused on the qualities of leadership, participants often identified leaders as those who were successful in negotiating, or helping others to navigate the complex, and sometimes conflicting, relationships among the girls in their class. Unlike the earlier work of Crockett et al. (1984), these girls seemed less concerned with the "popularity" of their leaders than with their leader's ability to advocate for and defend others (students new to the school, students who have low academic performance, students with difficulties at home, etc.). Teachers confirmed that six of the seven leaders identified by the largest number in each class were not necessarily those they would consider most "popular" among their peers. Instead, teachers referred to the girls most frequently identified as leaders as "compassionate" and "caring."

In the initial surveys, girls used terms and phrases such as "respectful," "treats people the way she wants to be treated," "kind-hearted," "helpful to others," and "listens to what other people have to say" to describe their nominees. In the interviews, one of the girls most frequently identified as a leader by her peers concluded, "I guess people think I'm a leader because I'm a good listener, um, not like just sitting there but, like being interested in what people think." Similarly, Aisha explained that Jessica did not just stick up for her, but for others as well. "If someone was making fun of another person's grades, she would try to help that person get their grades up and if it didn't work then she would just help the other person who was making fun of that person and try to tell them that, try to make them understand that it's not easy having good grades."

To a large extent, this theme can be dismissed as girls assuming traditional gendered roles as caregivers and nurturers—societal scripts that are written upon girls. Carter (1987), for example, suggests that children develop fairly rigid gender conceptualizations beginning in preadolescent years that develop into societal scripts by early adolescence. Such conclusions, however, fail to recognize that girls often both reside in and resist these societal scripts. Bird (1992) describes primary classrooms in New Zealand in which girls assume positions of power by taking on the authority of the teacher. Girls' power in the classroom, she notes, stems from their identification with the female teachers and their knowledge of the rules. Likewise, the girls interviewed in this study expressed a simultaneous understanding that they were expected to be "nice" to others and that, in doing so, it brought a certain recognition and sense of power among their peers.

Similarly, some feminists argue that the power of care as a leadership quality is underestimated. Tronto (1996) asserts that care is often rejected as part of the discourse on power and politics because it is seen as "prepolitical," "apolitical," and/or "above" politics. Tracing the first argument to Aristotle, she notes that care was among the "things that the statesmen must take for granted … (and) contribute in a preliminary way to the end of living a good life, which is the (real) concern of the political realm" (p. 140). Aristotle also considered care apolitical in that it was part of the domain of the woman and the household. "For Aristotle," Tronto explains, "the household cannot be part of political life because it necessarily involves relationships among superiors [the care receiver] and inferiors [the caregivers] rather than relationships among equals or potential equals" (p. 140). Aristotle concluded, then, "there is something inherent in banausic and domestic duties, in care activities, that makes someone who engages in them incapable of political life" (p. 141) or leadership.

Care is also often excluded from politics and leadership because it is considered "above" politics or some kind of "ideal." Tronto notes that positioning care as something above what is needed to lead means "those who routinely engage in altruistic, other-regarding acts are excluded from proper inclusion in the political world by their innocence and gullibility. [It is assumed] they will not know how to act when political action requires violence or coercion" (p. 141).

Fisher and Tronto (1990) suggest that care be redefined as a political concept, as "a species activity that includes everything that we do to maintain, continue, and repair 'our' world so that we can live in it as well as possible" (p. 40). Such a redefinition opens new possibilities for contesting boundaries that separate the personal from the public, care from politics, and feminine approaches to leadership from more traditional, masculine visions.

LEADERSHIP AS TALENT

Britney closed her eyes as she felt the music swell within her. She smiled. She loved the way she could feel the music from the ends of her long, dark ponytail to the tips of her tap shoes. Britney could tell that not all of the kids felt the music the way she did. For her, the musical notes were as natural as air. She breathed them in and let them fill her insides. She tried to be humble about her musical talents because she knew it wasn't polite to brag about things. Her mama told her people wouldn't like it if she started thinking she was better than anyone else. Britney laughed a little when she thought about her mama's concern that she not become "big headed." Most of the time, she felt awkward and ugly. Her frizzy hair was pulled into a ponytail so it didn't wind around and cover her face. Her developing breasts were slightly smaller than the bulge that emerged beneath them.

She knew she wasn't beautiful on the outside, still, Britney felt special when she was doing something involved with music. Just yesterday, the dance class had choreographed a new dance and everybody had voted for her to be the leader. Several of the girls in the class had whispered, "She has good ideas." Although their voices had been hushed, Britney had heard the compliment and felt proud. These girls were also in her class from school and there they didn't pay much attention to her. Sometimes they called her "fatty" and made fun her. She tried not to let their teasing affect her. She knew that, at least here, she had something to offer that the other girls didn't.

It was the same way in the church choir. The first time the director had asked her to sing in the youth choir, she was surprised. Britney loved to sing, but she'd never considered whether or not she was any good at it. Soon after she joined, she was singing solos, even though she was one of the youngest in the group. She remembered the first time one of the older girls had stopped her after rehearsal and asked what she thought about a new song. Britney felt the older girl waiting for her response and realized what she thought really seemed to matter to this older, middle school student.

"Imagine that," thought Britney as her feet started tapping out a complicated rhythm. "I don't get really good grades and I don't talk much at school but I'm still a good leader."

Heilman (1998) notes, "Postmodern theories of identity reject the concept of a stable self, and this seems particularly relevant for adolescent girls. For postmodern theorists, the self is understood as something fluid and changing, depending on the changing circumstances or discourse mode" (p. 189). Britney identified herself as a leader in the initial survey, though she was not nominated by anyone else in her class. When asked to explain why she thought she was a good leader, she described her talents in dance and choir. Britney was quick to make distinctions between her identity as a leader in dance class and the church choir and her identity as the "fat girl" at school. Whereas Britney exerted her leadership skills in one context, in her "other" life she demonstrated a struggle for self-definition in a world in which women are defined as passive objects (de Beauvoir, 1953).

Although none of the girls participating in the study identified physical appearance as a quality for being a good leader, Britney was quick to note this to be one of the reasons that she wasn't considered to be a leader by her peers. Though not extremely overweight, Britney's identity as a singer and dancer seemed to make her especially vulnerable to messages from the media about body image. Kilbourne (1995) notes, "Adolescents are particularly vulnerable because they are new and inexperienced consumers and are the prime targets of many advertisements" (cited in Heilman, 1998). Britney's notebook was covered with pictures of models, actresses, and singers. When asked to choose a pseudonym, a huge smile crossed her face as she squealed, "Britney!" (A scantily clad Britney Spears pictured on her notebook seemed smug with satisfaction.) An American Association of University Women Study (1991) noted that girls were most likely to prioritize the way they look—how closely they mirror the images that greet them on television, in magazines, and in movies. For Britney, this was part of her truth, but not all of it. While she talked about clothes, hair, and makeup, she seemed to embrace and reject their importance at the same time. She acknowledged her desire to "be" Britney, and then later mentioned that not all singers are "skinny." "Opera singers are really fat, well some of them are, and people still really look up to them."

Britney's identities as talented leader and unattractive outcast provided an interesting conflict. The fluidity of her identity marks the complexity of being female in a postmodern world—a world in which girls' identities are written and contested simultaneously. The sense of power and leadership Britney identified came from the interactions between her self and her talents, as well as her self and others. "Power must be understood as phenomena that exist dynamically and in relation to each other.... Power can only meaningfully be understood as something that happens in relation—in a girl's relation to herself or in her relationships with others" (Heilman, 1998, p. 199). Britney's sense of authority and power came both from within herself, and her understanding of her talent, and from the recognition she received from others because of these abilities.

DISPUTED SPACES

Whereas much of what has been studied and taught about leadership has been based on the experiences of White males (Fennell, 1999), researchers from various disciplines have argued "for studying leadership through women's eyes and experience, and through more than one perspective and lens" (p. 254). Gosetti and Rusch (1995) posit, "Multiple lenses help us focus in more than one way on how we view a concept like leadership and increase our chances of bringing embedded notions into view" (p. 14).

For children, and perhaps particularly for girls, considering leadership from multiple perspectives is essential if we are to gain insight into their experiences. Much of the formal curriculum related to leadership focuses on formal models of leadership, such as democratic education, conflict resolution, and academic excellence. Although some of these models were in place in the schools in which this study was conducted, the girls were more likely to identify themselves and others as informal leaders. "The distinction between formal leadership, in which the individual is either appointed or elected to a designated position of leadership, and informal leadership, in which individuals do not fill a formal role but are widely recognized as leaders among their peers, is significant" (Edwards, 1994, p. 920). Edwards cites a study conducted by Eagly and Johnson (1990) in which they found no evidences of differences between genders in the styles of formal leaders, but found significant differences in gender in the styles of people not selected for formal leadership roles.

When asked to talk about when and where they or others demonstrated the qualities of leadership, few of the participants focused on formal leadership positions resulting from academic skills and/or classroom behavior and responsibilities (as was frequently predicted by their teachers). Most of the spaces in which girls recognized leadership were in between their lives in the classrooms. The girls who talked about Jessica's leadership consistently described situations in the moments to and from school, on the playground, in the hallways, and, almost always, away from the supervision of adults. When asked, Jessica recognized her role in "taking care of people" when "teachers or whatever" weren't available.

For Britney, her construction of herself as a leader came from her talent for singing and dancing. Again, in neither of these contexts was she "elected" to lead. Instead, she concluded that her recognition from her peers in these spaces came through an unspoken agreement that she could make the group "look and sound" better because of her talents. When asked if she considered herself a leader at her school, Britney shook her head, almost violently, to the contrary. "No, I don't talk much in school. I'm kind of quiet and I just try to do my own work and stay out of trouble." It was in the hours after school, during choir practice and dance class, as well as on

Sunday mornings that Britney's visions of herself leading others, even girls who were older than she, were allowed to flourish.

Sibley (1995) describes boundaries from "the point of view of groups and individuals who erect boundaries but also of those who suffer or whose lives are constrained as a result of their [boundaries'] existence" (p. 32). For the girls surveyed and interviewed in this study, the spaces in which they identified themselves and others as leaders are often located in what Sibley would refer to as "zones of ambiguity in spatial and social categorizations" (p. 33). Their identities as leaders reside in the intersections between the regulated spaces of the classroom and the unsupervised spaces of the hallways, playground, and sidewalks to and from school; in the spaces between school and church; in the tensions between the concepts of formal and informal leaders; and, most important, in the zone of ambiguity between adult and child.

K. Jones (1996) suggests that leadership has been gendered in Western discourse in a way that recognizes only a stable, masculine vision of authority. Those looking for such leadership in these fifth-grade classrooms would fail to see the ways in which Jessica's quiet, compassionate, nurturing manner provides guidance for many of the girls her class, and would not recognize the fluidity of Brittany's identity as "fat girl" and "leader." As we look for ways to develop leaders among our girls and women, A. Jones (1993) provides us with some words of wisdom: "It seems to us that a discursive construction of women and girls as powerful, as producing their own subjectivities *within and against* the 'spaces' provided *is* useful in offering more possibilities for women and girls to develop and use a wider range of practices" (p. 164).

REFLECTIONS AND CONCLUSIONS

This study offered a valuable opportunity to meet adolescent girls in the spaces in which they construct and live out their lives and identities as leaders, and followers. We approached this space with the assumption that identity is contested and fluid. Instead of imposing the hegemonic definitions of leadership on to participants' lives, we encouraged them to construct and use their own language and understandings of what it means to be a leader. Their emphasis on informal leadership roles and more feminine definitions of what it means to be a good leader implies that much of the formal curriculum and language used to cultivate leadership among these groups fails to resonate with their lived experiences. This disjuncture demonstrates yet another space in which these adolescent girls' lives and the roles that are scripted for them differ. Listening to their "girl talk" about leadership opens new possibilities for understanding leadership, and power, in more interesting and complicated ways.

DISCUSSION QUESTIONS

1. Take a few moments to think about "leaders" that are portrayed in the media. What do these leaders have in common with one another? (You may want to consider race, class, gender, and other issues of identity.) What do these leaders have in common with the adolescent girls described in this chapter? What impact might these similarities and differences have on the girls' understanding of leadership?

2. Based on the findings presented in this chapter, what kind of leadership curriculum would you develop that might provide a more inclusive model of leadership and power? What would be the advantages and disadvantages of a broader discussion of leadership?

3. The authors of this chapter operate on the assumption that challenging the hegemony of leadership and power leads to positive results. What arguments could be made for encouraging these, and other, adolescent girls to embrace more traditional models of leadership?

REFERENCES

Adler, P. (1995). Dynamics of inclusion and exclusion in preadolescent cliques. *Social Psychology Quarterly, 58*, 145–162.

American Association of University Women. (1991). *Shortchanging girls, shortchanging America: Executive summary*. Washington, DC: Author.

Bernard, J. (1981). *The female world*. New York: The Free Press.

Bird, L. (1992). Girls and positions of authority at primary schools. In S. Middleton & A. Jones (Eds.), *Women and education in Aotearoa* (Vol. 2., pp. 149–168). Wellington, New Zealand: Bridget Williams Books.

Carter, B. D. (1987). *Current conceptions of sex roles and stereotyping: Theory and research*. New York: Praeger.

Crockett, L., Losoff, M., & Peterson, J. (1984). Perceptions of the peer group in early adolescence. *Journal of Early Adolescence, 4*, 15–18.

de Beauvoir, S. (1953). *The second sex* (H. M. Pashley, Trans.). New York: Knopf.

Eagly, A., & Johnson, B. (1990). Gender and leadership style: A meta-analysis. *Psychological Bulletin, 108*, 233–256.

Eder, D. (1990). Serious and playful disputes: Variation in conflict talk among female adolescents. *Sociology of Education, 58*, 154–165.

Edwards, C. A. (1994). Leadership in groups of school-age girls. *Developmental Psychology, 30*(6), 920–927.

Fennell, H. (1999). Feminine faces of leadership: Beyond structural-functionalism? *Journal of School Leadership, 9*, 254–285.

Fisher, B., & Tronto, J. (1990). Toward a feminist theory of caring. In E. Abel & M. Nelson (Eds.), *Circles of care: Work and identity in women's lives* (pp. 35–62). Albany: State University of New York Press.

Foucault, M. (1979). *Discipline and punish: The birth of prison*. New York: Vintage Books.

Foucault, M. (1991). Politics and the study of discourse. In G. Burchell, C. Gordon, & P. Miller (Eds.), *The Foucault effect: Studies in governmentality* (pp. 53–72). London: Harvester Wheatsheaf.

Glaser, B., & Strauss, A. (1967). *The discovery of grounded theory*. Chicago: Aldine.

Goodson, I. (1998). Storying the self. In W. Pinar (Ed.), *Curriculum: Towards new identities* (pp. 3–20). New York: Garland.

Gosetti, P., & Rusch, E. (1995). Reexamining educational leadership: Challenging assumptions. In D. Dunlap & P. Schmunk (Eds.), *Women leading in education* (pp. 1–10). Albany: State University of New York Press.

Gough, N. (1998). Beyond Eurocentrism in science education: Promises and problematics from a feminist poststructuralist perspective. In W. Pinar (Ed.), *Curriculum: Towards new identities* (pp. 185–210). New York: Garland.

Heilman, E. (1998). The struggle for self: Power and identity in adolescent girls. *Youth and Society, 30*(2), 182–208.

Hughes, L. (1988). Beyond the rules of the game: Why are rookie rules nice? In F. Manning (Ed.), *The world of play* (pp. 188–199). West Point, NY: Leisure Press.

Jones, A. (1993). Becoming a 'girl': Post-structural suggestions for educational research. *Gender & Education, 5*(2), 157–164.

Jones, K. (1996). What is authority's gender? In N. Hirschmann & C. DiStefano (Eds.), *Revisioning the political* (pp. 117–138). Boulder, CO: Westview Press.

Kilbourne, J. (1995). Beauty and the beast of advertising. In G. Dines & J. M. Humez (Eds.), *Gender, race and class in media* (pp. 112–125). Thousand Oaks, CA: Sage.

Kvale, S. (1997). *InterViews*. Thousand Oaks, CA: Sage.

McDowell, L. (1999). *Gender, identity, and place: Understanding feminist geographies*. Minneapolis: University of Minnesota Press.

Merten, D. (1997). The meaning of meanness: Popularity, competition, and conflict among junior high school girls. *Sociology of Education, 70*, 175–191.

Morris, G. B. (1991). Perceptions of leadership traits: Comparison of adolescent and adult school leaders. *Psychological Reports, 69*, 723–727.

Richardson, L. (1994). Writing: A method of inquiry. In N. Denzin & Y. Lincoln (Eds.), *Handbook of qualitative research* (pp. 516–529). Thousand Oaks, CA: Sage.

Shinew, D. (2001). Disrupt, transgress, and invent possibilities. *Theory and Research in Social Education, 29*(3), 488–516.

Sibley, D. (1995). *Geographies of exclusion: Society and difference in the West*. London: Routledge.

Strauss, A., & Corbin, J. (1990). *Basics of qualitative research*. Newbury Park, CA: Sage.

Tierney, W. G. (1997). Lost in translation: Time and voice in qualitative research. In W. G. Tierney & Y. S. Lincoln (Eds.), *Representation and the text: Reframing the narrative voice* (pp. 23–36). Albany: State University of New York Press.

Tronto, J. (1996). Care as a political concept. In N. Hirschmann & C. DiStefano (Eds.), *Revisioning the political* (pp. 117–138). Boulder, CO: Westview Press.

Chapter 5

Girls in Groups:
The Preps and the Sex Mob
Try Out for Womanhood

Pamela J. Bettis
Washington State University

Debra Jordan
Oklahoma State University

Diane Montgomery
Oklahoma State University

Interviewer: So what does it take to be a member of the Preps?

Chastity: Just, you know—you gotta wear preppy clothes and think they're better than everybody else and they, you know, they make straight As in school.

Interviewer: So what do you have to do to be in your group [i.e., Sex Mob]?

Chastity: You have to be a friend. That's it.

Chastity, a seventh-grade African American girl, explained the different requirements for belonging to the Preps and the Sex Mob, two peer groups found in a Midwestern middle school. Peer groups are a fixture of the landscape of girlhood literally. They tell girls where to sit at lunch, what to wear, where and with whom to hang out between classes (Wexler, 1992), and how to "be" as Chastity notes. In a sense, girls in peer groups construct collective female identities because they are colearners (Lave & Wenger, 1991) in the

69

important ritual of trying out for womanhood. For members of the Preps and the Sex Mob, these collective female identities diverged significantly.

This ethnography of a multiracial (15% Native American; 5% Hispanic; 5% African American; 75% White) middle school, which drew from field observations made 4 days a week during the fall semester and 2 days a week during the spring semester along with 93 interviews, revealed that different female peer groups tried out for womanhood in different ways. Race, ethnicity, and social class intertwined with peer affiliation to create different routes for becoming women. "There is not one masculinity or one femininity, but many versions of each both within and across class and cultural boundaries" (Davies, 1993, p. x). Although there are a variety of femininities, only a few versions are deemed appropriate in the larger society, and all girls feel the pressure to conform to these appropriate gender roles (Brown & Gilligan, 1992; Fordham, 1993; Orenstein, 1994; Pipher, 1994). However, girls themselves are actively involved in constructing multiple and often contradictory ways of being female (Davies, 1989, 1993, 2000; Jones, 1993; Kenway & Willis, 1998; Walkerdine, 1990, 1993). For middle school girls, much of this gender work is performed within peer groups, which provide collective spaces for practicing what it means to be a woman.

Peer groups have been the subject of 50 years of sociological research, and that research has consistently documented social stratification among peer groups and the existence of popular groups, deviant groups and ostracized groups, (e.g., Adler & Adler, 1995, 1998; Adler, Kless, & Adler, 1992; Coleman, 1961; Eckert, 1989; Eder, 1995; Evans & Eder, 1993; Hollingshead, 1949; Merten, 1996, 1997). But, peer group stratification and relations of power are not mere sociological abstractions; they are lived every day (J. B. Thompson, 1990). For adolescents, it is often the peer group that embodies these relations of power. In this chapter we extend the work of Eckert (1989), Wexler (1992), and Merten (1996, 1997) on peer groups as well as feminist scholars of girl culture (e.g., Brumberg, 1997; Budgeon, 1998; Inness, 1999; Lemish, 1998; McRobbie, 1993) by exploring how peer group membership shapes girls' gendered identities. If gender is a performance (Walkerdine, 1993), that performance takes on different dimensions in a collective setting where a group creates its own story and identity within the larger landscape of school privilege and power. We argue that these middle school girls are constructing and trying out their femininity and "becoming somebody" (Wexler, 1992) through the groups with which they identified, those they critiqued, and those to which they aspired. For this chapter, we explore two very different groups of girls: the Preps and the Sex Mob and what belonging to these groups meant to how girls understood, learned about, and enacted female identity.

THE PREPS: PRIVILEGE, POWER, AND THE MANTRA OF NICENESS

The Preps were the only universally identified peer group in this school, and those girls who comprised the Preps were typically popular, White, and middle class. Although only a small minority of students actually belonged to the Preps (approximately 20–25 girls), it was still a powerful group because it acted symbolically in defining appropriate roles and identities in school (Eckert, 1989). "Prepness" also operated as a gendered marker for describing a particular feminine look and way of being that was reflective of dominant notions of ideal femininity and adult success. Prepness dominated the discourse of femininity through which all girls constituted themselves as females.

That Preps were consistently named and described at this school should not be surprising because Preps have been consistently identified as a peer group that enjoys high status in schools across the United States (Bettis & Adams, 2003; Brantlinger, 1993; Durham, 1999; Kinney, 1999; Merten, 1996). Preps represent mainstream notions of success and publicly conduct themselves in ways that are deemed appropriate by adults in their world (Eckert, 1989). For example, Preps espouse the belief that good grades pay off in terms of future economic and social success; they participate in school activities as preparation for adult life; and if they engage in inappropriate social behaviors such as drinking or having sex, they do not advertise these activities to adults. Furthermore, adults such as teachers, usually recognize Preps' "appropriate" behaviors and reward them with leadership positions in schools. The Prep group in this particular middle school was no different. When asked which students would be selected as the leaders of the school by the teachers, almost every student replied that members of the Preps would be selected. Daneka, a Native American non-Prep explained, "Since all the Preps suck up, it'd probably have to be a Prep."

When asked to describe the various peer groups, girl after girl began her discussion with a detailed description of the Preps, often in very positive terms. Anna, a White Prep girl, attempts to explain why the Prep girls are good at everything:

Interviewer: How does that come about? How are the Prep girls good at almost everything?

Anna: They're ... just the ones that are Preppy; the ones that are all cool and everybody wants to be like them; they're good at everything; they're pretty ... they're cute [slight laughter].

Besides being cute, cool, and good at everything, Preps were "nice." Nice was an adjective that was used repeatedly by all girls in describing other girls; however, it had the most salience for members of the Preps. Niceness was closely aligned with Prepness and permeated many girls' discussions of female identity. At this middle school, Prep girls delineated three markers of niceness: Girls were to dress in a particular manner, be sexually appropriate, and be friendly to everyone. Anna included all three criteria in her discussion of what it meant to be a Prep: "We dress nice and we don't wear anything inappropriate … like shorts too short or spaghetti strap shirts. Me, I try to be nice to other people so no one will think I'm a snob." Dressing "nice" and being "nice" were the Preps' cherished principles of femininity. Prep girls' biggest fear was being labeled a snob, as Anna noted, which was a common critique of the Preps provided by many non-Prep girls.

Dressing and Acting Nice

At the time, Doc Marten shoes, Lucky jeans, and sweater vests with long-sleeved white blouses were examples of the appropriate fashion for Preps, and certainly some of these name brands were expensive. Jennifer, a member of the Preps, explained her Prep identity through her clothing: "They consider me a Prep because they think I have nicer clothes 'cause you can just tell who the people that like, have good parents and stuff. They provide better clothes for them." Jennifer's comments weave together social class, morality, and parenting. Preps had "good parents" as opposed to other girls' parents who were not willing or able to purchase the "better clothes." Selena, a White non-Prep, was the most succinct in her description of the Preps and their finances: "Like Preps, they have the money and everything in their pockets. They have money, every time you turn around." Although non-Prep girls typically pointed out that most Prep girls came from wealthy families, Preps themselves did not necessarily acknowledge family wealth.

However, Prep fashion sense was more than just sporting the elite brand names as Tracey, a former member of the Preps, pointed out: "They [Preps] dress really neat. They dress like, they wear like Lucky Jeans or Tommy Jeans and like Doc Martens and like little tops and they're tucked in with their belts on and their hair will be all curled." One quick perusal of the Prep table at lunchtime would indeed reveal a row of similarly clad girls with curled hair in pony tails tied with white ribbons.

Undergirding the Prep style of dress was an implicit rule against sexually inappropriate clothing and makeup. Just like Anna warned, Preps did not wear "short shorts or spaghetti strap shirts." Tight clothes, dirty clothes, and too much makeup or the wrong kind of makeup were also frowned upon. Here Connie, a White Prep, described the dress of skanks who were considered sexually promiscuous and/or dirty. Not surprisingly, promiscuity and being unclean were inextricably woven together (Douglass, 1966; Sibley, 1995): "Some of the skanks like dress sloppy like with baggy jeans and dirty T-shirts. I wouldn't say that people don't like them because of that but that has something to do with it usually. The skanks wear belly shirts and really really short shorts and get sent home for it and the black lipstick."

Furthermore, Prep girls were disdainful of girls who engaged in "dirty dancing" and so-called slutty behaviors. Typically, Prep girls would provide generalizations about what not to do but did not specifically name others who might exemplify some of these activities. They indeed presented themselves as too nice to critique others specifically. Terry, a White Prep girl, explained the difference between skanks and Preps: "For some girls here, it's they like to sleep around and stuff like that and that's like bad—they can get you like a really bad reputation; and a good reputation's like straight As and Bs and you're always doing your studies and you have like a boyfriend like not all the time. You don't have to have, like, one constantly." Wearing the appropriate clothing and avoiding a skanky and slutty reputation were two important facets of being nice. However, Prep girls had to attend to acting nice as well.

Acting and/or Being Nice

Prep girls worked hard at acting nice, which meant that they talked with everyone, even those who were not Preps and were not popular, and did not act snobbish. In day-to-day life of this middle school, acting nice meant that a girl said "hello" or acknowledged everyone while passing them in the hallway. Moreover, it meant a willingness to interact with non-Preps in class, for example in physical education where girls talked during breaks in the action. Being nice to everyone was an important facet of being nice and a Prep, which we heard over and over in our interviews. In describing her own actions as a member of the most popular peer group, Suzi, focuses on being nice:

> I try to be nice to everybody and I try to be nice to the people that don't, like Brad. Like Steve and Paul and them always kind make fun of Brad 'cause Brad is really really smart and like everybody else always makes fun of him. So me and Laurie and Lisa [all Prep girls] always go up to him and say Hi and try to be nice to, like, them people. We try to be nice to everybody.

Being nice, a ubiquitous adjective for White middle-class girls and women in this culture and certainly for the Prep girls in this study, was a contradictory space in which to be situated (Brown & Gilligan, 1992). Being nice to everyone ensured popularity, and popularity bestowed status and power. The irony was that popular girls were not allowed to demonstrate that power publicly (Merten, 1997). In other words, they still had to be nice to everyone and not slight or neglect anyone; for if they did, they became suspect of becoming a snob, one of the most reviled descriptors of girls at this age and a factor in losing popularity.

No doubt, the Preps enjoyed many obvious privileges in this school. In the following exchange, Lisa, one of the acknowledged Prep leaders, describes the pleasures of being a Prep:

Interviewer: Do you like your identity now?

Lisa: I do. I love it so much; it is so much fun. I can go shopping with my friends and we can buy outfits that are similar and we wear them and people are like, "Oh, you look so cute today," and people used to say, "Your hair looks pathetic," and now I have my hair fixed every day.

Lisa describes a way of being and looking that is admired by others and considered ideal. But there is clearly a price to pay when group membership mandates a particular look and way of being female. In the following exchange, Angelica, a White Prep, comments on that price.

Interviewer: What do you not have as much confidence in yourself about?

Angelica: Um sports and being outgoing. I used to be really outgoing and at school around certain people, I am not as open. There are a lot of girls in school who are just really pretty and and skinny and I feel so weird getting up by them.

Interviewer: Really?

Angelica: I feel really judged.... Your looks, your popularity, what people think of you is a big thing.... My whole life is centered around what people think of me.

Angelica details the difficulties of this particular female identity, one in which girls are constantly judged and compared to others in body shape, clothing, and ultimately their way of being female.

It would be easy to characterize the Preps as an ideal example of the regulation of female behavior. Certainly, their uniform clothing, hairstyles, and focus on being "nice" appear to conform to dominant notions of femininity. At times they appeared to be locked into a monolithic and standardized space of femininity that did not allow the fluidity of movement and trying on of different female identities that one would hope would be possible during adolescence. Prep girls could not necessarily say what they wanted or thought. If adolescence is supposedly a time to try out different ways of being, then the Prep girls were inhibited from doing just that task.

However, membership into the exclusive Prep group granted many privileges as well. Teachers and administrators paid attention to them and when possible, granted them leadership positions. The average seventh-grade girl at this middle school studied their clothing and hair style and generally admired them. Furthermore, Prep girls occupied the most visible public space for girls in school, that of cheerleading, which brought with it the interest of popular boys. Being a Prep meant that these adolescent girls were somebody; it signified that they embodied the dominant notion of American womanhood.

THE SEX MOB: PERFORMANCE, PLAY, AND "SOMEONE TO RECKON WITH"

The Prep focus on and desire for uniformity of appearance and thought, and the group's lack of racial and ethnic diversity was what drove one Prep girl to curtail her Prep status. Tracey, a White middle-class 12-year-old who had been a Prep in her elementary school and had joined the Sex Mob during seventh grade, was explicit about why she wanted to belong to this group.

> My school that I went to last year, it was mainly White, Preppy kids so there was one Black girl and that was it. And we all had White kids and that was it. This year I wanted to explore. I never really got to know anyone else and this year I just wanted to see what everybody else was like. You know I was like the biggest Prep last year and now I am not. I met all my different friends like Joelle [African American] and they aren't Preps, so I changed my ways.

The Sex Mob was a group of 8 to 12 girls who were African American, Native American, and White. Although they were predominantly working class, several middle-class girls, like Tracey, were members of the group as well. Whereas the Prep girls worked hard at dressing appropriately and being and looking nice, the Sex Mob members utilized their more ambiguous social position to try out a wider range of female identities. Part of the group's membership was fairly fluid with girls considered "in" at times and "out" at other times. Only about eight core members of the Sex Mob actually called it that name. One of the leaders of that core group, Brittney, had coined the name, and others thought it was funny. The name was kept in house and unknown by those outside the group.

But the adult-sounding Sex Mob was only one way that members identified themselves. Members also created their own individual pet names, all of which were affiliated with the more childlike bear motif. Individual members called themselves Teddie Bear, Mama Bear, Grizzly Bear, Pooh Bear, Nervey Bear, and Sugar Bear; each name alluded to a unique personality characteristic embodied by the individual girl. For example, Sugar Bear was a White working-class girl who was known for her flirtatious and some would say "slutty" behavior. She was also was known as a girlie girl and a terrible fighter, and other members of the group, like Grizzly Bear Brittney, an African American girl who was known as the leader of the group, were willing to intervene for her. In fact, Grizzly Bear Brittney prided herself on being the "meanest" and "baddest" bear of the group. Grizzly Bear, the fighter, and Sugar Bear, the lover, were both an integral part of the Sex Mob, and although Sugar Bear was chastised for her flirtatious behavior and Grizzly Bear for the fear she invoked, both girls' versions of femininity were acknowledged openly and accepted. Members of the Sex Mob were able to construct a space in which being female was fluid and diverse. The names of the group as a whole and for individual members spoke to this openness to difference and the loyalty engendered by the group.

From Prep to Fighter to Slut: Diverse Ways of Being Female

Contrary to Wexler's (1992) and Eckert's (1989) findings that peer groups sometimes are formed in opposition to each other, the Sex Mob embraced some facets of Prepness. In fact, many Sex Mob members asserted some form of relationship with the popular group. For example, Tracey, a former Prep who had joined the Sex Mob during her seventh-grade year, alluded to this relationship:

Interviewer: And what would you call your group?
Tracey: Sometimes Preppy. [slight laughter]. Sometimes just don't care.
Interviewer: And how would, how would another student describe your group? How would the Preps see it?
Tracey: They'd think we were Preps.

Tracey's last comment was not accurate. Not a single member of the Prep group ever claimed that members of the Sex Mob were also Preps; however, several Preps commented that they were friends with some of these girls within the school setting.

Sex Mob members clearly saw themselves in a more substantive relationship with the Preps. Some Sex Mob members followed Prep fashion criteria at times. Brittney, Tracey, Randi, and Joanie all wore jeans with sweater vests and white blouses at least once during a typical week and would sometimes comment that they were dressed like Preps. Besides dressing like Preps, five members of the Sex Mob enrolled in the cheerleading elective class to prepare for spring cheerleading tryouts. Although none of the five eventually tried out for the squad, their presence in the class and comments made during interviews indicated a desire to be a cheerleader with its accompanying privileges.

However, for most members of the Sex Mob, acting like a Prep was a temporary way of being. Sex Mob girls were actively involved in how, why, and under what contexts they chose to appropriate Prepness. They chose to dress like Preps sometimes and associate with members of the Prep group; it appeared that they saw it as enhancing their status. At other times, they were disdainful of the position and power that Preps held and even made fun of them. Dana, a White working-class girl who moved in and out of the Sex Mob, described how the assistant principal called her group "thugs" but how he still tried to bring the various school cliques together: "Mr. Connors, like always tryin' to get us to come together and we can't. Because, I mean if you get a whole bunch of Preppy people around the thugs, then Preppy people are gonna be like freakin' out because they don't know what we are talking about."

Dana was probably right. Members of the Sex Mob did not adhere to the Preps' cherished principles of femininity, that of being, talking, and dressing nice and being sexually appropriate. Furthermore, members of the Sex Mob played with and dramatized sexuality, power, racial, and class antagonisms. They literally tried out different versions of womanhood, many of which were not considered appropriate by Prep and dominant standards. The girls of the Sex Mob did not denigrate the "niceness" principle, but it was not central to who they were. When they talked about the members of their group, they talked about the importance of relationship, loyalty, and power, not about how nice they were. For example, when asked who the leaders of the Sex Mob were, every girl named Brittney as one of the leaders, if not the only one. But descriptions of Brittney did not adhere to the "she's so sweet and nice" common refrain of the Preps description of their leaders. Sex Mob members were effusive in their praise of Brittney's loyalty to them, no matter what the problem, and her willingness to chastise them when necessary. For example, several girls commented on the fact that Brittney kept them from skipping class, and they appreciated her efforts.

As A. Thompson (1998) explained, the "black cultural model for womanhood is ... not about being nice, or being a lady, or not upsetting people.... It's about being capable and competent. It's about being someone to reckon with" (p. 536). Although fewer than half of the Sex Mob's members were African American, Thompson's description was an appropriate one for the group and its members. They were girls to be reckoned with; they said what they thought and did not try to appease everyone. Indeed, they were not necessarily nice.

Not Nice

Nice was not an adjective used to describe many of the members of the Sex Mob. Whereas it was a coveted trait among the Preps, it did not hold value in a group, which at times challenged school authority and dominant views of femininity. Furthermore, some Sex Mob members were openly critical of the focus on niceness that so many Prep girls embraced. For example, they did not necessarily support the importance of the perennial smile that many of the Preps adopted to maintain their "nice" image and to accompany their cheerleading persona. Chas, an African American Sex Mob member who was also enrolled in the cheer prep class, remarked that the required cheerleading smile was not natural for her. "Sometimes I have a smile on my face; sometimes I don't. Sometimes my attitude's good; sometimes it's not. You know, people get on my nerves, like the boys do." In line with Chas' comments, Sex Mob members openly displayed their emotions and perspectives on a wide variety of topics. Tracey, a White Sex Mob member, called the vice principal "a dick," and other group members used strong language in describing particular individuals. Moreover, Sex Mob members did not just denigrate adults and other adolescents; they also talked about each other's strengths and weaknesses. They critiqued specific girls for their slutty behaviors. Furthermore, they railed against perceived injustices such as racial slurs, social-class conflicts, and female stereotypes. They named names as opposed to the Prep girls. Here Randi, a White working-class girl, acts as a moral gatekeeper in considering the actions of another Sex Mob member, Joanie, a White working-class girl. She explains that Joanie is a slut:

Interviewer: So why is she considered a slut?

Randi: Because she flaunts herself too much.

Interviewer: Okay. And flaunt meaning?

Randi: The things she does, the way she acts. She goes up and hugs all the boys, and acts too hyper all the time. And she's nasty, and then she's—I don't know. She just wears like little skimpy clothes … And the makeup—gotta go.

Randi, like several other Sex Mob members, was so concerned with Joanie's behaviors that she chastised her publicly during a physical education class and in front of other girls. Joanie cried but did not protest the critique. At the same time that some Sex Mob members regulated some of the "slutty" behaviors of some of its members, the group provided a space for girls to critique that kind of group and self-regulation. Here Gina, a Native American girl, challenged the stereotype of dressing inappropriately:

Gina: Because everyone was always thinking that me and Myra are wild just cause of the way we dress when we're uptown. They think of us as easy girls to get with.

Interviewer: Because of the way you dress?

Gina: Yea well, 'Cause we'll wear those spaghetti strap shirts and
              shorts and everybody is like 'Well, that's the way a ho would
              dress.' And I'm like, how would a ho dress? Someone could be
              all suited up in a full set of clothes and she can be a ho. I don't
              get that.

Gina's comments spoke to the narrow dress code that the Preps had perpetuated for girls at this middle school. Members of the Sex Mob wore a wide
range of clothing styles from athletic apparel to the Prep style to short
shorts. A few Sex Mob members' style appeared to center around getting to
school on time. Other Sex Mob members were as fastidious as the Preps
were about their hair and makeup but followed their own fashion dictates.

Besides being critical of dominant notions of dress and femininity, members of the Sex Mob playfully critiqued various raced and classed identities
as well. As Shameeka commented about herself and two other Sex Mob
members, "We're not, like, afraid to speak up or say anything, like most of
the time if something's to be said, we're the ones that say it ...." For example, members of the Sex Mob confronted in a very public way fellow students whom they found to be oppressive.

During several different observations of a seventh-grade math class,
members of the Sex Mob addressed social-class privilege when they tar-
geted one of the wealthiest girls in the school, Caroline, in an impromptu
collective response to her continual references to wealth. Tracey, a White
Sex mob member, complained that when she was friends with Caroline during sixth grade, Caroline had always emphasized how much money her
home cost. But what was annoying and confounded members of the Sex
Mob was that Caroline displayed poor fashion sense even though she was
wealthy. During one class session when there was a lull in the curriculum,
three members of the Sex Mob (one African American and two Whites)
raised their pants to "highwater" levels and then raised their legs as if water
was rising quickly in the classroom. The girls called out, "Where's the
flood?" to their fellow classmates. Then the three stood up and walked
around still holding up their pants to a "highwater" mark. The drama was
meant to highlight the fact Caroline was wearing pants whose length was
unfashionably above her clogs. During one of these performances, a Prep
girl clued us in on what was taking place and appeared to be supportive of
the critique. However, she did not participate in the silly but biting har-
rangue of Caroline. It wouldn't be nice.

Sex Mob members did not embrace the mantra of niceness. As demonstrated in the preceding example, they were not nice to Caroline; in fact,
some might consider their actions the opposite of nice, that of being mean.

They criticized each other openly, they occasionally engaged in fights, and they harassed particular students such as Caroline. They did not dress uniformly or always appropriately by Prep standards. Moreover, they sometimes challenged the normative assumptions regarding female sexuality, social class, and race.

Although members of the Sex Mob demonstrated a strong commitment to the group through their group rituals, names, and the fact that individual members would occasionally fight for each other, that commitment did not engender, however, the uniformity of dress and behavior that was part of the Prep experience. Within the ranks of the Sex Mob, instead, there was great variation in dress, acceptable behavior, and ways of being female. No doubt, part of that diversity emanated from the varied social class and racial positions of group members. However, we think that this diversity and fluidity of identity represents more than differences of class and race. In commenting on an African American propensity for improvisation in daily life in order to survive successfully in a racist society, Fordham (1993) argues "symmetry is obtained not through uniformity but through diversity" (p. 13). Fordham's description seems fitting for the Sex Mob's group dynamics and the multiple ways of being female that they engendered. The Sex Mob girls were privileged in their opportunities to try on different ways of becoming women. The "tyranny of niceness" (Brown & Gilligan, 1992) did not envelop them as it did Preps.

Certainly, Sex Mob girls did not have the privileges of the Preps, including the endorsement of their teachers and peers in school. They did not represent ideal femininity. Because of their race/ethnicity and social class, many members of the Sex Mob also faced uncertain futures (Walkerdine, Lucey, & Melody, 2001). However, they did have the opportunity to reinvent themselves and to try on new ways of being female. Furthermore, being a member of a group that possesses no structural visibility offered a space to critique dominant ideology of what constitutes the ideal female. Although members of the Sex Mob were not recognized as popular, they learned skills that would serve them well as adult women in a society that still struggles with gender equity. Many Sex Mob members were "outspeakin' " and "someone to be reckoned with," traits that would serve all girls well as they transition into womanhood.

A CURRICULUM OF NICE, SLUT, AND OUTSPEAKIN'

What does belonging to the Preps and the Sex Mob mean to the teachers and the administrators who work with these girls every day? How do these adults help adolescents negotiate this time of trying out for womanhood? Or do they? Many teachers and administrators are unaware of or uninterested in the social lives of students unless it impacts directly on the academic culture of their classrooms. This is unfortunate because adolescents live the daily realities, both materially and discursively, of being a member of the Preps or Sex Mob. These peer group identities were infused in how these adolescent girls understood themselves. It is who they were at that moment in their lives.

Adolescents possess little economic or political power in the school setting, but the "one kind of power they do have is the ability to create peer status systems. So it's not accidental that teenagers come to be obsessed with status systems" (Milner, 2001, p. 6). Although "obsessed" might not be the adjective describing all the girls we interviewed, it certainly is reflective of most of the girls' attention to the local peer status system. Why not use that "obsession" and attention pedagogically through helping girls imagine the possibilities for trying on new and different ways of being female. Using the girls' words—nice, outspeakin', and slut—teachers, along with students, could construct a curriculum that explored the complexities of female adolescence identity. Instead of reinforcing the norms of femininity as seen in the imperative of "niceness" that enveloped the Preps and that was the standard for normative femininity in this particular school, adults could offer alternative vehicles on which to focus such as Thompson's notion of "competence," Fordham's "improvisation," and/or Shameeka's "outspeakin.' " A curriculum that grew from students' own words and understandings of what it means to female could provide a powerful vehicle to move into larger social issues surrounding gender, heterosexuality, and race.

Furthermore, the meaning of nice could be interrogated so that all girls understood its power in both privileging them and circumscribing their choices and their lives. A curriculum that made explicit the privileges and limitations associated with membership in groups like the Preps and the Sex Mob would be a curriculum about the everyday lives and everyday identity work in which these girls were so passionately engaged.

DISCUSSION QUESTIONS

1. Consider and provide examples of the multiple meanings of *nice*. Why and how do these meanings become associated with femininity and not masculinity? What does it mean to be a nice boy or man and how is that different or the same as a nice girl or woman? What does a focus on niceness do to/for girls and women?

2. How do the Preps and the Sex Mob both support and contradict reproductionist theories of schooling?

3. What do you think of Milner's assertion that adolescents become "obsessed" with peer status systems because it is the one kind of power that they do have in their day-to-day lives? How are other types of peer groups lived in schools?

REFERENCES

Adler P., & Adler, P. (1995). Dynamics of inclusion and exclusion in preadolescent cliques. *Social Psychology Quarterly, 58*, 145–162.

Adler P., & Adler, P. (1998). *Peer power: Preadolescent culture and identity.* New Brunswick, NJ: Rutgers University Press.

Adler P., Kless, S., & Adler, P. (1992). Socialization to gender roles: Popularity among elementary school boys and girls. *Sociology of Education, 65*, 169–187.

Bettis, P. J., & Adams, N. G. (2003). The power of the Preps and a cheerleading equity policy. *Sociology of Education, 76*(2), 128–142.

Brantlinger, E. (1993). *The politics of social class in secondary schools: Views of affluent and impoverished youth.* New York: Teachers College Press.

Brown, L., & Gilligan, C. (1992). *Meeting at the crossroads: Women's psychology and girls' development.* New York: Ballantine Books.

Brumberg, J. (1997). *The body project: An intimate history of American girls.* New York: Random House.

Budgeon, S. (1998). "I'll tell you what I really, really want": Girl Power and self-identity in Britain. In S. Inness (Ed.), *Millennium girls* (pp. 115–143). Lanham, MD: Rowman & Littlefield.

Coleman, J. S. (1961). *The adolescent society.* Glencoe, IL: The Free Press.

Davies, B. (1989). *Frogs and snails and feminist tales.* Sydney, Australia: Allen & Unwin.

Davies, B. (1993). *Shards of glass: Children reading and writing beyond gendered identity.* Cresskill, NJ: Hampton Press.

Davies, B. (2000). *A body of writing 1990–1999.* New York: AltaMira Press.

Douglas, M. (1966). *Purity and danger. An analysis of concepts of pollution and taboo.* New York: Praeger.

Durham, M. G. (1999). Girls, media and the negotiation of sexuality: A study of race, class, and gender in adolescent peer groups. *Journalism and Mass Communication Quarterly, 76*, 193–216.

Eckert, P. (1989). *Jocks and burnouts: Social categories and identity in the high school.* New York: Teachers College Press.

Eder, D. (1995). *School talk: Gender and adolescent culture.* New Brunswick, NJ: Rutgers University Press.

Evans, C., & Eder, D. (1993). "No exit": Processes of social isolation in the middle school. *Journal of Contemporary Ethnography, 22*, 139–170.

Fordham, S. (1993). "Those loud Black girls": (Black) women, silence and gender "passing" in the academy. *Anthropology and Education Quarterly, 24*(1), 3–32.

Hollingshead, A. B. (1949). *Elmstown youth.* New York: Wiley.

Inness, S. (1999). *Tough girls: Women warriors and wonder women in popular culture.* Philadelphia: University of Pennsylvania Press.

Jones, A. (1993). Becoming a "girl": Post-structural suggestions for educational research. *Gender and Education, 5*(2), 157–164.

Kenway, J., & Willis, S. (1998). *Answering back: Girls, boys and feminism in schools.* London: Routledge.

Kinney, D. (1999). From "Headbangers" to "Hippies": Delineating adolescent active attempts to form alternative peer culture. *New Directions for Child and Adolescent Development, 84*, 21–35.

Lave, J., & Wenger, E. (1991). *Situated learning: Legitimate peripheral participation*. New York: Cambridge University Press.

Lemish, D. (1998). Spice Girls' talk: A case study of the development of gendered identity. In S. Inness (Ed.), *Millennium girls* (pp. 145–167). Lanham, MD: Rowman & Littlefield.

McRobbie, A. (1993). Shut up and dance: Youth culture and changing modes of femininity. *Cultural Studies, 7*(3), 406–426.

Merten, D. (1996). Burnout as cheerleader: The cultural basis for prestige and privilege in junior high school. *Anthropology and Education, 27*(1), 51–70.

Merten, D. (1997). The meaning of meanness: Popularity, competition, and conflict among junior high school girls. *Sociology of Education, 70,* 175–191.

Milner, M. (2001). Murray Milner on status systems among American teenagers: Fellow interview. *Insight.* Charlottesville: University of Virginia Institute of Advanced Studies in Culture.

Orenstein, P. (1994). *Schoolgirls: Young women, self-esteem, and the confidence gap.* New York: Doubleday.

Pipher, M. (1994). *Reviving Ophelia: Saving the selves of adolescent girls.* New York: Ballantine.

Sibley, D. (1995). *Geographies of exclusion.* New York: Routledge.

Thompson, A. (1998). Not the color purple: Black feminist lessons for educational caring. *Harvard Educational Review, 68*(4), 522–544.

Thompson, J. B. (1990). *Ideology and modern culture: Critical social theory in the era of mass communication.* Stanford, CA: Stanford University Press.

Walkerdine, V. (1990). *Schoolgirl fictions.* London: Verso.

Walkerdine, V. (1993). Girlhood through the looking glass. In M. de Ras & M. Lunenberg (Eds.), *Girls, girlhood and girls' studies in transition* (pp. 9–24). Amsterdam: Het Spinhuis.

Walkerdine, V., Lucey, H., & Melody, J. (2001). *Growing up girl: Psychosocial explorations of gender and class.* New York: New York University Press.

Wexler, P. (1992). *Becoming somebody: Toward a social psychology of school.* London: Falmer Press.

Chapter 6

"The Beauty Walk" as a Social Space for Messages About the Female Body: Toward Transformative Collaboration

Rosary Lalik
Virginia Tech

Kimberly L. Oliver
New Mexico State University

> *Transformation is the development of a critical perspective through which individuals can begin to see how social practices are organized to support certain interests. It is also the process whereby this understanding is used as the basis for active political intervention directed toward social change, with the intent to disempower relations of inequality.*
>
> —Lewis (1992, p. 168)

Our work with adolescents has been directed toward the goal of transformation. That is, we are interested in helping adolescents understand how social practices serve various interests and how adults and adolescents can collaborate to change inequitable practices and conditions. Our pedagogy is committed to both "ways of knowing" and "ways of acting in the world" (Brodkey & Fine, 1992, p. 80). Such work requires two types of language (Giroux, 1992)—a language of critique and a language of possibility. Giroux argued that educators are wise to collaborate with students to examine the etiology of unjust relations, while also defining and justifying "the nature of the good life we want to defend and how do we do that" (p. 25). Toward those dual ends, we have engaged adolescents in studies of cultural messages of the female body. These messages together with the social spaces in which they occur have become a focal point for our teaching and research.

As has been explained by Walkerdine (1990), images of the female body are both persistent and ubiquitous. They appear and reappear in a wide variety of forms and in the many shifting and varied spaces of social life and are part of wider discursive practices through which meaning and subjectivity are produced (Weedon, 1987). Through these images and the messages they imply, female bodies have been used to support unequal gender relations in society. Through them, the female body has been pathologized (Foucault as cited in Weedon, 1987), as in images of the welfare mother (McDade, 1992). It has been found insufficiently developed for sophisticated reasoning, as in images of the dumb blonde. It has been "hystericized and medicalized" (Walkerdine, 1990, p. 33), as in images of the middle-class wife dependent on prescription drugs for emotional stability.

Girls' bodies have not been spared from the ravages of these oppressive processes. Within popular media, girls' bodies have been fetishized as at once innocent and erotic (Walkerdine, 1997). Thus all too frequently images of young girls are disseminated together with rhetoric that constructs the young female as simultaneously manipulative seducer and innocent victim. Recently, this social construction has become painfully obvious in the exploitation of Jon Benet Ramsey by the mass media in the United States.

Most girls are keenly aware of these messages, as well as the concomitant oppressive surveillance and regulation of the female body. During a series of conversations with researchers (Fine & Macpherson, 1992), four adolescent informants explained that, "[girls] are often reminded of their bodies as a public site (gone right or wrong), commented on and monitored by others—male and female" (p. 185). Furthermore, Black girls reported especially disturbing experiences of the body, revealing the pain they experienced due to "the violence of racism on the female body" (p. 190). Thus Fine and Macpherson explained that gender as well as race and other social constructions influence how girls experience the body:

> Gender determines that the young women are subject to external surveillance and responsible for internal body management, and it is their gender that makes them feel vulnerable to male sexual threat and assault. Culture [race] and class determine how—that is, the norms of body and the codes of surveillance, management, threat, assault, and resistance available to them. (pp. 185–186)

Thus, it appears that for Black girls to be successful, they must overcome stereotypes related to both gender and race.

As Kim worked with girls in a yearlong effort at transformation, one particular social space came to her attention—a space in which the female body served as focal point. That space was annually created in the form of a school event known locally as the Beauty Walk. Kim learned about this event when she encountered a billboard advertising it. Later, Kim learned that the Beauty Walk was a long-standing school-sponsored fund-raising event that followed the general format of a beauty pageant. Appalled that schools would sponsor an event that she interpreted as oppressive to girls and women, Kim vowed to include this event as a topic for critique in her work with adolescents.

In this chapter we examine what Kim and the girls learned about whose interests were supported and whose overlooked or damaged by this school-based social practice. We also examine the extent to which the girls, with Kim's support, were able to use their emerging critique as a basis for political action. We believe that such research has potential for helping girls learn processes that they can use for pursuing healthy lives in a variety of contexts within and beyond school.

METHOD

Our four collaborators, Destiny, Brandi, Alexandria, and Jaylnn, self-identified as Black.[1] The girls attended Landview Middle School, an all-eighth-grade school located in the southeastern region of the United States. This particular grade arrangement was a result of efforts to integrate the historically racially segregated city schools. At the time of this collaboration, 70% of the Landview students were classified as African American in official school documents. In contrast, both of us identified as White. Kim grew up in an upper-middle-class family in the western United States, whereas Rosary was a member of a working-class immigrant family. Both of us now work as professors in major universities in the United States.

Kim met with the girls 1 day per week for 60 minutes. Kim and the girls completed 26 sessions together between September 1998 and May 1999. Kim began the sessions by inviting the girls to develop personal biographies, and she supported their completion of these biographies using a series of questions about matters such as their home lives and personal interests. She also asked the girls to create personal maps of where and with whom they spent their time. Next, Kim asked the girls to complete a series of magazine explorations and critiques that focused on selecting and analyzing pictures that sent messages to girls about their bodies (Oliver, 2001).

---

[1]We use the word *Black* as a racial identifier to remain true to our informants' use of the term.

Kim also gave the girls journals and asked them to document the times they noticed their bodies. She encouraged the girls to write about what they were doing when they noticed their bodies, as well as what they were thinking and what they were feeling. Finally, she asked them to photograph places where they received messages about their bodies. In addition, Kim involved the girls in an inquiry project. The inquiry project was designed to help the girls critically examine some aspect of their culture that implicated girls' bodies. This chapter draws exclusively on the data from the girls' inquiry project.

For the first part of the inquiry, Kim and the girls designed a survey to learn about how other adolescent girls perceived the Beauty Walk. With Kim's help, the girls created 12 survey questions designed to evoke comment and critique of the Beauty Walk. These included among others: Do you think the Beauty Walk is a popularity contest; why does Landview Middle School have a Beauty Walk; and what do girls who are in the Beauty Walk have to do to prepare for the "Walk"?

To learn more about the Beauty Walk, two of our four collaborators, Alexandria and Brandi, attended the event with Kim as participant observers. They took field notes recording their observations about contestant and audience behavior. Throughout the event the girls talked with Kim about their observations and reactions.

During the weeks immediately following the Beauty Walk, Kim helped the girls distribute their survey in two girls' physical education classes. Each of our four collaborators also interviewed two survey respondents asking for clarification and elaboration of their written comments. While our collaborators were conducting interviews with their peers, Kim interviewed Kemya, a Beauty Walk participant who self-identified racially as "mixed."

With Kim's help, Destiny, Jaylnn, Alexandria, and Brandi analyzed the survey data focusing their analysis on how the Beauty Walk affected girls. As part of analysis, the girls discussed how respondents described the unfairness and discrimination involved in the Beauty Walk. During the final phase of the inquiry, Kim helped the girls synthesize their learning about girls' perceptions of the Beauty Walk. Finally, to simulate a form of political action, Kim asked the girls to express their learning in the form of a letter to the editor of a local newspaper.

Data Sources and Analysis

Data sources for this study included audio recordings with transcriptions of each work session in which time was used for the inquiry project. Data also included researcher-generated and student-generated products relevant to the inquiry such as written instructions that Kim developed, surveys created by the girls, and letters the girls created. Kim's field notes provided an additional source of data. In all, we analyzed 13 audiotapes, 325 pages of transcriptions of audio recordings, 80 documents, and 35 pages of field notes.

To analyze the data, we two researchers, working alone and together, carefully read and reread all transcripts, listened repeatedly to the session recordings, and examined all documents. We used our data sources to construct a narrative analysis[2] (Oliver, 1998) of the Beauty Walk. We developed a set of successive drafts, working each time to more clearly articulate, elaborate, and refine our narrative so that it faithfully accounted for the data (Alvermann, O'Brien, & Dillon, 1996).

In the section that follows we draw on field notes, interviews, and student responses to illustrate what the girls learned about the interests associated with the Beauty Walk and whether the girls were able to take political action in the form of a letter to the editor. In keeping with our analytical processes, we present our learning using narrative style as a means for making the girls' experiences of the Beauty Walk palpable for our readers.

THE BEAUTY WALK

The month of February is known throughout this region for its Beauty Walk contests. In kindergarten through the 12th grade, girls are given the "opportunity" to participate in Beauty Walks. Whereas the "official" school intent for these events is to raise money for Parent Teacher Organizations (PTOs), the students use the Beauty Walk as a time and space where some girls can try on their notions of femininity and sexuality (read heterosexuality). Although the contests are held in February, the buzz begins with the "nominations" in January.

According to school policy, any girl is eligible to participate if she has at least a 2.0 grade point average and has not been suspended from school during the academic year. In practice this eligibility was somewhat more restrictive because each homeroom selected a girl who served as its official representative. Though girls not selected in this manner could self-nominate as a way to participate, few choose to use this alternative route to participation.

Most homerooms consisted of both girls and boys, and both participated in the voting process. One exception to mixed-gender homerooms occurred for students who took physical education during first period. These students met for homeroom in a same-sex group in the locker room prior to first period, thus creating an all-girls' homeroom and an all-boys' homeroom. The all-girls' homeroom was one of the groups with which Kim worked extensively and regularly described in her field notes.

---

[2]For a detailed description of narrative analysis, please see Oliver (1998).

Nomination Day: An Excerpt From Kim's Field Notes

It is 7:45 a.m. on Friday morning in late January. I walked through the locker room door to find students from the 1st period homeroom sitting in chairs and on benches awaiting Mrs. Smith to begin the Beauty Walk nominations. Today was the day that students at Landview Middle School were going to vote on which girls they wanted to represent their homeroom class in the up-coming Beauty Walk competition. The chatter in the locker room was more focused than usual. The girls were whispering about who they thought would win the nomination within their homeroom, as well as in other homerooms. Mrs. Smith began by reminding the girls of the rules for eligibility before asking for nominations.

Immediately hands shot into the air and names were yelled out. After getting the girls settled a bit more, Mrs. Smith began to call on each girl whose hand was in the air. As a name was suggested Mrs. Smith would first ask the girl being nominated if she were "interested and willing" to participate in the Beauty Walk. If the girl answered "yes," Mrs. Smith would write her name on a piece of poster board. Six girls were nominated and four accepted the nomination, while two declined. Next, Mrs. Smith handed out pieces of paper and each girl was given a chance to vote on who she wanted to represent her homeroom.

Kemya was the winner for Mrs. Smith's homeroom class. As Kemya's name was read from the tallied votes, the heads of the other three nominees dropped low signaling some level of disappointment or perhaps even shame. Kemya's face gleamed with pride. She expressed delight to have been selected and eagerness to represent her homeroom in the Beauty Walk. For her part, Mrs. Smith reminded the girls that even if they had not been se-lected as the homeroom representative, they were still eligible to participate.

"A Night Among the Stars":
Two Girls Become Participant Observers

Three weeks after the nominations, the day of the big event arrived. Student conversations focused on the Beauty Walk, as students expressed their support for various participants and predicted final outcomes. Many partic-ipants checked out of school early to get to hair and makeup appointments.

That evening, Brandi, Alexandria, and Kim met at the front of the gym-nasium to attend the event and take field notes for their inquiry project. As they entered a side door of the gym, Mrs. Smith greeted them and walked them over to where the contestants were standing in line waiting for the event to begin.

The room was filled with excitement. Some of the girls were giggling and talking among themselves; others were making last-minute adjustments to their dresses and to the dresses of others. A few were applying a last coat of lipstick. Brandi and Alexandria commented on how "grown-up" and "beautiful" the contestants looked in their long, fancy gowns. Most of the White girls were arrayed in long white gowns conveying an aura of demure innocence. The Black girls wore more colorful gowns—gowns that blended like a fresh rainbow of colors from delicate pastels to deep and vibrant hues.

After visiting with the contestants, the three observers reentered the gymnasium through the main door. Two students, serving as ushers, greeted them and handed each a program entitled, "A Night Among the Stars." Depicted on the cover was an image of a young White woman with long hair, wearing a fancy dress, pearl earrings, necklace, and bracelet.

The three found seats among several Black students attending the event. They noted that the majority of those attending were Black. Most of these audience members were students, though a few were adults who had come to support contestants. There was also a small group of White students in the audience, as well as a group of White parents and family members of Beauty Walk contestants. Three female judges sat in the front of the gym under the stage; two were Black and one was White.

While looking through the program, Alexandria and Brandi identified the race of each participant. In a school with a student population that was reportedly 70% African American, one might have expected that, if all things were equal, about 70% of the participants would have been African American. Nevertheless, of the 37 Beauty Walk participants, only 46% (17 girls) were persons of color, whereas 54% (20 girls) were White. These numbers reminded Alexandria and Brandi of a claim they had considered during inquiry sessions with Kim. "A lot of Black girls don't want to be in it because White girls always win." They noted that the racial composition of this group made them suspect that there might be more truth to this assertion than they earlier believed.

Shortly, the lights dimmed and the program began with the "parade of the beautiful students." During this time all 37 girls paraded out onto the stage in a single-file line to form a semicircle at the back of the stage facing the audience. Once the girls were in place on stage, each contestant took a turn walking to the front and center of the stage, turning around so that her back was facing the audience, waiting 3 seconds in that position, and then walking to the far side of the stage before returning to her original position. As each girl walked, she was introduced by name and, if appropriate, by the homeroom that had nominated her. For example, the announcer called out, "Kemya Reeves from Mrs. Smith's homeroom," as Kemya took her turn walking across the stage. The announcer also reported each girl's age, the name(s) of her parent(s), her preferred activities, and her favorite television show. In her field notes, Brandi recorded her assessment of the audience response. "The Black girls received more applause from the audience than the White girls."

Next, the three judges selected the top 11 contestants. Typically only 10 girls were selected, but on this evening two girls tied for the number 10 position resulting in a "top 11."

The only apparent criteria informing the judges' selections were how the girls looked and how they walked across the stage. As the names of the top 11 contestants were called, each stepped forward to form a line at the front of the stage. Thus two lines of girls were formed. The girls remaining in the back line were those who had not been selected to advance to the next level of competition.

While observing the formation of the two lines of girls, Brandi, Alexandria, and Kim each commented on the racial composition of each line noting that the "majority of the girls" in the back line—those who had been eliminated from further consideration—were "Black." In contrast, the "majority of girls" in the front line—those who would continue to "walk in beauty" in this competition—were "White." Brandi made a record in her notes to describe the successful girls: "Eight were White girls, 2 were Black girls, and 1 girl was interracial."

The next phase of the competition involved each of the "top 11" girls answering the judges' question, "Who do you admire most and why?" As each semifinalist took her turn, the girls who had not been selected remained standing at the back of the stage. Typical responses were "mom" and "grandmother." A few girls named a celebrity. Once answers had been supplied, the judges announced the top three contestants, as well as the girl to be designated as "Ms. Congeniality."

The second runner-up was a light-skinned interracial girl, Rachel. Rachel had long brownish black hair and hazel eyes. She wore a long peach dress. She was approximately 5 feet 4 inches tall and weighed about 105 pounds. The first runner-up was a White girl, Carol. Carol had long blond hair and green eyes. She was about the same size as Rachel but dressed in a White gown. Ms. Congeniality was also a White girl, Amie. Like Carol, Amie, too, was blond and dressed in a white gown. The Beauty Walk winner was Mary Anne. Mary Anne was a short, thin, blond, White girl. As well, she was the daughter of the school's PTO president. She, too, was dressed in a white gown. Brandi described the winner by exclaiming, "Mary Anne looks like a Barbie doll!"

As the winner was announced the response from the audience was dramatic. There was almost no applause. Most students rose quickly yet silently from their chairs and exited the building.

Kemya's Beauty Walk Experience: An Interview

Kemya Reeves described herself as a 13-year-old "mixed" (half White, half African American) girl. On several occasions prior to the Beauty Walk she had talked with Kim about her excitement to be a participant as she described a variety of ways she'd been preparing for the event. She had told Kim that she had participated in several school-sponsored Beauty Walk competitions in her past, as well as other beauty pageants throughout the community. She described how she "loved to get dressed up and be onstage at the center of attention." When Kim interviewed Kemya following the contest, her views had shifted noticeably:

> Okay. When I first left school I was really happy, and my dress had just got back from the cleaners 'cause it had to be pressed. And I was so excited, and I went to get my hair done. And I was gonna get my nails done, but I didn't think that was, you know, they wouldn't see my hands that much. And I got my hair done, and I thought it was just so cute, and then I got home and it started to fall and I was like, "Oh my God, oh my God!" I was going crazy. And then I went to McRae's [department store] and this lady did a beautiful job on my makeup. I loved it. I thought it was so cute. And I practiced my walk like it was nothin'. Like this is my stage, it's my walk.... And I feel that I should have made at least the top 11.... I didn't think it was fair ... because most of the girls that won, it's not necessarily a racial part, but you know, every girl that was up there [in the top 11] was blonde hair and green eyes, blond hair and blue eyes. And Rachel, I don't even think they [the judges] knew that she was a mixed, or had Black in her because her skin was so light ... and then [when the winner was announced] the thing that was so funny, it wasn't necessarily funny.... It was total silence in there [in the auditorium]. Total silence! After Mary Anne [the winner] started walking, everybody got up and left. I couldn't believe it! I was like, "Oh my god!" It was funny, but you know I think it kinda hurt her feelings. She was like "Why is everybody leaving?" I think she kinda felt bad about it. And there were like all of these rumors going around ... Her mother knew the judges—all that type of stuff.... Her mom is the PTO president.

"Doing Us a Favor":
Theorizing the Role of Race in the Beauty Walk

When we first began the inquiry into the Beauty Walk, Destiny, Jaylnn, Alexandria, and Brandi expressed doubts that race played any part in the competition. They reasoned that because "both White and Black girls were allowed to participate" the event should be considered to be fair. Nonetheless, after observing the event and surveying other girls' perceptions of the Beauty Walk, they became rather skeptical about the fairness of the event with respect to both race and social influence.

When our collaborators analyzed the survey responses and interview data, they were somewhat surprised at what they found. In particular, they noticed the concerns about racial inequity expressed by many respondents. For example, one survey response regarding race captured the girls' attention and prompted much discussion about what role race might play in the selection process: "If the judges are White, a White girl **will** win. If the judges are Black, a Black girl **might** win." As an expression of probability (the actual voting panel consisted of two Black judges and one White judge) this assertion expressed the existence of inequitable power relations—a belief that became increasingly compelling to the girls as they pursued the inquiry.

After Brandi and Alexandria finished interviewing other girls about their survey responses, they joined Kim and Kemya, who were considering the role of race in the Beauty Walk. Together the girls and Kim began to theorize about how race operated within the school event. As part of their analysis, they noted that student influence in selecting a winner for the Beauty Walk was limited because, unlike in the selection of homecoming queen, students did not have a final vote. They also questioned the motives of the Black judges who participated in this contest:

Kemya: [There were] eight White girls, two Black girls, and one inter-racial girl. That's 11.

Brandi: I think if the Black judges picked mostly White [girls] so they could probably could get in with the, [pause] so they could fit in.

Kim: And of the Black girls [selected for the top 11] that were up there, only one had dark skin.

Kemya: You couldn't tell Rachel was Black.... Ashley's not that dark either; she's a little bit darker than me, but she's not really dark.

Brandi: They could have at least had one Black [dark-skinned] girl, but they didn't have any. Maybe they thought since Rachel was kinda mixed, maybe they thought they were doin' us a favor since she was mixed.

Alexandria: My mama says that since a Black girl won homecoming queen, you can just forget about the Beauty Walk.

Brandi: But see, we voted [for homecoming queen], it was our [student] choice.

Alexandria: In most Beauty Walks or pageants it is said that the White girls always win.

"No Need for Such a Bad Fund-Raiser": Taking Social Action

After the girls and Kim had finished analyzing the survey responses and interviews, the girls worked in pairs to prepare a letter to the editor of a local paper. This was an important task from Kim's viewpoint because letter writing can be a politically powerful strategy. To support their letter writing, Kim asked the girls to work in pairs to write a letter that synthesized what they had learned about the Beauty Walk. Both pairs were able to finish a letter to the editor. Both letters expressed quite similar views and focused on concerns the girls had about the Beauty Walk. The letter written by Destiny and Jaylnn is illustrative:

> To Whom It May Concern:
>
> Concerned students say Beauty Walk (B.W.) discriminates, is unfair, and is almost equal to prostitution. The B.W. is an event that sells tickets to students, parents, and friends to see 8th grade young women parade around on the stage in pretty, expensive, and fancy gowns. According to 8th grade girls, B.W. is "unfair" because girls are judged by their looks not by character, talent, or any other quality. Also B.W. costs too much money. Therefore, girls that do not have enough money can't afford to participate. Girls have to get their nails & hair done, buy a dress & shoes.... Most girls don't have enough money for those kinds of things. They don't have to do these things, but they are afraid if they come as themselves, the everyday person that they are, that they really won't win. That lowers most girls' self-esteem .... Also because only one girl wins and that makes every other girl feel "not so beautiful." ... Some of the girls say that the B.W. discriminates by race because most of the time it's a white girl that wins.... They also say that most of the people that are judges are White. The 8th grade girls say that's "racist" because the judges are White[3] and the girl that wins or the girls in the top 10 are White.... What I'm trying to say is that there's no need for a school to have such a "bad" fundraiser for school. It makes girls feel bad about themselves.
>
> Sincerely, Destiny and Jaylnn (8th grade girls)

DISCUSSION

With Kim's support the girls were able to develop a "language of critique." For example, they were able to identify how gender inequity was structured in the social space of the Beauty Walk. As the letter by Destiny and Jaylnn explained, "BW is unfair because girls are judged by their looks not by their character, talent, or other quality." Thus these girls were beginning to challenge the way that beauty is featured discursively as an essential and even primary goal for a girl to pursue. Their assertion of unfairness suggests awareness that gender is not a fact to be lived with so much as it is one of many "social constructions we have learned to live by" (Brodkey & Fine, 1992, p. 80).

---

[3]This statement is not a representation of the events in the actual Beauty Walk that occurred.

The girls were also able to note the inequities of social class evident in the costs associated with the clothes and services that contestants in the Beauty Walk believed were essential for participation. The girls addressed this issue in their letters to the editor. Although they did not raise the issue of social class explicitly, they astutely explained the underlying inequity. "Most girls don't have enough money for these kinds of things." These insights are consistent with many available in the literature on critical pedagogy. For example, Arnot (1992) argued that the influence of social class, though often ignored in capitalistic societies, has enormous range. "It affects the shape of educational careers, the nature of schooling and training received, and the possibility of higher education after compulsory schooling. It does this for both men and women, for all ethnic groups, and for individuals in all geographic regions within that [capitalistic] society" (p. 28).

Besides pointing to inequities due to gender and social class, the girls adamantly expressed concern about racial inequity. That is, they frequently raised the issue of racial inequity, pointing to an unfairness of the competition for the Black contestants. Brandi and Alexandria took particular note of the racial identity of the contestants on the stage, highlighting how the relatively low level of participation by Black girls was exacerbated by the even more drastic discrepancy in the racial makeup of the group of semifinalists. As the girls and Kim noted, of the top 11 contestants only 3 were non-Whites. In a school where 70% of the students were registered as African American, this pattern of success captured the girls' attention and evoked their discontent.

Kemya developed the idea of racial inequity even while disavowing its existence. "Most of the girls that won, it's not necessarily a racial part, but you know, every girl that was up there was blond hair and green eyes, blond hair and blue eyes. And Rachel, I don't even think they [the judges] knew that she was mixed or had Black in her." Brandi theorized about the behavior of Black judges, suggesting that they were seeking acceptance or affiliation: "I think if the Black judges picked mostly White [girls] so they could probably could get in with the, [pause] so they could fit in." Brandi's explanation of the judges' decisions reflects simmering emotion and identification as a Black person. "Maybe, they thought since Rachel was kinda mixed, maybe they thought they were doin' us a favor."

The girls' theories of racial inequity were not confined to those of our four collaborators. Such theories appeared in numerous survey comments written by other students. For example, one respondent stated, "If the judges are White, a White girl **will** win. If the judges are Black a Black girl **might** win." Thus the respondent suggested a broad-based skepticism among Black students about the fairness of the Beauty Walk. Such skepticism would help to explain the behavior of the audience when the winner was announced as a form of social protest. It could also account for Alexandria's report of her mother's view: "My mama says that since a Black girl won homecoming queen, you can just forget about the Beauty Walk."

This analysis of the racial inequity structured within the social space of the Beauty Walk is consistent with recommendations from Ladson-Billings and Tate (1995), who have argued that race remains "a central construct for organizing inequity" (p. 50) and thus should not be subsumed as gender or ethnicity. It also supports the view of Collins (1998) that critical feminist work is likely to be distorted and limiting when it does not take into account the views and issues developed through non-White standpoints. Had we included only White girls as collaborators, the critique of the Beauty Walk would more easily have overlooked, downplayed, or dismissed a consideration of racial inequity.

The girls were able to theorize about ways that gender, class, and race figured into the social space of the Beauty Walk. That is, they were able to see how interests of girls, of nonaffluent girls, and of Black girls were not well served by the Beauty Walk. Nevertheless, they did not question the construction of sexuality structured within that social space. Rather their analysis maintained the perspective of heteronormativity—the unquestioned expectation that heterosexuality is the normal human experience and perspective.

The absence of alternative sexual perspectives is not surprising within discussions that occur at school where the official discursive practices around sexuality, whether through instruction in physical education or through family life curriculum and pedagogy, have been marked by distortion and omission and directed toward control of the adolescent body. These practices are typically rooted in a logic that "the control of bodily instincts enables the activities of the mind to flourish" (McDade, 1992, p. 52). Nevertheless this omission is a significant one because as Sumara and Davis (1999) suggest, pedagogy is heterosexualized and linked to "all other knowledges and all other forms of knowing" (p. 201). Thus by interrogating the sexuality in pedagogy we can gain insight on how we and others come to know. This analytical lens represents a challenge for us as we continue to develop and examine analytical processes intended to be transformative.

Even within a context of presumed heterosexuality, the girls talked little about their own sexual desires and how these related to the Beauty Walk. One exception is the allusion to pleasure apparent in Kemya's account of her experience: "And then I went to McRae's [department store] and this lady did a beautiful job on my makeup. I loved it. I thought it was so cute. And I practiced my walk like it was nothin'. Like this is my stage, it's my walk." Nevertheless, Kemya did not elaborate on her pleasure nor did Kim elicit further discussion. This omission is significant in part because pleasure and desire are central in the development of subjectivity "the site of the consensual regulation of individuals ... through the identification by the individual to particular subject positions within discourses" (Weedon, 1987, p. 112). More attention to the role of pleasure and desire in the development of transformative pedagogy represents another important challenge for future work.

Besides examining the girls' "language of critique," this research also focused on the girls' use of a "language of possibility." That is, we wanted to know whether the girls could use their critique as a basis for pursuing some form of action. In this study it was Kim who suggested that the girls write a letter to the editor. She introduced this task at a lively point in the girls' discussion of the Beauty Walk, and it was met with enthusiastic response. The girls also pursued the survey design, analysis of survey responses, and interviewing with enthusiasm. For example, they eagerly worked on practicing interviews and identifying themes in the survey data. They produced letters to the editor that included many of the arguments that they developed during data analysis and discussion. The letters, if disseminated in the community, could potentially have influenced public opinion about the school event. However, once they finished the letters, the girls seemed exhausted and expressed disinterest in pursuing the topic further.

Because our work with girls is rooted in a belief in the importance of following girls' interests (Oliver & Lalik, in press), Kim moved on to a related project in which the girls took pictures of places where they received messages about their bodies. We do not see Kim's shift in the direction of the girls' expressed wishes as a shortcoming of our work. Rather, we recognize that by assuming the subject position as teachers, we are "implicated in the very structures we wish to change" (Ellsworth, 1992, p. 101). By accepting the girls' disinterest and moving to an allied but different project, we were attempting to mitigate the typical asymmetrical power relations between teachers and students that contribute to oppression.

In retrospect, we might have pursued the action part of this collaboration by using the girls' interests as a springboard for action. Thus in future work, we (and others) may wish to invite girls to design their own initiatives for action. That is, rather than asking girls to pursue some form of action that we teacher/researchers construe, we might ask them to brainstorm various types of possible action, imagine ways to conduct the actions they identify, and select plans for actions they deem worthy enough and compelling enough to pursue, perhaps with assistance from adult collaborators. The girls might have much more intellectual and creative energy available to them if they are engaged in action plans of their own design.

As part of a more learner-centered approach to a "language of possibility," we might also wish to help girls analyze various types of actions they imagine and consider. For example, certain types of action might be considered "palliative" insofar as they operate to relieve the pain inflicted on targets of inequitable relations. Other forms of action might be considered "systemic" insofar as they alter systems of relations that operate to produce conditions of inequity.[4] Time spent considering types of action might help both adolescent and adult collaborators make more judicious choices for action.

Perhaps what will be most important in developing a more learner-centered approach to the "language of possibility" is relying on the principle that the choice of action should remain largely with the adolescents. Their choices may be different from those of their adult collaborators, but by helping them to pursue those choices adults may provide adolescents with opportunities to participate as actors in the world—actors aware of both the power that is possible when they act in concert to influence their world and the responsibility such power carries with it.

In sum, these girls were able to develop a "language of critique" that included considerations of how social constructions of gender, class, and race differentially affected participation and success in the Beauty Walk. They were able to develop a "language of possibility" insofar as at Kim's suggestion they produced a text that had potential to influence community opinion. Yet given the limitations in their critique and in our ability to support that critique and given the limitation in their approach to social action, we can see that there is much work ahead if we persist in this agenda toward transformation. Given our belief that such efforts have considerable potential for increasing the life chances (New London Group, 1996) of adolescents, it is likely that our work will continue.

DISCUSSION QUESTIONS

1. How can we inspire critique and social action without dominating the very learners we wish to support?

2. How might teachers and researchers initiate dialogue on heteronormative practices in schools?

3. What approaches would you take if you wanted to help adolescents participate in critique and social action?

REFERENCES

Alvermann, D. E., O'Brien, D. G., & Dillon, D. R. (1996). On writing qualitative research. *Reading Research Quarterly, 31*(1), 114–120.

Arnot, M. (1992). Schools and families: A feminist perspective. In K. Weiler & C. Mitchell (Eds.), *What schools can do: Critical pedagogy and practice* (pp. 27–48). Albany: State University of New York Press.

Brodkey, L., & Fine, M. (1992). Presence of mind in the absence of body. In K. Weiler & C. Mitchell (Eds.), *What schools can do: Critical pedagogy and practice* (pp. 75–94). Albany: State University of New York Press.

---

[4]These categories of action are not intended to be mutually exclusive.

Collins, P. H. (1998). *Fighting words: Black women and the search for justice*. Minneapolis: University of Minnesota Press.

Ellsworth, E. (1992). Why doesn't this feel empowering? Working through the repressive myths of critical pedagogy. In C. Luke & J. Gore (Eds.), *Feminisms and critical pedagogy* (pp. 90–119). New York: Routledge.

Fine, M., & Macpherson, P. (1992). Over dinner: Feminism and adolescent female bodies. In M. Fine (Ed.), *Disruptive voices: The possibilities of feminist research* (pp. 175–202). Ann Arbor: University of Michigan Press.

Giroux, H. (1992). The hope of radical education. In K. Weiler & C. Mitchell (Eds.), *What schools can do: Critical pedagogy and practice* (pp. 13–26). Albany: State University of New York Press.

Ladson-Billings, G., & Tate, W. (1995). Toward a critical race theory of education. *Teachers College Record, 97*(1), 47–68.

Lewis, M. (1992). Interrupting patriarchy. In C. Luke & J. Gore (Eds.), *Feminisms and critical pedagogy* (pp. 167–191). New York: Routledge.

McDade, L. (1992). Sex, pregnancy, and schooling: Obstacles to a critical teaching of the body. In K. Weiler & C. Mitchell (Eds.), *What schools can do: Critical pedagogy and practice* (pp. 49–74). Albany: State University of New York Press.

New London Group. (1996). A pedagogy of multiliteracies: Designing social futures. *Harvard Educational Review, 66*, 60–92.

Oliver, K. L. (1998). A journey into narrative analysis: A methodology for discovering meanings. *Journal of Teaching in Physical Education, 17*(2), 244–259.

Oliver, K. L. (2001). Images of the body from popular culture: Engaging adolescent girls in critical inquiry. *Sport, Education, & Society, 6*(2), 143–164.

Oliver, K. L., & Lalik, R. (in press). "The Beauty Walk, this ain't my topic": Learning about critical inquiry with adolescent girls. *The Journal of Curriculum Studies*.

Sumara, D., & Davis, B. (1999). Interrupting heteronormativity: Toward a queer curriculum theory. *Curriculum Inquiry, 29*(2), 191–208.

Walkerdine, V. (1990). *Schoolgirl fictions*. New York: Verso.

Walkerdine, V. (1997). *Daddy's girl: Young girls and popular culture*. Cambridge, MA: Harvard University Press.

Weedon, C. (1987). *Feminist practice and poststructuralist theory*. New York: Basil Blackwell.

Chapter 7

Fighters and Cheerleaders: Disrupting the Discourse of "Girl Power" in the New Millennium

Natalie G. Adams
The University of Alabama

Girl Power is a term found in both academic and popular-press writing to describe the recent girl empowerment movement sweeping the United States, Britain, Israel, and other industrialized nations.[1] Girl Power has been used to explain everything from the proliferation of girls in sports (Dickson, 1999; Solomon, 1999), the takeover of girls in pop music (Schoemer, 1997; Wener, 1998), the enormous power girls exert on what sells on TV and at the box office (Labi, 1998), the increase in violent crimes committed by girls (Carroll, 1998; Fowler, 1999; " 'Girl Power' Fuels Bullying," 1998), the perceived masculinity crisis among boys (Arlidge, 1999), and the "most positive public health trend in this country" (Roan, 1999). Lemish (1998) asserts that Girl Power, as understood by the middle-class Jewish Israeli girls in her study, is an "expression of independence, strength, success, and self-worth" (p. 153). Melanie Chisolm, one of the former Spice Girls, whose mantra was "Girl Power," defines Girl Power

---

[1]Girl Power appeared in newspaper headlines in 1944 to describe the rioting of 30,000 girls who, after being informed that the Frank Sinatra concert was sold out, "mobbed the streets, broke shop windows, and destroyed the Paramount ticket booth" (Munk, 1997). Police hand to be called in to subdue the unruly girls. Girl power was also used in conjunction with the "riot grrl" movement begun in the late 1980s and early 1990s in the Pacific Northwest.

101

as "being able to do things just as well as the boys—if not better—and being who you wannabe" (McFarland, 1998). Jane Pratt, the editor of *Jane* magazine, defines Girl Power as "mean[ing] something different from feminism. It means finding the strength and expressing the strength that's girlie—everything from the way that girls talk to each other to having fun with makeup. And, most important, it refers to girls or women supporting each other or choosing not to put a man first" (Hall, 1998). Or defined another way by several preteen girls, "Girl Power means that girls can do everything that boys can do. That we're as good as boys and sometimes better. It means that your friends will always be there for you, no matter what happens" (McFarland, 1998). Whether Girl Power is being used to sell Gatorade, red meat, Soft & Dri deodorant, the new CosmoGirl, or to describe the recent good news about girls in schools and in athletics, Girl Power signifies a cultural shift in describing what constitutes today's ideal girl.

However, for those of us who are parents, teachers, and advocates of adolescent girls, we must look deeper into this new construction of girlhood and ask: Who is the "girl" being sold in this seemingly new discourse of girlhood? And, more important, what kinds of "power" are afforded to girls in the 21st century and at what costs? In this chapter, I draw upon the everyday world of early-adolescent girls to look at how girlhood and girl empowerment plays out in the discursive practices of two activities involving girls—cheerleading and fighting. On the surface, one may find it difficult to discern any identifiable similarities between the two. Certainly, cheerleading since its takeover by females in the 1950s, has become a cultural icon for representing ideal girlhood (Adams & Bettis, 2003). Hanson (1995) notes that the cheerleader is an "instantly recognized symbol of youthful prestige, wholesome attractiveness, peer leadership and popularity" (p. 2). In fact, cheerleaders are often described as the "all-American" girl or the "girl next door." Adler and Adler (1995) and others (Eder, 1985; Merten, 1996) have documented that in schools cheerleaders represent the highest status position for girls. On the other hand, fighting has been viewed as a quintessential masculine activity. Typically, girls who fight are seen as exhibiting gender deviancy and thus viewed as abnormal or freakish (Adams, 1999).[2] Peruse any issue of *The American Cheerleader* or watch any of the nationally televised cheerleading competitions and what becomes readily apparent is that cheerleading is associated with Whiteness and middle to high socioeco-

---

[2]However, with the well-publicized entrance of the daughters of Ali, Frazier, and Foreman into the world of boxing as well as the recent plethora of movies featuring girls and women who fight (e.g., *Shrek*, *Crouching Tiger, Hidden Dragon*, *Lara Croft: Tombfinder*, *Enough*, and *Girl Fight*), the phenomenon of women fighting has begun to receive some favorable attention.

nomic status. Read any account of girls fighting in popular or academic writing and the image is almost always that of poor girls and/or girls of color. Drawing from two ethnographic studies conducted in two different middle schools (one in the Midwest and one in the Deep South), I argue in this chapter that similar discursive practices operate in both the practice of cheerleading and the practice of fighting, although the participants of these practices differ with cheerleaders being primarily White and middle class and fighters being primarily poor and/or non-White. Hence, the implications of how these two groups of girls are situated differently within the discourse of normative girlhood at their school challenges us to disrupt the normalization of girlhood, even in the supposedly liberatory discourse of Girl Power.

ATHLETICISM, STRENGTH, AND ASSERTIVENESS AS GIRL POWER

There is no question that cheerleading has changed as a result not only of the recent Girl Power movement but as a result of several pro-female policies (e.g., Title IX and the move to recognize cheerleading as a sport in approximately 20 states). Varsity Cheerleading, one of the leading cheerleading companies in the United States, captures the spirit of Girl Power in their opening poem for their 1999 catalog:

I am not arrogant.
I am confident.
I am not a daredevil.
I am daring.
I am not a beauty queen,
I am an athlete.
I am not a stereotype.
I am my own person.
I am not interested in the past.
I am living for the future.
I am not afraid of success.
I am afraid of nothing.
I am not another face in the crowd.
I am the one others wish they could be.

What we learn about Girl Power in this poem is that cheerleaders, as personification of the ideal girl, are daring athletes, not silly beauty queens. They are also independent, future oriented, success oriented, fearless, dominant, and the envy of others.

As we listen to the following conversation among five middle school girls who are known at their school as fighters, we hear similar references to confidence, fearlessness, dominance, independence, and the need to prove they are "not another face in the crowd":

Interviewer:	Tell me some reasons why you fight.
India (African American):	I'll fight somebody if they're being messy with my boyfriend.
Chasity (African American):	If someone talks about my family or my friends, I'll fight them.
India (African American):	I'll fight for money or if someone tries to steal something from me.
Trisha (White):	I'll fight if someone hits me first.
Kerry African American):	Or if someone calls me a bad name.
Sharon (White):	I fight for rulership, to show that I'm somebody.

Both cheerleading and fighting are social practices that allow girls a space to demonstrate the valued characteristics of today's ideal girl—self-determination and assertiveness. In both practices, girls are often demonstrating that they are rational thinkers in charge of their bodies and their lives. Take for example, Sharon, a poor White girl who has in the past been involved in relationships with abusive men. She has learned to fight as a way to demonstrate that she alone is responsible for her own well-being:

> After I got in a fight with his ex-girlfriend, me and him [a boyfriend] got into a fight 'cause he say, "Sharon, why did you hit that girl? You didn't have to hit her." And he came back and hit me and I was drinking a 40-ounce and I took it and cracked it on his TV and I said, "You want some of me?" He backed off and said, "We don't have to do all that."

> You do with your body what you want to do. You don't let nobody do nothing to you unless you want it. Like sometimes, I'll be standing at my locker and some boy will come grab my butt. I'll turn around and he'll be standing here, and I slap him and say, "Leave me alone you chip-tooth mother fucker."

Similarly, Julie, Lisa, and Patti, three White, middle-class girls recently selected junior high cheerleaders, talk about how cheerleading offers them the opportunity to demonstrate control of self and others:

Patti:	Most of us are loud and we like to cheer because we like to draw attention to ourselves at school and stuff.
Lisa:	Cheerleading's just neat 'cause you get to tumble and you get to be some of the stars of the game.... It's just you want to be one of the main focuses of the game instead of the players. And you want to get people's attention.

Julie: I like getting up in front of people and, like, being the one in charge.

Girls who cheer and girls who fight are, in many ways, contesting stereotypical images of the passive, inert female body because both social practices require girls to demonstrate a degree of athleticism, aggressiveness, and power. Woodmansee (1993) illuminates how cheerleading has evolved in the last 20 years:

> No longer are cheerleaders merely the most popular girls with the prettiest teeth; today, both men and women who practice cheerleading are finely conditioned athletes who are selected for their skills rather than the number of friends they have at school. Cheerleaders today train alongside football players in the weight room, adhere to special diets, and devote exhausting hours to wind-sprints, calisthenics, and intense choreography. (p. 18)

Georgia All-Star Cheerleading coach Julie Parrish notes that cheerleading has "evolved in recent years into more of a dangerous sport than recreation … Everything has changed so much in this sport. These kids are athletes. We don't even own a pair of pompoms or megaphones" (Alpert, 1999, p. JG-11).

In the cheerleading preparation class observed as part of this study, cheerleading as an athletic endeavor was emphasized repeatedly. In preparation for trying out in front of three judges, Ms. Stone, the cheerleader sponsor, instructed the girls continuously to show off their muscular bodies:

> All right, girls, make your muscles tight so the judges can see them.
> Tight across the shoulders. Tomorrow you should hurt.
> Legs are tight. This is a great time to show off your muscles.

In addition to having a muscular, fit body, the ability to tumble and maintain "tight motion technique," which alluded to rigid body movements that some would characterize as almost militaristic in style, were also critical to making the squad. Lisa, a petite blonde who scored the highest number of points at tryouts, explains the importance of being "tight": "Like when you cheer, your arms have to be tight, and your emotions are like aggressive, not like to where you're going to punch someone, just like when they're tight. Like when I get up there, I'm like [hard snapping noise] push my arms down and slap them." This aggressive attitude was encouraged by Ms. Stone whose language during practices was replete with militaristic jargon. "Command the room" was a phrase she frequently used to motivate the girls into maintaining an aggressive attitude toward the judges and audience. In teaching proper motion techniques, she instructed them, "punch forward—don't swing your arms. Keep everything close to your body. Think close. Tight, tight, tight." Much like a drill sergeant, Ms. Stone while working with the girls on motion technique yelled: "Chins up, shoulders back, smiles. Hit the motion. Hit. Hit. Hit. 1, 2, 3, hit. 1, 2, 3, hit. When I say Hit, do a V. When I say Hit, do a down V. Hit L; Hit V; Hit Down V." At one point, she advised the girls, "don't be afraid to push through the floor. Smash—power off your toes." At another time, she told the girls, "attack those jumps even if you don't like the side we're doing." In addition to robotic, tight motions, cheers were to be yelled in a deep masculine voice.

Just as cheerleading offers girls an opportunity to exhibit a powerful body, fighting also offer girls the opportunity to demonstrate power and aggression. Unlike the cheerleaders in this study, who paid for formal training in order to perfect their ability to execute aggressive movements (i.e., cheer classes, tumbling classes), the girl fighters in this study learned their techniques from family members who view fighting as necessary for survival:

Brittney (African American): My daddy and my oldest brother, they used to pick on me, and they used to give me boxing gloves and tell me to punch a bag or punch the wall. I still do it, see, bruise my knuckles.

Tilley (Native American): My mom says to never fight unless the person that you're mad at throws a first hit and then you defend yourself.

Kerry (African American): When I fight, I don't stop fighting until I see blood or something. I don't pull no hair, I don't scratch, I just be hitting, I just go for the face first. My brother used to beat me up all the time, so he just taught me how to fight.

India (African American): I don't do the windmill on nobody and stand there and just swing my arms. I fight like my brother, my brother, most of my brothers taught me how to fight, and when I fight I fight until I see blood. If I don't see blood, I'm going to fight you until I see some. I learned that from my brothers.

The girls who fight and the girls who cheer both talk about how they train their bodies to withstand pain through perseverance and discipline. This often involves risk taking in the face of danger and fear. The cheerleaders do this by participating in grueling, physically exhausting tumbling and cheering classes in which they must master difficult tumbling moves (e.g., back tucks), jumps that require them to contort their bodies in unusual ways, and pyramid and stunt building, which require some girls to fall backward off pyramids 8 or more feet high. In the following excerpts India, a fighter, and Lisa, a cheerleader, tell similar stories about how they emerged as victors, in very different contexts, by overcoming pain through the disciplining of their bodies and emotions:

India: Most of my fights be with boys, and they might knock me out, knock me down, but I'm going to get up and I'm going to fight back until I hurt them; they're not going to take advantage of me.

Lisa: On the day of tryouts I had 104 degrees fever; I had pneumonia. I had been sick for days and lost 6 pounds before tryouts. I wasn't going to let that stop me. At tryouts, I fell on my head during my back handspring. It was like my wrists just collapsed, but I got back up. I scored number 1.

The physicality of both fighting and cheerleading allows girls the opportunity to engage in a formal system of persuasion, invincibility, and power, thus gaining entrance into a spiritual and psychological realm usually reserved for males. Their bodies become a source of strength and subjectivity. They are able to move from an object to a subject through the use of their bodies. Very few writers talk about how fighting can be viewed as a form of transcendence. Simone de Beauvoir (1952), writing 50 years ago in *The Second Sex*, is a notable exception in that she talks about fighting in ways that do not pathologize those who fight. She even makes an interesting differentiation between sports and fighting, saying "sports does not provide information on the world and the self as intimately as does a free fight, an unpremeditated climb" (p. 330). Although she, like many people, assumes that only boys fight, her critique of fighting opens up the possibility of reading girls' fighting in ways that move beyond deficiency theories, victimization theories, and gendered theories based on essentialized notions of femininity and masculinity. She argues that the physical use of one's fists and muscles offers boys and men an avenue to "assert one's sovereignty over the world" (p. 330). She notes that feeling rage in one's body and being able to express it in a physical way is a form of transcendence for males:

> For a man to feel in his fists his will to self-affirmation is enough to reassure him of his sovereignty. Against any insult, any attempt to reduce him to the status of object, the male has recourse to his fists, to exposure of himself to blows: he does not let himself be transcended by others, he is himself at the heart of his subjectivity. Violence is the authentic proof of one's loyalty to himself, to his passions, to his own will; radically to deny this will is to deny oneself any objective truth, it is to will oneself up in an abstract subjectivity; anger or revolt that does not get into the muscles remains a figment of the imagination. (pp. 330–331)

As de Beauvoir (1952) notes, girls, however, have been denied this avenue of transcendence. This inability of girls to affirm themselves through
their fists has significant consequences on the development of girls' psy-
ches. According to de Beauvoir, "This lack of physical power leads to a more
general timidity: she has no faith in a force she has not experienced in her
body; she does not dare to be enterprising, to revolt, to invent; doomed to
docility, to resignation, she can take in society only a place already made for
her. She regards the existing state of affairs as something fixed" (p. 331).
Yet, the girls in this study who engaged in physical fighting viewed the affirmation of themselves through their fists as a way to demonstrate their own
sense of agency and control of their environment, or as Sharon explained,
"I fight to show that I am somebody."

GIRL POWER: REAFFIRMING THE "GIRL" IN GIRL POWER

As illuminated in the preceding section, cheering and fighting afford girls a
space to exhibit physicality, power, and aggression, thus embodying the
ideas behind Girl Power that suggest that anything a boy can do, a girl can
do (and perhaps do better). In many ways, cheerleading and fighting also
demonstrate another important feature of Girl Power—that is, girls value
their relationships with others and are loyal, particularly to their girlfriends
and their families. As the girls in the opening section stated, "Girl Power
means that your friends will always be there for you, no matter what happens" (McFarland, 1998).

One of the primary reasons why girls fight is to prove their loyalty to a
friend, boyfriend, or family. In this way, they are demonstrating "the importance of friendship, unity, and togetherness" (Lemish, 1998, p. 160):

Denise (White):	When one of us ever hear of a fight, we always there backing our friends, just in case someone tries to jump them.
Sharon (White):	If Monica wants to fight India, I'm going to be India's back. I'll beat Monica up 'cause India's my baby's godmother; I don't want nobody hurting her 'cause if something happens to me, my baby going straight to her.
India (African American):	Me and Sharon got the relationship of a lifetime. I really don't think nothing could break me and Sharon's relationship. Because if I'm ready to fight somebody, Sharon's got to say, "Don't fight them. I'll handle it." She'll fight for me. Sharon will get suspended for me.

Shameka (African American):	All the Black girls and the White girls that hang out with the Black girls are gonna jump this one girl and some of her friends because she calls the Black people "niggers" and the White girls who hang out with them "nigger lovers." I gotta hurry up and get outside so I can try to keep my friends from fighting.

Cheerleading has long been seen as a space for girls to forge friendships and develop unity and togetherness. As any cheerleader can attest, long hours, both at cheerleading camp and at team practices, are devoted to building loyalty, trust, and harmony. The Cheerleading Constitution, which all cheerleaders at the site of this study must sign, speaks to the importance of loyalty and unity: "The primary purpose of cheerleading is to promote unity, sportsmanship, and school spirit at school and school events…. The primary function of cheerleading program is to support interscholastic athletics." One of the main reasons why the cheerleaders in this study wanted to be cheerleader was to have the opportunity to make new friends, to bond with other girls, and to have fun with each other. It was a space for them to publicly act "hyper" and "silly," and to "get crazy" with their girlfriends.

However, this emphasis on the importance of girlfriends in their lives should not be mistaken for opening up in the discourse of normative girlhood to other forms of sexual identity. The discourse of Girl Power is still very much couched in the expectation that only one sexual orientation is appropriate for ideal girls—that is, heterosexual. In many ways, fighting and cheerleading can both be read as an affirmation of heterosexualized femininity. Fighting to either preserve or earn the position of some boy's girlfriend was often cited as one of the reasons why girls fight:

Trisha (White):	Last weekend, I got in a fight over my boyfriend, 'cause I liked him and another girl who lives in my neighborhood is a slut, and she wanted to go out with him, and I told her she wasn't going to get him, so we fought.
Kerry (African American):	I was with my boyfriend one day and we were at the mall and his ex-girlfriend came up to him and asked him something, and I asked him what she say, and she started talking crazy, so I just punched her in her face. She ain't going to take my man away.

Similarly, cheerleading was attractive to many of the girls because it of-fered a quick route, they thought, to gaining a boyfriend:

Milea (Native American):	Boys like cheerleaders so that makes you popular. I want more boys to like me.
Shanna (Native American):	Some girls think the boys will like you if you're a cheerleader 'cause boys like the cheeriest people.
Daneka (Native American and White):	Girls want to be cheerleaders because they believe that guys will like them more—they will see them as cute women in short skirts.

CONCLUSION

Norms of femininity have changed, and in many ways ideal girlhood in the 21st century is in a liminal state, allowing girls to assume both signifi-ers of traditional femininity and masculinity. Girl Power can be read in some ways as a positive move away from the Girl in Crisis discourse of the 1990s. Certainly more girls are playing sports today than before Title IX; the achievement gap between boys and girls in some areas has less-ened (Phillips, 1998); and female protagonists on televisions and movies provide accessible portrayals of girls as active, take-charge individuals who do not need boys to be fulfilled. Certainly, a powerful component of the discourse of Girl Power is that girls and young women are being urged to adopt many of the traits once associated primarily with norma-tive masculinity. Entrance into these masculine spheres, girls are being told, will give them a form of power not experienced by the majority of girls in previous generations. However, the success of Girl Power as a selling tool of ideal girlhood is based on another significant component of the discourse; that is, girls are not being asked to give up their femi-ninity, but rather are being given a cultural script for today's version of ideal girlhood that says it is desirable to assume some of the signifiers of masculinity as long as they remain feminine. Susan Douglas (1997) de-scribes this liminal state of contemporary girlhood: "Girls today are being urged, simultaneously, to be independent, assertive, and achieve-ment-oriented, yet also demure, attractive, soft-spoken, fifteen pounds underweight, and deferential to men." Or put more simply by a group of early-adolescent girls: "A girl could be anyone—as long as she is pretty" (Lemish, 1998, p. 162).

But the context for how and to what degree this gender blending can occur greatly determines who will be constructed as "normal" within the discourse of Girl Power and who gets constructed as "abnormal." Hence, the opportunity to perform idealized girlhood is available to only a select few girls. For example, when athleticism, assertiveness, and competitiveness is acceptable for girls only in certain contexts (e.g., cheerleading, soccer, gymnastics), a large majority of girls are left outside the parameters of acceptable gendered behavior for girls. Girls have to figure out for themselves how far they can go in pushing the boundaries of acceptable feminine behavior. At the schools where these two studies took place, it was quite evident that the cheerleaders (i.e., White, middle-class girls) were viewed as possessing and embodying desirable traits for girls, thus being inside the discourse of Girl Power. Cheerleading offered a select few girls a space to "play" with some of the traditional markers of masculinity, such as athleticism, risk taking, and self-discipline, without transgressing clearly demarcated gendered boundaries. As Candance Berry, coach of a Kentucky cheerleading squad that has won many national competitions, states, "cheerleading offers budding young women something that girls' basketball, track, soccer, softball can't offer: lessons in how to be a *lady*, how to be tough without imitating men" (McElroy, 1999, p. 119).

On the other hand, the girls (i.e., poor and/or non-White girls) who were known at their school as fighters were perceived as performing femininity in ways that take Girl Power too far as Sharon was reminded one day, when after a slight skirmish with a boy outside the classroom, her teacher asked her, "Why can't you act like a proper little lady?" These girls were considered gendered abnormalities in that they disrupt normative beliefs about ideal femininity by going too far in imitating men and assuming too many masculine signifiers. Sherri Inness (1999) explains that patriarchal society can allow some flexibility in redefining what constitutes normative femininity as long as men's power and privilege is not challenged. Girls who fight threaten mainstream society too much; thus, their behavior must be regulated by situating them outside the discourse of Girl Power and within a discourse of gender deviancy.

Girl Power may have opened some athletic fields to some girls; it may have encouraged some girls to enter spheres once reserved solely for boys because they can do "things just as well as the boys"; and it may have taught some girls the importance of putting their girlfriends first in their lives. But the discourse of Girl Power continues to sell many girls short, leaving them on the margins of society where normative femininity is still determined by White, patriarchal, capitalist norms. For Girl Power to be a truly progressive step in rewriting the cultural scripts for girls in the new millennium, the continuance of a narrowly defined construction of girlhood must be challenged, and multiple ways of being a "normal" girl must be encouraged. Only then will all girls, regardless of their race, class, or sexual orientation, have the opportunity to experience what it means to be a self-actualized, emotionally healthy, socially competent woman.

DISCUSSION QUESTIONS

1. Think about the recent trend in Hollywood to portray women engaging in physical fighting. What characteristics do these women fighters or "princess warriors" have in common? What message does this trend send to adolescent girls? Is this a healthy or unhealthy message?

2. Develop a list of characteristics describing the "ideal girl" of the 21st century. Which of these traits would be considered "masculine"? Which would be considered "feminine"? Which traits of the ideal girl have not changed over the years? Why?

3. Many people argue that sports is an avenue for girls to merge the cheerleader image with the fighter image. Do you agree? Do you think sports is a more liberatory space for girls than cheerleading or fighting?

REFERENCES

Adams, N. (1999). Fighting to be somebody: The discursive practices of adolescent girls' fighting. *Educational Studies, 30*(2), 115–139.

Adams, N., & Bettis, P. (2003). *Cheerleader! An American icon.* New York: Palgrave/Macmillan Press.

Adler, P., & Adler, P. (1995). Dynamics of inclusion and exclusion in preadolescent cliques. *Social Psychology Quarterly, 58*(3), 145–162.

Alpert, M. (1999, January 21). As cheering gains respect: Georgia keeps producing champions. *The Atlanta Journal,* p. JG-11.

Arlidge, J. (1999, March 14). Girl power gives boys a crisis of confidence. *The Observer* [online], p. 3. Retrieved October 13, 2000, from http://proquest.umi.com/pqdweb?TS=97144Ymt=3&Sid=1&Idx=220&Deli=1&RQT=309&Dtp=1

Carroll, R. (1998, July 22). Gangs put boot into old ideas of femininity: The violent side of girl power. *The Guardian* [online]. Retrieved October 13, 2000, from http://proquest.umi.com/pqdweb?TS=97144...mt=3&Sid=1&Idx=355&Deli=1&RQT=309&Dtp=1

de Beauvoir, S. (1952). *The second sex.* New York: Vintage Books.

Dickson, M. (1999, July 9). The impact of the U.S. Women's World Cup soccer team. *Houston Chronicle* [online], p. __. Retrieved October 13, 2000, from http://proquest.umi.com/pqdweb?TS=97144...mt=3&Sid=1&Idx=154&Deli=1&RQT=309&Dtp=1

Douglas, S. (1997, August 25). Girls 'n' spice: All things nice? *Nation* [online], *265*(6), 21. Retrieved October 16, 2000, from wysiwyg://bodyframe.5/http://ehostvgw13...=39&booleanTerm=Girl%20Power&fuzzyTerm=

Eder, D. (1985). The cycle of popularity: Interpersonal relations among female adolescents. *Sociology of Education, 58,* 154–165.

Fowler, R. (1999, July 12). Women: When girl power packs a punch. *The Guardian* [online], p. T-6. Retrieved October 13, 2000, from http://proquest.umi.com/pqdweb?TS=97144...mt=3&Sid=1&Idx=152&Deli=1&RQT=309&Dtp=1

"Girl power" fuels bullying, study says. (1998, March 30). *Christian Science Monitor, 90*(85), 7.

Hall, C. (1998, January 11). The "girls" are back, jiving and joshing. *Seattles Times* [online], p. L3. Retrieved October 13, 2000, from http://proquest.umi.com/pqdweb?TS=97145...mt=3&Sid=1&Idx=531&Deli=1&RQT=309&Dtp=1

Hanson, M. E. (1995). *Go! Fight! Win! Cheerleading in American culture.* Bowling Green, OH: Bowling Green University Press.

Hass, N. (2000, October 2). When women step into the ring. *The New York Times*, p. B8.

Inness, S. (1999). *Tough girls: Women warriors and wonder women in popular culture.* Philadelphia: University of Pennsylvania Press.

Labi, N. (1998, July 29). Girl power. *Time* [online], *151*(25), 60–62. Retrieved October 13, 2000, from http://proquest.umi.com/pqdweb?TS=97144...mt=3&Sid=1&Idx=369&Deli=1&RQT=309&Dtp =1

Lemish, D. (1998). Spice Girls' talk: A case study in the development of gendered identity. In S. Inness (Ed.), *Millennium girls: Today's girls around the world* (pp. 145–167). Lanham, MD: Rowman & Littlefield.

McElroy, J. (1999). *We've got spirit: The life and times of America's greatest cheerleading team.* New York: Simon & Schuster.

McFarland, M. (1998, October 9). Girl Power! A new form of sisterhood flexes its muscle in the marketplace. *Greensboro New Record* [online], p. D1. Retrieved October 13, 2000, from http://proquest.umi.com/pqdweb?TS=97144...mt=3&Sid=1&Idx=296&Deli=1&RQT=309&Dtp=1

Merten, D. (1996). Burnout as cheerleader: The cultural basis for prestige and priviledge in junior high school. *Anthropology and Education, 27*(1), 51–70.

Munk, N. (1997, December 8). Girl Power! *Fortune, 136*(11). [online]. Retrieved October 16, 2000, from wysiwyg://bodyframe.5/http://ehostvgw13...=35&boolean.Girl%20Power&fuzzyTerm=

Phillips, L. (1998). *The girls report: What we know and need to know about growing up female.* New York: The National Council for Research on Women.

Roan, S. (1999, November 29). Say "aaah": Media mix: Guidance on tapping into that girl power. *The Los Angeles Times* [online], p. 2. Retrieved October 13, 2000, from http://proquest.umi.com/pqdweb?TS=97144...Fmt=3&Sid=1&Idx=90&Deli=1&RQT=309&Dtp=1

Schoemer, K. (1997, December 29). The selling of girl power. *Newsweek, 131*(1), 90.

Solomon, A. (1999, April 27). Girl power? *The Village Voice* [online], *44*(16), 59–63. Retrieved October 13, 2000, from http://proquest.umi.com/pqdweb?TS=97144...mt=4&Sid=1&Idx=196&Deli=1&RQT=309&Dtp=1

Villarosa, L. (2000, October 3). Cheerleading changes and injuries increase. *The New York Times*, p. F8.

Wener, B. (1998, December 31). Girl power rules in 1998. *Houston Chronicle* [online], p. 3. Retrieved October 13, 2000, from http://proquest.umi.com/pqdweb?TS=97144...mt=3&Sid=1&Idx=252&Deli=1&RQT=309&Dtp=1

Woodmansee, K. (1993). Cheers! Jeff Webb's multicolored world wide spirit machine. *Memphis Business, 3*(7), 14–19.

Chapter 8

"Only 4-Minute Passing Periods!" Private and Public Menstrual Identities in School

Laura Fingerson
University of Wisconsin–Milwaukee

As girls start to menstruate, they must learn how to incorporate a menstruating body into their everyday lives and into their identities. A large part of this everyday life is spent in school, a place where girls have little control over their schedule and with whom they interact. By high school, girls have experience with menstruation in their private lives, yet they are still learning how to manage menstruation in public spaces. In high school, the girls move from being children concealing their new menstrual status to adults taking on a public menstrual identity. They are in a liminal space betwixt and between childhood (as nonmenstruants) and adulthood (as menstruants). In this chapter, I explore how high school age girls manage the practicalities of menstruation and their social interactions surrounding menstruation in the schools. I then turn to the tension girls experience between a private menstrual identity and public menstrual identity where menstruation is talked about and experienced in social interactions.

THINKING ABOUT THE BODY AND MENSTRUATION

The body is a hybrid of sorts. Torn between the realm of the physiological and the social, the body encompasses both but is entirely neither. Whereas biological reductionists risk losing the social in their physical renditions of

115

the body, pure social constructionist approaches focus too heavily on the construction and thus often lose the surface upon which the meanings are inscribed (Connell, 1995; Prout, 2000). Some theorists argue that there are two bodies, the social and the physical (Douglas, 1970); however, following an embodied sociology, I find that the materiality and the sociality of the body are intertwined and cannot be separated.

We are immersed in a world that has a bodily dimension, yet is not biologically determined. The body, both physical and symbolic, is dependent on the social, discursive, historical, and physical context in which it resides (Scheper-Hughes & Lock, 1987). There is a reciprocal relationship between the body's materiality and the social interactions and interpretations with which it is shaped and given meaning (James, 2000; Nettleton & Watson, 1998). We experience the "lived body" in a fundamentally social way (Leder, 1992b) and our identities hinge on the experience of our bodies.

The body is not static, but is constantly changing and shifting such as through sickness or injury. For example, when our bodies are ill, our social worlds and social interactions are subsequently altered and transformed. This is particularly true for children, whose bodies change even more dramatically and quickly than adults' through growth and puberty (James, 2000). We are *embodied* social agents: When something changes about our bodies, it changes the way we interact with it and thus we reconceptualize the body itself (Nettleton & Watson, 1998). The body is a focus of our human experience, and we experience our bodies differently daily and at different points in our life spans (Lorber, 1993).

Coinciding with a popular interest in women's and girls' self- and body image shown in news magazines and popular press-books (Ehrenreich, 1999; Pipher, 1994), there is an increasing scholarly literature on the sociology of the body and body politics, which focuses on the body in its social context (e.g., Brumberg, 1997; Leder, 1992a; Martin, 1992; Weitz, 1998). With this increased interest in women's bodies comes an interest in a central experience for women: menstruation. Menstruation is often seen as an individual "woman-issue" and not legitimate for sociological study or even everyday conversation. Given the large theoretical literature on the body and sexuality, it is surprising that menstruation, an integral and continuing event in women's lives (particularly pubertal teens' lives) that has significant implications for women's health and well-being over the life course, is still considered a taboo topic and has generally been neglected in mainstream social research (Martin, 1992; Prendergast, 2000). People tend to be uncomfortable around the topic of menstruation. It is seen as not relevant to social life. However, *all* women, whether they menstruate or not, deal with menstruation in one form or another. Women who menstruate, menstruate for approximately half of their lives. *All* men who have any interaction with women deal with menstruation in one form or another.

Existing research and writing on menstruation and menstrual issues have explored the cultural history of menstruation, women's stories about menstruation, and ways of honoring and celebrating menstruation. In addition, research has examined girls' attitudes toward menarche and menstruation, sources of information about menstruation, and the psychological impact and meanings of menarche and menstruation.[1] In dominant culture, and indeed in most cultures, menstruation is seen as dirty, gross, messy, toxic, and overall a nuisance (Delaney, Lupton, & Toth, 1988). For example, Lee (1994) found that women remembering menarche said their first menstruation made them feel dirty, unclean, ashamed, and even fearful. Amann-Gainotti (1986) found that almost half of post menarcheal girls had a negative evaluation of menstruation. Kowalski and Chapple (2000) found that women perceived themselves as stigmatized by males if they were menstruating as compared to if they were not menstruating. Some researchers have attributed these attitudes to lack of information (Amann-Gainotti, 1986; Ruble & Brooks-Gunn, 1982) or the cultural stereotypes and beliefs about menstruation (Brooks-Gunn & Ruble, 1982; Lee & Sasser-Coen, 1996).

As this literature reflects, much of the research on the body has focused on women's and girls' bodies as passive and negatively viewed. The literature has concentrated on the physical aspects of menstruation, such as the frustrations of menstruating. Previous literature has not explored the social side of menstruation that takes places among girls' and boys' interactions.

The existing literature has also lacked an emphasis on children's experiences with the body and menstruation. It is important to hear stories, thoughts, and interpretations from children and adolescents themselves and how their attitudes are important in their lives *now*, not only from memories of adults (Christensen & James, 2000). Following the "new sociology of childhood," children must be the center of analysis in researching children's experiences and children's bodies (Christensen & James 2000; Prout, 2000; Qvortrup, 1994). I extend this analysis by including adolescents in the new sociology of childhood, and I argue that adolescence is a unique "liminal" period in time where girls and boys are poised physically, emotionally, and socially between being children and being adults. A focus

---

[1]For more on the cultural history of menstruation, women's stories about menstruation, and ways of honoring and celebrating menstruation, see Delaney, Lupton, and Toth (1988); Grahn (1993); Houppert (1999); Hughes and Wolf (1997); Lee and Sasser-Coen (1996); and Owen (1998). For more on girls' attitudes toward menarche and menstruation, see Amann-Gainotti (1986); Brooks-Gunn and Ruble (1982); and Moore (1995). For more on sources of information about menstruation, see Amann-Gainotti (1986); Brooks-Gunn and Ruble (1982); Koff and Rierdan (1995); Moore (1995); and Rierdan, Koff, and Flaherty (1985). For more on the psychological impact and meanings of menarche and menstruation, see Koff, Rierdan, and Jacobson (1981); Kowalski and Chapple (2000); Lee and Sasser-Coen (1996); Moore (1995); and Usmiani and Daniluk (1997).

on adolescence is particularly important in issues of the body. Teens have mostly completed puberty and have the height and frame of adults, yet they are under the age of emancipation and are bound by adult rules and structures, such as required schooling and limits on paid work.

Previous research has also ignored collective interpretations and discussions of menstruation, which can uncover the social experiences of menstruation. Prior research has been based on individual interviews only and focus on either adult experiences or adult memories and reflections of menstruation. Most researchers have also restricted their observations to girls (notable exceptions include Amann-Gainotti, 1986, and Lovering, 1995) and mention boys only in terms of their changing sexual relationships to girls when they begin to menstruate (Lee, 1994; Lee & Sasser-Coen, 1996).

In this chapter, I address the intersections between the body and social interaction by exploring how girls negotiate their shifting identities as menstruants. How do girls manage menstruation in school? How do girls negotiate their menstrual identities in school? How does the school structure, both temporally and spatially, affect girls' menstrual identities? Answering these questions can help us address larger issues in childhood research such as how teens can negotiate their identities in school and how teens can use, inhabit, control, and be limited by space and structure in school. As I show, the girls' identities as menstruants are flexible and changing as the school setting forces a shift from private to public.

METHODS AND DATA

I employed group and individual interviews with high school–age girls and boys to explore their body and menstrual talk. Individual interviews allowed me to investigate each teen's[2] understanding of menstruation and their experiences with menstruation. I was able to learn about their worlds listening to their own language. It was also vital to understand their individual contexts and make a personal connection with each participant in order to interpret the collective discussions in which the teens engaged with their peer groups (Fingerson, 1999).

Many of the teen beliefs about life including the body and menstruation are culturally based and transmitted through social discourse. In terms of general health and sickness, Christensen and Prout (1999) showed that children talk to each other about bodily phenomena and attempt to understand their own experiences with the body through collective talk. Similarly, teens learn about the mechanics and experience of menstruation from each other, joke about it, and form beliefs about the menstruation

---

[2]I use term *teen* instead of *adolescent* as it is not only shorter, but it (and *teenager*) is preferred in teens' own language and culture.

process through social talk (Fingerson, 2001, in press). Group interviews grow directly out of peer culture as the participants construct their meanings collectively with their peers (Eder & Fingerson, 2002). In group interviews, participants build on each other's talk and discuss a wider range of experiences and opinions than may develop in individual interviews as they build their talk together, pick up on each other's ideas, and collectively respond to members' thoughts (Morgan, 1993).

After conducting pilot groups to test the questions and format of the interviews, my male research assistant, Paul, and I conducted individual and single-gender group interviews among teens, ages 14 through 19 participating in on going community groups in central and southern Indiana representing six different schools. I conducted the girls' interviews, and Paul conducted the boys' interviews. By using on going groups, the group interviews were composed of teens who knew each other and had a shared history of experiences. Twenty-six girls participated in this research with 7 group interviews and 23 individual interviews. Eleven boys participated in 2 group interviews and 11 individual interviews. The size of the group interviews ranged from two to nine participants. Most of the teens were White and were from both working and middle classes. Two were biracial, and one was a Korean immigrant. In the individual and group interviews we first asked questions about how they felt about their bodies, weight, strength, and athleticism, and then we explored how they felt about menstruation, what they knew about menstruation, and their experiences with menstruation.

My thematic analysis followed a grounded theory approach with constant comparison. Through repeated readings of the transcripts (the interviews were transcribed in full), I marked patterns that recurred in the data, particularly interesting quotes, or issues discussed in existing literature and theory. I developed analytic themes based on those patterns. Through each reading of the transcripts, I continued to revise and develop new codes as themes continually emerged, and I found new ways of organizing the information and refining my theoretical ideas.

MANAGING MENSTRUATION AT SCHOOL

Prendergast (2000) describes the work involved for a girl when she has her period:

> Most basically she must know in advance that her period is likely to start that day, and be prepared with appropriate supplies. She must learn how to keep these in a safe place so that they are both readily accessible but not likely to be found, deliberately or accidentally. After that she must judge the appropriate time to change in order that no accidents happen, timing this with lesson breaks, and finding a toilet that has the facilities that she needs. If a girl has

any kind of negative effects from menstruation (which, as we have seen, they commonly do) she must assess how she is likely to feel and be appropriately prepared (for pain, for example) in order to stay alert and complete school tasks successfully. She must have considered the day's lessons, and brought a note if she wishes to be excused from any of them. (p. 117)

This list explains the difficulty in managing menstruation during the school day for girls. The work involved to maintain invisibility in public space highlights the fact that the lived menstrual experience is often a secret and constraining event. Following the norm in childhood culture of being un-noticed and part of the group (Simpson, 2000), many girls do not want to call attention to themselves and their menstrual cycle and thus prefer to hide their bodies and slip to the bathroom unnoticed.

Prendergast (2000) found that the structure of schools in particular failed to provide conditions for girls where menstruation can be experi-enced adequately, much less positively. The work of menstruation is similar for adult women, but many adults do not have the additional and significant constraint of negotiating an institution, such as a school, run by those so much higher in the power structure, such as the teachers and principal. School, a central feature of children's lived experience, is a spatial context that is dedicated to the control and regulation of the child's body and mind (James, Jenks, & Prout, 1998). Not only do menstruating girls have to worry about other kids finding out their situation, they have to do this while negotiating the adult-run world (Backett-Milburn, 2000).

The girls interviewed agreed that schools failed to provide conditions for girls where menstruation could be managed easily. Schools were limited in both their physical space and their timed schedules to which students must adhere. In short, schools ignored menstruation. They pretended it does not happen by making only rare and insufficient accommodations for menstru-ating girls. The adults running schools preferred to keep menstruation pri-vate, concealed, and out of the public discourse. Thus, girls have to do a lot of work to not only care for their period but do it in a concealing and secre-tive manner in this public space. Imagine the frustration and anxiety for Kasey[3] when she got her very first period in "the first week of seventh grade, the first week in a new school, first week with a new schedule, first week with 45-minute class periods, and with only 4-minute passing periods!"

MENSTRUATING IN PUBLIC

A primary worry for girls is the fear of leaking through their clothes. Leak-ing not only gives evidence of the "secret," but also makes a mess that is dif-

---

[3]All names of respondents have been changed to protect confidentiality.

ficult to clean up at school where girls do not have access to bathing facilities or a clean change of clothes. Ally showed concern about leaking when she said, "I've heard people talking about girls that have, like, bled through their pants or something. And I've always been terrified of doing that, because they're like, making fun of her." Ally keeps a sweatshirt in her locker to wear around her waist just in case she does leak through. Marcia described in her group interview how she helped her menstruating friend: "I had a friend in middle school; she kept making me check her butt to make sure she wasn't leaking through."

Leaking is a concern because girls are not exactly sure when their periods are going to come, particularly because as teenagers, their cycles may not have stabilized yet. Being aware of their bodies and being prepared for their periods is an important part of managing menstruation. The girls in one group interview talked about how important it was to try and keep track of when their periods were coming. They said that in an ideal world, they would know "to the second" when their periods would start. They were frustrated that the timing of menstruation was so out of their control and talked about how their periods "attack" them when they were in public and not always prepared.

Many girls said bathroom breaks were difficult because time between classes was so short. Girls planned to go before school, during lunch break, and after school, and they hoped that was all they needed. However, just as with leaking, the girls rose to the challenge of this responsibility and employed various strategies for managing menstruation. This management highlighted how menstruation is a personal bodily phenomenon that is experienced in social contexts and interactions (Prendergast, 2000). Using strategies for managing menstruation, they must negotiate their time, the adult world telling them when to go to the bathroom, and their menstrual supplies. Greta said that "you really have to plan ahead for it" and that having "more time in school to be able to go to the bathroom" would make things much easier. Andrea said that during her period, she tries to "stay close to a bathroom ... 'cause, just in case there's an accident." Alyssa described the difficulties and frustrations of managing bathroom breaks, saying that in "high school, you have like hour classes and you have, like 5 minutes of passing period, and you can't even go to the bathroom and change it, and it's like, really hard."

For some girls, the public nature of menstruating in school was frustrating. Unlike managing menstruation at home, schools are public places where girls go to the bathroom in packs. Although being a part of a pack can be empowering, girls can also be embarrassed to expose themselves in front of others. In one of the girls' groups, the girls shared an extended discussion on tampon use and how, when they were younger, they did not know how to use them.

Kassie then told a story about how in school, she was in the bathroom with a peer, and she did not know how to put a tampon in (the italicized speaker is the interviewer, either Laura or Paul):[4]

Kassie (16):   I had never put in a tampon before. I didn't know how.

Leslie (16):   Ooh.

Kassie: I wasn't sure. It was a big one. No, no listen to this, it was Jenny, do you guys remember her? Julie Weerd.

Leslie: Oh, Ward.

Kassie: And I didn't want her to know that I didn't know how to put a tampon in, because I didn't want to, you know, seem uncool. So, I was like, "You can do this." I pulled the thing, like, I took the plastic part off, and I was like [makes confused face]. [group laughs] And so, then, I pulled the tampon part out, and I was like, "What is this for?" Like- [makes motion as if tossing tampon] [group laughs] And it went out and on the floor. And I just, like, I did, and so I take it and I'm like, "OK," you know. And like, that much [with index and thumb close together] of it goes in. I'm like, "This feels kind of weird." And, like, it really starts to hurt later. And, like, and, like, I'm walking like this [ ] in pain, 'cause like I—

Laura: *You put this much of a tampon in?*

Kassie: Yeah. And like, when I go to sit down, I'm like [ ]. Awful. It was horrible. And, so, like, and then I'm like in giant pain, and I'm just like, "Something is seriously wrong." I didn't want to, like, tell anybody. And I had Mr. Kabel for English.

Leslie: Oh. [group laughs]

Kassie: And he was like, "You okay?" And I was like, "Can I use the phone."

Korrine (15):   He's a really weird guy.

Kassie: Anyway, so I'm like, "I need to use the phone." So, I call my mom, and my mom was at her office, and I'm talking to her. I'm like, "There's something seriously wrong." She was like, "What's wrong?" And I was like, "I put a tampon in and some-

---

[4]Transcribing conventions:
   ... omitted text for clarity
   - word that was cut off by next speaker
   [overlapping speech
   = continued speech/latching
   [word] explanatory information for reader
   ( ) inaudible speech
   (word) barely audible speech with guessed word

thing's bad." And, so- and my mom was, like, in Indy [India-napolis], so she comes to the school. Like, my mom's like dr- I barely know this woman, and, like, brings me clothes, think-ing that I had, like, spilled blood all over me, and, like, I had to tell her it was just-

Laura: *Oh.*

Kassie: She was like, "What?" [in screeching voice]

The other girls collectively laughed and commiserated with Kassie as she shared this embarrassing early moment. Kassie was unprepared for the public nature of using tampons at school, even in the girls' bathroom. She did not want to appear ignorant in front of her peer and did not ask for help. Then, when things went wrong, she did not want to tell her male teacher or friends what happened but instead called her mom, a private re-source, for help. In this case, Kassie removed herself from the public school setting (by calling her mom) to deal with the problem.

CROSS-GENDER INTERACTIONS

Not only must girls manage the school schedule and physical structure of school, but they must also manage the cross-gendered interactional space created by the schools. In one of the group interviews, the girls shared sto-ries about how boys rifled through the girls' school backpacks and embar-rassed girls about the menstrual products they found:

Leslie (16):   The funny thing is, they'll [boys] be going through your back-pack or something, they'll be like, "What's this? Oh my god!"

Kassie (16):   Yeah.

Greta (15):   Don't go there, especially when it's in a separate little part. Oh, [boys] persists to open [the little bags] up.

Kassie: It's like there's a bigger world in there, and you're like, "No, just pads and tampons."

Korrine (15): Elizabeth keeps hers in her purse.

Leslie: Or there's, like, some little flowered little Clinique bag, and they know it's not your makeup bag. And they're like, "So, is your makeup in here?" I was like, "No."

Lacey (16):   No.

Leslie: It's like, "Is there where you keep your pencils?" I have this small little pocket, inside at the bottom of my bag, you know. I'd stick in the front part, but, you know-

The boys were in a more powerful position as they violated the girls' personal space by rifling through the girls' backpacks. The boys were interested in pads and tampons and were interested in teasing the girls about their menstrual status, something most of the girls in this story would rather keep private. Kassie, however, seemed to have come to terms with the public nature of girls' menstrual status and said that pads and tampons are not that big of a deal. She masterfully regained control of the situation as the boys, then, lost the power to tease her.

Some of the girls talked about ways that they could conceal pads and tampons from the public view in school. Kasey and Jane said that one of the difficult things about menstruation is buying menstrual products and keeping them organized and hidden at school:

Kasey (13):   Having to go to the store and buy your own pads and having to go through the line with like male cashiers.

Jane (14):   Yeah. That is, like, totally embarrassing. I think we should just create a women's store. Women can go there and have, like, and have, like, like we'd help the guys that had no clue that were coming in there.

Kasey: Or during each time during school, and then you have to, like, write a pass out of class, and go through all this junk in the bathroom, and those really thick things that they have in the bathroom. It's just annoying.

Jane: I think we should have a place in the lockers, like, where you can, like, have a little compartment.

Kasey: I do, now.

Jane: But there is like nothing ( ).

Kasey: I keep them in my backpack, like in the bottom, and my locker.

Kasey and Jane did not want others, especially males, to know they are menstruating. By presenting ways that would make it easier for a girl to obtain and store menstrual products, they shared their preference for keeping menstruation private and shared only among women even while at the store or at school. These girls were not ready to make their menstrual identities public.

Some girls said that in a perfect world, they would get to stay home during the first days of their periods. At home, the girls did not have to negotiate potential teasing, ask to go to the bathroom during class, or worry about how often to take bathroom breaks. These girls wanted to retain their private menstrual identities. When I asked what would make it easier for a girl to menstruate, Katie and Jennifer suggested time off from school in their group interview:

Katie (14):   Well, in a perfect world, we would have like, at least 2 days where we could stay home, like, whenever we wanted to during our period. 'Cause like, when you're on your period you're really lethargic, and it's like, "I just don't wanna go to school today." So like, have 2 days during your period when you were allowed to stay home. So not necessarily during the whole—whole thing, but just like, days when you could like, take time off, read books, eat chocolate. Heh heh.

Jennifer (14): Yeah, my friend always has to stay home sick when she starts her period 'cause she gets migraines and cramps and everything and she's just like, sometimes she starts throwing up and, so for her, it's just like, nasty nasty time of the month!

These girls wanted more control over their time and how they managed menstrual symptoms. At school, the girls did not have access to their own resources such as a change of clothes, unlimited bathroom access, and pain medication. In the following example, the girls talked about how hard it can be to manage their symptoms in school:

Laura: *Is there anything, any changes that would make it easier to be a girl menstruating?*

Ally (17):   No cramps.

Ellen (17):   Yeah, that would be nice.

Laura: *No cramps.*

Ally: They have a cure for impotence, but they don't have a cure for cramps. That's about the dumbest thing I've ever heard of.

Ellen: The only thing they do is they have Midol, which is supposed to take care of cramps.

Ally: But they don't have that at the school. They're not allowed to give us anything but Tylenol.

Laura: *Why not?*

Ally: Because our school's ran by a bunch of guys- no, I'm serious. They say that we don't have the money to stock our medicine cabinet with something like that, because it's not extremely important.

Laura: *Really?*

Ally: Well, like half the school needs that stuff, you know.

These girls saw a lack of sympathy about their symptoms of menstruation and believed that it was based in gender politics. They recognized that the medical problems of males, such as impotence relating to the FDA-approved and heavily marketed Viagra pill, were given priority in medical research and funds over female issues such as menstrual cramps. Ellen and Ally saw these same gender politics working in their school. Midol, which they thought was a more effective drug for cramps than the school-stocked Tylenol, was not handed out because menstruation was seen as "not extremely important."

The classroom was a place where girls cannot avoid interaction with boys, and teachers and girls must deal with the potentially public nature of their menstrual identities. Because everyone knew the girls were menstruating, girls used various strategies to deal with this collective knowledge and awareness of menstruation. For example, girls who wanted to keep their menstrual status private concealed their supplies to limit this collective awareness, as described by Kasey and Jane in a group interview:

Kasey (13):   Everybody can tell when a girl is on her period, because most of them, they won't carry a purse, and then they'll carry a purse that week.

Jane (14):   Yeah.

Laura: *Oh really?*

Kasey: And it's like totally obvious. That's why I never carry a purse.

In another group interview Jennifer referenced the larger group awareness of menstruation by saying that just leaving the room during class was cause for notice and speculation:

Jennifer (14):   Sometimes you'll hear like a girl leave the room and you'll hear a whisper around the room like, "it's a girl thing and it got out of control" and everyone will be like, "oh, her period started and she wasn't ready." Heh heh.

Similarly, Leslie told about how boys noticed when she left her classroom to go to the bathroom. She said, "When you leave class, like, in the middle of class to go to the bathroom to change your pad or tampon, and there happen to be immature guys in class and- like, 'Why are you leaving with your backpack on?' [in nasal voice]." Leslie said she wanted to turn the tables on the boy and respond with "Why do you have to be such an immature jerk?" Whereas Kasey, worked to keep her menstrual identity private, Leslie recognized the public nature of menstruation and wanted to retort back, but admitted she did not do so.

Those girls who wanted to keep their menstrual status a secret were more susceptible to boys' teasing than those who saw it as not a big deal. In my interview with Lacey, she said she wished that guys could menstruate so they would understand the experience and then not pick on her: "I wish guys could go through it for a day ... bleed through the day, get cramps for the day, be moody for the day, everything ... and be like, 'OK, now you want to pick on me?'" This issue was particularly salient for Lacey because she added this comment at the end of the interview, not in response to any specific question I asked.

Girls must also interact with their teachers, who are often male. Male teachers do not want to discuss or deal with menstruation, some girls said. They attempted to silence menstrual discourse and not let it enter their classrooms. This may be due to teacher discomfort or to the threat of parental lawsuits or discipline from the school district if such issues are discussed outside of health class. Regardless, by not allowing menstrual discussions or talk about girls' needs, these teachers devalued girls' bodily experiences and tried to retain control over classroom interactions.

In the following group interview, the girls talked about how their male teachers are "so scared of" menstruation and how they found this funny:

Lacey (16): Yeah. If I ever get to class, like, you know, late, and my teacher's, like, "Where were you?" He doesn't li- he hates my guts, mostly-

Linda (16): Who?

Lacey: Mr. Pease. I was like, "I was at the nurse." He was, like, "Where's your purs- your pass?" I was like, "I had to get something." "Oh, OK."

Leslie (16): They're scared of it. It's so funny.

Kassie (16): Oh, I know. It's like your defense toward any male teacher.

Leslie: If they're like, "Why did you skip class?" "I lost the string." [group laughs]

Kassie (16): Yeah. No, seriously, that's what Mr. Brinstein, I came in, like, 20 minutes late one day, and he was like, "Where have you been?" And he hated me, and I was just, like, "I had a female problem." He said, "OK." [group laughs]

Leslie: But one day, he was like, I was like, "Can I go to the bathroom?" He was like, "Why do you have to go to the bathroom?" I was like, "Because I have to go to the bathroom." He was like, "Oh my gosh, OK," and he, like, throws the pass at me, and he's like, "Go, go." [insistently]

Kassie: When they know you're on your period, they're, like, afraid to make eye contact with you, like they're going to catch it or something.

Korrine (15): It's contagious.

Greta (15): Contagious PMS.

Lacey: This girl that sits behind me in journalism, she said that one of her teachers wouldn't let her go. She was like, "If you don't let me go, I'll bleed all over your classroom." [group laughs]

This example showed not only how male teachers negatively responded to menstruating girls, but also how the girls used this negative response to gain interactional power. In some instances such as these, the girls, because of their menstrual identities, have more power in the interactions than the male teachers do. Kasey and Jennifer, in the previous examples, worked to conceal evidence of their menstrual identity. In this last example, some of these girls were comfortable with a public menstrual identity, and they talked about menstruation on their own terms and in the open. In the last line, they showed that they admired those who retort back to male questions, just as earlier Leslie wishes she herself could by calling boys "immature jerks." By embracing menstruation on their own terms, these girls prevented boys and others from having the power to ease or embarrass them.

SHIFTING FROM PRIVATE
TO PUBLIC MENSTRUAL IDENTITIES

There was a tension between girls' public and private menstrual identities. Many of the girls wanted to keep their menstrual status private even though by high school those around them, including boys, knew that they were menstruating. The schools—spatially, interactionally, and temporally—supported this private menstrual identity as schools do not acknowledge or openly offer support to menstruating girls. At the same time, because they are in public space, schools forced menstruation into the public realm. Other girls began to accept and even embrace their public menstrual identities by openly discussing menstruation and handling menstrual products. In the following group interview, the girls shared an embarrassing story about unsuccessfully concealing their menstrual products in the classroom:

Greta (15):   Wasn't like Sue Heinz or Allison or somebody that was in eighth-grade algebra, and-

Leslie (16):   That would be me.

Lacey (16):   And, in her folder-

Leslie: Tell it.

Lacey: I almost forgot about that.

Greta: Who was I talking to-

Lacey: I don't know, but it was-

Greta: Sue was, like, "Can I have the English notes?" or something. I was like, "Sure." So, I rip out my folder, and my pad had somehow, it was just loose in the bag, it had gotten stuck in the folder. So, I was li- I think there was somebody between me and Sue. I think it was a guy, too, and I was like, "Can you pass this to Sue?" And it, like, falls out. It hit her in the head, too, it, like, it just flew to her forehead.

Lacey: I was looking ( ). And I was like, "Well, here it is," pull out my pad, and it flies across, "That's mine." I had to, like, go over, like, pick it up. It was so embarrassing.

Kassie (16): You know what they did to ( ) freshman year. She was sending one to me, so I was like, "That's it." So, I reached in my bag, and it was in Mr. Berry's room. And, like, someone, I don't know, we were sitting there doing classwork or something, and I pulled it out, and I threw a pad across the room, and it landed on her desk. She was like [ ], but, like, no one else around her noticed. And, then, remember that when I pulled that pad out, and I was just like, "Pa-ching."

Leslie: You got me.

Kassie: Oh, did it hit you?

Leslie: No, it hit my desk or- and I was like, "Here."

Kassie: Yeah, and then everyone was like, "What the-?" It was funny.

The first story in this story-telling sequence was particularly embarrassing. It showed instances when pads or tampons end up where they are not supposed to be: in public space. However, in the second story, Kassie challenged the nonpublic nature of menstrual products and tossed a pad to a friend during class. She laughed at the incident precisely because she broke prevailing social norms. In both of these stories, the girls together decided if having pads in public spaces was embarrassing (as Lacey evaluated the first story) or funny (as Kassie evaluated the second story). In contrast to Lacey's feelings, Kassie thought that having pads out in public should not be embarrassing and actively resisted this embarrassment. This example highlighted the tensions between the public and private natures of menstruation and their relationship to the girls' menstrual identities.

Another way girls expressed their public menstrual identities was through talking about menstruation at school in front of others, both girls and boys. In one group interview, the girls who were very talkative said that if I had come just a year or 2 earlier, they would not have had nearly as much to say. Some of the boys interviewed also said that it was not until high school that they heard girls talking about menstruation openly in the halls and that boys could talk with girls about menstruation. Younger girls were not as comfortable with menstruation and wanted to keep their menstrual identities private.

A few of the boys mentioned learning about menstruation from other girls at school. Brian learned about menstruation "at lunch." He said, "In seventh grade I'd always eat lunch with four girls, maybe like five or six girls, and that's what they talk about at lunch sometimes. So I just kinda listened to that." This example was unusual in that the girls were only in seventh grade, yet were comfortable talking about it in front of him. But, Brian did not engage in the discussion or question the girls; he just listened quietly. Dave also recalled overhearing "girls bitch about it" in middle school. He added that girls talk about menstruation, "more so now than middle school 'cause they were still a bit ashamed of it I guess. But now in theater, or not theater, but around the halls they'll be like 'damn it, not again!' and I'll see just people like bend over in the halls and be like, 'oh shit.' I find it kind of amusing."

In Dave's group interview, the boys were interested in learning about menstruation, not simply teasing and embarrassing girls about it. Elsewhere in their discussion, these boys said they try to stay away from the subject by leaving the area or trying to change the topic of conversation when it comes up. But, at the same time, as we see here, they said that they learned about menstruation and menstrual products from their female friends:

Dave (15): People at school sometimes are very open.

Curt (15): A little too open.

Jim (18): Detailed.

Paul: *More than you want to know?*

Dave: Yeah, pretty much, heh heh.

Paul: *Well you said, actually we were talking about, you said the one's at school suck because your girlfriend told you?*

Dave: Yeah, she says they're made out of cardboard.

Jim: Yeah they are. I know the nurse personally and she tells me all this stuff when I'm in the office. So she like oh yeah they stink. I'm like didn't want to know that but all right.

Dave: My friend Kristin explained how to put on, put in a tampon, he he. She's like this is the hole, this is the tampon, and it goes in like this.

Jim: And you pull the string. Push it through, push it in like that and it stays up there and you pull the applicator out, he he. Don't ask me how I know, I just know, heh heh. Trust me I just know.

The boys first said that the girls were "a little too open" about menstruation in their conversations in school, but the boys clearly learned about menstrual products from these interactions and shared this rather detailed knowledge in the group interview with each other. The boys were learning from girls who were more comfortable with their public menstrual identities and were talking about it openly.

CONCLUSIONS

From these interviews, we learn the importance of the body in social life. Teens use menstruation and the body as resources in their everyday social interactions. The body is a gendered social phenomenon as it is discussed, interpreted, and lived in embodied social interaction. Menstruation, in particular, is not merely a physical process that girls experience individually. Rather, these girls are embodied beings as they use menstruation as a social event and discuss menstruation through sharing experiences, strategies, and support. Additionally, menstruation is not just a "woman's issue." Menstruation enters boys' social lives through talk with other boys and in their social interactions with girls. We have also seen the importance of the bodily experience as teens experience the world through their bodies. A girl's menstrual status and experience can be an important focus of her everyday interactions.

Embodiment focuses on the body as the site for social experience (Williams & Bendelow, 1998). Our realities are indeed socially mediated, but we experience reality by living in and through our physical bodies. Additionally, our views on our own bodies may affect our interactions with others and how we understand and interpret those interactions (Nettleton & Watson, 1998). For example, any changes in our bodies, such as menstruation, can affect how we interact with others and can produce shifting and changing identities. We can also express our identities through our bodies such as body modification, tattooing, clothes, and style. Thus, the body is a social creation dependent on the social, discursive, and physical context in which it resides. Embodiment is a way of reconciling the material body (essentialism) with the socially constructed body (social constructionism).

As shown in this chapter, these high school age–girls are in a liminal space betwixt and between childhood, as nonmenstruants, and adulthood, as menstruants. In the interactive space of school, they are with others constantly, including other girls, boys, and adults. Schools offer a unique and unavoidable public space in which the girls must negotiate this liminality. The social context and discursive practices in school thus influence how girls construct their public identities as menstruants. Girls enter school with a private menstrual identity, which the schools ostensibly support by ignoring menstruation and trying to keep it private. Nevertheless, schools are inherently public spaces and the girls realize that a private menstrual identity is impossible because their peers and teachers know that girls of their age are menstruating. In my data, girls both accepted norms of keeping menstruation a secret in school, yet they also resisted this norm and used menstruation as a way to confront teachers and boys in the classroom. The girls created a public menstrual identity for themselves that was in contrast to the dominant norms of secrecy and their wish as younger girls to keep their menstrual identity private. Rather than being susceptible to having boys define menstruation (e.g., through teasing), those girls embracing a public menstrual identity have the power to define menstruation and their bodies on their own terms.

How can schools help girls negotiate menstruation? First, school schedules should be flexible enough to allow girls time to go to the bathroom between classes. In some schools, the girls tell me that the halls are so crowded that students can barely wedge their way directly to class on time. Relatedly, schools can ensure that restrooms are clean, and private, and that pad and tampon dispensers are well stocked with modern products at minimal cost. If a girl starts her period, she should have a safe place to go to get supplies and keep clean. Third, school nurses can stock Midol or other medications specifically geared toward alleviating menstrual symptoms. Finally, teachers, both male and female, can be sensitive to girls' menstrual needs. Teachers can be aware of the range of emotions girls have about their periods and whether girls are comfortable with a private or public menstrual identity. Teens learn by modeling adults. Teens and adults must see girls and treat girls' bodies with respect. Schools must not ignore menstruation but must acknowledge and accommodate it.

What else can we do with these findings? We can support teens by encouraging their explorations of their worlds, answering their questions about their bodies, and giving them space to be with other teens to develop their own understandings of social life. We can offer girls support of their bodies and their maturity by celebrating menstruation and celebrating impending womanhood. We can ensure that they have the knowledge about their bodies to promote sexual agency. Without knowledge and language, girls cannot respond to sexual situations in the safest manner. An engaged and open understanding of the body is crucial to how girls respond to social situations and to their own emotions, psychology, and bodily needs.

How might we develop a conception of menstruation that highlights the positive and prosocial aspects of menstruation for teens? A conception that celebrates girls' bodies? A conception that fosters self-esteem for girls? A conception that recognizes that we are all embodied selves? Several authors have recently suggested new cultural traditions that would celebrate menarche and menstruation to redefine the experience as a positive event. For example, upon menarche we could give girls a material token, such as flowers, to show the girl that something wonderful and positive has happened. Such a token can be discreet, which would respect a girl's possible wishes to keep her reaction and the event a private, yet a celebrated moment in her life.

In her book titled *Honoring Menstruation: A Time of Self-Renewal*, Lara Owen (1998) discussed how she thinks we need to pay attention to our bodies, notice when we menstruate, and take the appropriate time off for self-reflection and renewal. She contended that dominant cultural biases against menstruation and negative feelings are detrimental to women's health and psychological well-being. She strongly believed, and I agree, that if women were valued and celebrated for themselves and in their womanhood through puberty, many of the abuse and self-esteem problems in both women and girls might be significantly lessened. To increase respect, Owen advocated the development of rituals to honor menstruation and femininity. Rituals can also be designed around hysterectomy, menopause, and other female experiences. I am not arguing that we need to celebrate menstruation throughout the life course. But, I believe that by recognizing menstruation and its salience at certain points in girls' and women's lives, we recognize that we are embodied selves and the influence our bodies have in our social interactions.

ACKNOWLEDGMENTS

I thank the editors and the anonymous reviewer for their helpful comments on earlier drafts of this manuscript. This chapter benefited from conversations and collaborations with Donna Eder, Brian Powell, and Kris De Welde.

DISCUSSION QUESTIONS

1. How do the data presented illustrate the concept of embodiment?
2. What other areas of teen life in school can illustrate embodiment?
3. How can girls gain power in their social interactions by asserting a public menstrual identity? How can teen boys and/or girls assert power (using embodiment) in the areas discussed in Question 2?

REFERENCES

Amann-Gainotti, M. (1986). Sexual socialization during early adolescence: The menarche. *Adolescence, 21*(83), 703–710.

Backett-Milburn, K. (2000). Parents, children and the construction of the healthy Body in middle-class families. In A. Prout (Ed.), *The body, childhood and society* (pp. 79–100). Houndmills, England: Macmillan.

Brooks-Gunn, J., & Ruble, D. N. (1982). The development of menstrual-related beliefs and behaviors during early adolescence. *Child Development, 53*, 1567–1577.

Brumberg, J. J. (1997). *The body project: An intimate history of American girls*. New York: Vintage Books.

Christensen, P., & James, A. (Eds.). (2000). *Research with children: Perspectives and practices*. London: Falmer Press.

Christensen, P., & Prout, A. (1999, October 29). *The cultural performance of children's everyday sickness*. Paper presented at the Sociology Departmental Colloquium, Indiana University, Bloomington, Indiana.

Connell, R. W. (1995). *Masculinities*. Berkeley: University of California Press.

Delaney, J., Lupton, M. J., & Toth, E. (1988). *The curse: A cultural history of menstruation*. Chicago: University of Illinois Press.

Douglas, M. (1970). *Natural symbols: Explorations in cosmology*. New York: Pantheon.

Eder, D., & Fingerson, L. (2002). Interviewing children and adolescents. In J. F. Gubrium & J. A. Holstein (Eds.), *Handbook of interview research* (pp. 181–201). Thousand Oaks, CA: Sage.

Ehrenreich, B. (1999, March 8). The real truth about the female body. *Time, 153,* 56–69.

Fingerson, L. (1999). Active viewing: Girls' interpretations of family television programs. *Journal of Contemporary Ethnography, 28*(4), 389–418.

Fingerson, L. (2001). *Social construction, power, and agency in adolescent menstrual talk*. Unpublished doctoral dissertation, Indiana University, Bloomington.

Fingerson, L. (in press). Agency and the body in adolescent menstrual talk. *Childhood*.

Grahn, J. (1993). *Blood, bread, and roses: How menstruation created the world*. Boston: Beacon Press.

Houppert, K. (1999). *The curse: Confronting the last unmentionable taboo, menstruation*. New York: Farrar, Straus & Giroux.

Hughes, K. W., & Wolf, L. (1997). *Daughters of the moon, sisters of the sun: Young women and mentors on the transition to womanhood*. Gabriola Island, British Columbia: New Society Publishers.

James, A. (2000). Embodied being(s): Understanding the self and the body in childhood. In A. Prout (Ed.), *The body, childhood and society* (pp. 19–37). Houndmills, England: Macmillan.

James, A., Jenks, C., & Prout, A. (1998). *Theorizing childhood*. New York: Teachers College Press.

Koff, E., & Rierdan, J. (1995). Preparing girls for menstruation: Recommendations from adolescent girls. *Adolescence, 30*(120), 795–811.

Koff, E., Rierdan, J., & Jacobson, S. (1981). The personal and interpersonal significance of menarche. *Journal of the American Academy of Child Psychiatry, 20*(1), 148–158.

Kowalski, R. M., & Chapple, T. (2000). The social stigma of menstruation: Fact or fiction? *Psychology of Women Quarterly, 24*(1), 74–80.

Leder, D. (Ed.). (1992a). *The body in medical thought and practice*. Dordrecht, Netherlands: Kluwer Academic.

Leder, D. (1992b). Introduction. In D. Leder (Ed.), *The body in medical thought and practice*. Dordrecht, Netherlands: Kluwer Academic.

Lee, J. (1994). Menarche and the (hetero)sexualization of the female body. *Gender & Society, 8*(3), 343–362.

Lee, J., & Sasser-Coen, J. (1996). *Blood stories: Menarche and the politics of the female body in contemporary society*. New York: Routledge.

Lorber, J. (1993). Believing is seeing: Biology as ideology. *Gender & Society, 7*, 568–581.

Lovering, K. M. (1995). The bleeding body: Adolescents talk about menstruation. In S. Wilkinson & C. Kitzinger (Eds.), *Feminism and discourse: Psychological perspectives.* London: Sage.

Martin, E. (1992). *The woman in the body.* Boston: Beacon Press.

Moore, S. M. (1995). Girls' understanding and social constructions of menarche. *Journal of Adolescence, 18*(1), 87–104.

Morgan, D. L. (1993). Future directions for focus groups. In D. L. Morgan (Ed.), *Successful focus groups: Advancing the state of the art* (pp. 225–244). Newbury Park, CA: Sage.

Nettleton, S., & Watson, J. (1998). The body in everyday life: An introduction. In S. Nettleton & J. Watson (Eds.), *The body in everyday life* (pp. 1–24). London: Routledge.

Owen, L. (1998). *Honoring menstruation: A time of self-renewal.* Freedom, CA: Crossing Press.

Pipher, M. (1994). *Reviving Ophelia: Saving the selves of adolescent girls.* New York: Ballantine Books.

Prendergast, S. (2000). "To become dizzy in our turning": Girls, body-maps and gender as childhood ends. In A. Prout (Ed.), *The body, childhood and society* (pp. 101–124). Houndmills, England: Macmillan.

Prout, A. (2000). Childhood bodies: Construction, agency and hybridity. In A. Prout (Ed.), *The body, childhood and society* (pp. 1–18). Houndmills, England: Macmillan.

Qvortrup, J. (1994). Childhood matters: An introduction. In J. Qvortrup, M. Bardy, G. Sgritta, & H. Wintersberger (Eds.), *Childhood matters: Social theory, practice and politics* (Vol. 14, pp. 1–24). Aldershot, England: Avebury.

Rierdan, J., Koff, E., & Flaherty, J. (1985). Conceptions and misconceptions of menstruation. *Women and Health, 86*(10), 33–45.

Ruble, D. N., & Brooks-Gunn, J. (1982). The experience of menarche. *Child Development, 53*, 1557–1566.

Scheper-Hughes, N., & Lock, M. M. (1987). The mindful body: A prolegomenon to future work in medical anthropology. *Medical Anthropology Quarterly, 1*(1), 6–41.

Simpson, B. (2000). Regulation and resistance: Children's embodiment during the primary-secondary school transition. In A. Prout (Ed.), *The body, childhood and society* (pp. 60–78). Houndmills, England: Macmillan.

Usmiani, S., & Daniluk, J. (1997). Mothers and their adolescent daughters: Relationship between self-esteem, gender role identity, and body image. *Journal of Youth and Adolescence, 26*(1), 45–62.

Weitz, R. (Ed.). (1998). *The politics of women's bodies: Sexuality, appearance, and behavior.* New York: Oxford University Press.

Williams, S. J., & Bendelow, G. (1998). *The lived body: Sociological themes, embodied issues.* London: Routledge.

Chapter 9

In the World But Not of It: Gendered Religious Socialization at a Christian School

Stacey Elsasser
The College of Saint Rose

> *You see the girls wanted to have that respect that you're supposed to treat*
> *women with in the church, but they didn't want to have that, the other.*
> *They didn't like the domineering. And actually, when it first happened,*
> *they were so happy that the boys stood up and said, We are the spiritual*
> *leaders of this school. We're never going to be blessed until we take our*
> *male authority; until we volunteer to pray.*
> —Mrs. Hunter, English teacher

Mrs. Hunter, an English teacher at Charity School, a nondenominational Christian high school located in south central United States, is speaking to a recent shift in power from the female students to the male students. Although the girls had prayed that the boys would take their "rightful place" as the spiritual leaders, they had mixed feelings about their loss of power to the boys. Becky and Susan explain:

Becky (senior): You hear a guy say "Well, I'm a guy and you need to listen to me."

Susan (junior): They'll [boys] come right up to a girl and say, "You must submit to me because I'm a man."

137

As illustrated by these girls' comments, the boys' domination was justified through the use of biblical theology that situated women as submissive to men. Hence, female students were pressured to conform to this theology by their peers, their teachers, their principal, and the culture, curriculum, and practices at Charity. This theology of submission shaped their school identities, yet gave them little ownership over the exact way this theology was ab/used. Within the context of the Christian school, the two distinct ideas of religious and gendered socialization were shown within this study to merge together into one force that shaped the realities and lived experiences of these "young women of Christ."

This study considers gendered religious socialization of girls at an evangelical Christian school during a dynamic period of growth and "revival" at the school. Students were getting closer to God, and therefore, more interested in the spiritual dynamics of their relationships. This led to conflict between the boys and girls over issues of leadership in their rapidly expanding school. What quickly became the focus of this study were the complex ways in which the language and attitudes of the larger evangelical debate regarding the submission of women played out in the everyday lives of high school Christian girls. Embedded within this gendered religious socialization was a strange dichotomy that asked the girls to be in the world—as strong, confident women—but not of it—as submissive, silenced Christians.

GIRLS AT A HOLY CROSSROAD: THE CONTEXT OF CHARITY

This chapter is based on a case study of a Christian school, conducted during the spring of 1999, and draws primarily from teacher and student interviews at the high school level, Grades 9–12. Charity Christian School had an enrollment of approximately 150, prekindergarten through 12th grade, with a high school population of 21: 12 girls and 9 boys. The only nonpublic school in a city located in the south central United States, Charity was 14 years old and supported with students from 22 evangelical churches in the city and surrounding area. This represented approximately 50% to 60% of the area churches. The school board consisted of male members from four different churches.

Charity was housed within a Southern Baptist church, a denomination that believes in the authority of the church and disallows female pastors. Unique to this study was that this same church practices Pentecostalism, a segment of evangelicalism that places more authority in the Holy Spirit's work in a believer's life than in the church's (Balmer, 1994). This contradiction of having a Southern Baptist church observe Pentecostal practices is representative of the denominational boundary crossing researched by Bollar-Wagner (1997) in which schools governed by a single church, and adhering only to their beliefs, are less evident in today's society.

Bollar-Wagner found that most Christian schools adhere to more ecumenical beliefs to "recruit" more students. This suggestion of ecumenicalism led to doctrinal confusion at Charity and created a space where differing notions of submission theology could flourish. This in turn gave the students less definitive boundaries in which to practice their religion and led to the reinterpretation of many of their fundamental beliefs.

Because I had previously taught at the school and identify myself as an evangelical Christian, I understood the language, expectations, and attitudes present in the school. Certainly I was not an "objective" observer; however, Lous Heshusius (1994) offers a counter to the ideal of objectivity in research with the notion of participatory consciousness and "somatic knowledge." Certainly my somatic knowledge of the school itself and evangelical Christianity in general positioned me as an insider–researcher, but as a graduate student steeped in feminism and critical theory, I was also able to make sense of those experience-near knowledges to create a narrative that both explains and critiques an aspect of schooling typically not discussed in the literature.

Though studies regarding gender and churches (e.g., Gallagher & Smith, 1999; Griffith, 1997; Stacey & Gerard, 1990) and gender and schooling (e.g., American Association of University Women [AAUW], 1992, 1999; Eitzen & Zinn, 1992; Sadker & Sadker, 1994) abound, research looking at aspects of evangelical Christian education includes only a few: Peshkin's (1986) "total world" of a fundamental Christian school and Michelle Bollar-Wagner's (1990) look at the interdenominational aspects of Christian schools. Yet the 11,000-plus evangelical Christian schools, serving 1.5 million students (Bollar-Wagner, 1997), occupy a significant place in the educational landscape of the United States. With claims of truth, righteousness, and freedom as their calling cards, evangelical Christian school families pay as much $5,000 per year to have their children shaped by evangelical doctrines and beliefs.

Focusing on the specific "institution within an institution," called Christian schools, a microcosmic example of gender emerged from the socializing force of the macrocosm, the evangelical church. The girls involved in this study were placed in a tenuous position where leadership within the school was an entitlement for boys but doled out to girls if they were either deserving enough—through their adoption of traditional Christian female roles—or there were no other choices—for example, no boy to volunteer.

SUBMISSION THEOLOGY

Central to understanding this study was the evangelical doctrinal notion of submission theology; that the wife has less authority, specifically spiritual, than her husband (Gallagher & Smith, 1999). This belief comes from a passage in Ephesians 5:23 of the New Testament of the Christian Bible (New King James Version, 1983) that states "the husband is the head of the wife." Other verses that support this theology include Genesis 3:16, which says the man shall rule over his wife, and I Corinthians 11:3, which restates Genesis 3:16. There are two extreme positions regarding submission theology: One is described by ultratraditionalists as the belief that women should not teach men or hold governmental positions whereas egalitarians believe that there is neither male nor female in function, both in the church or home (Jacobs, 1998). Most evangelicals hold a neo-traditionalist view in which women are seen as subordinate, but not unequal to men, much like the army's definition of positionality among the ranks (Gallagher & Smith, 1999).

Gallagher and Smith (1999) explain that the evangelicals' gender ideology focuses on differences in family responsibilities, which is based on the ideal of separate spheres for women and men that emerged during the late 19th century. Evangelicals argue that men and women have natural, even God-given essences inherent to each sex; examples include masculine aggression, worldly wisdom, and rationality for men and feminine submission, purity, piety, and domesticity for women. Due to the family's increasing reliance on women's income and because the impact of feminism on evangelical discourse has been "profound and diffuse" (p. 215), evangelicals are beginning to see in their lived experiences what Gallagher and Smith call pragmatic egalitarianism. In this arrangement, submission theology is considered a rarely used "trump card" that is mostly symbolic and not a practical reality in the lives of modern evangelicals who face the commitments of a postindustrial economy. Gallagher and Smith describe the negotiation of gender within the evangelical church this way:

> It is in this slippery area between ideals and resources, intended and experienced, that we find gender negotiated, managed, and lived. In these processes, evangelicals negotiate gender in much the same way others of different or no religious world views do—borrowing from, resisting, and participating in the larger structures of which they are a part. (p. 231)

According to Gallagher and Smith (1999), women in the evangelical church are moving toward a more egalitarian and pragmatic role, yet there still remains the frustration and anxiety associated with a major social change. The girls at Charity also participated in this change; the submission of women was, indeed, a slippery area for the girls in this study. Their position regarding submission remained in a state of flux, moving between attitudes of equity and docile submission. They were caught between a religious doctrine they ambivalently embraced that told them that "good Christian girls" submit to the authority of their male peers and a secular world that taught women that strength, confidence, and assertiveness were desirable ideals. Hence, they struggled to be in the secular world, partaking of the collective identity women are making as equal and unsubmissive, yet not of this world as they tried to remain true to religious beliefs that ask them to be unequal and submissive.

The remainder of the chapter examines how the issue of the submission of women became a pronounced theme in the lives of the girls and boys at Charity. In particular, I look at how notions of submission were found in their explanation of leadership, in the teasing and interactions among students themselves and between the students and faculty, by the example set through the lack of doctrinal absolutes, and through the favoritism shown by faculty toward males. Finally, this chapter explores the implications for evangelical girls caught between being in the world, but not of it.

RIGHTFUL LEADERS AND ANSWERED PRAYERS

> Her dreams were so outrageous they could fill the sky.
> —from a short story by Nancy, (sophomore)

This study is situated during the 1998–1999 school year, the year when it was collectively agreed that "the boys took over." Prior to this academic year, the girls outnumbered the boys more dramatically and were considered the leaders, academically and spiritually, of the school. Starting with the 1997–1998 school year, the girls and the faculty "agreed in prayer" to ask God for spiritually stronger males. Mrs. Hunter, the English teacher, describes it this way:

> We have prayed and prayed and prayed and prayed and the girls have done it too, so they deserve it. They prayed so hard that the boys at the school would take spiritual leadership and be the leaders because they got sick of being the police. They got sick of "Now, boys, you're not supposed to spit and cuss at the lockers and you're supposed to be nice to us 'cause we're girls. You're supposed to not say things like Aooh, ooh, look at your boobs"; literally. It was so bad about 3 years ago because our boys had no Christian leadership at all. No Christian respect. They did not ... You see the girls wanted to have that respect that you're supposed to treat women within the church, but they didn't want to have that, the other. They didn't like the domineering. And actually, when it first happened, they were so happy that the boys stood up and said, "We are the spiritual leaders of this school. We're never going to be blessed until we take our male authority; until we volunteer to pray." I never had a guy pray the first whole year for lunch because we take volunteers to do lunch. Then the boys had this little minirevival. Then, they took over and they got swelled heads this year.

The idea of "rightful leader" is part of the discourse of the Promise Keepers and their push to get men to "step up to the plate" (Messner, 1997). Both of these phrases were used more than once in reference to the turnover of power from girls to boys and the prevalent submission theology in general. The timing of the girls beginning to pray for more male leadership coincided with the peak of the Promise Keepers movement, around 1997. Although Promise Keepers is on a downward trend and fewer men are attending their rallies (Associated Press Wire Service, 1999), the effects were still being felt throughout the evangelical community at this time and were definitely still felt at Charity. Reminiscent of the old adage, "Be careful what you wish for, you just may get it," the girls got what they prayed for, strong males.

The issue of leadership at Charity centered on Tom and Bob, both sophomores, who were the recognized leaders of the senior high. They received this recognition from the other students, themselves, but mainly through favoritism shown by teachers and the principal. Tom and Bob took charge of many situations where they were either given leadership by authority or leadership was surrendered by the girls. During observations, Tom and Bob especially liked to use their power to get out of class frequently and spend long hours with Mr. Lincoln, the principal, in his office, making sure that other students were aware of this. The boys would also take over class events such as group projects and presentations even when it was obvious the girls in their group had a better grasp of the material. They were observed often using the girls for information and then directing the work of the group. When Tom and Bob were asked about their roles as leaders, they defended it as a God-given right:

Tom:	I think it's easier [at this school] to be a boy. People look to guys a lot more for leadership.
Researcher:	Why?
Tom:	Because that's the way it's supposed to be. They try to follow the biblical standards.
Researcher:	What in the Bible tells you that?
Tom:	The man is supposed to be the head. They [the girls] look more toward us.
Researcher:	Where do you learn that men are supposed to be the head of the household?
Tom:	Mr. Lincoln. He's really pushed for guys. I know myself and Bob, he's really pushed for guys to take leadership.
Researcher:	I called you in because everyone, boys and girls, when I asked who were the leaders, they would always say you two. Because you are more spiritual and more outgoing. What do you think when you hear that?

Bob: That it's God. I don't want people to see me, I want them to
                 see Jesus.

Mr. Lincoln, the principal, was central to situating Tom and Bob in leadership positions. His favoritism was obvious in everything he did that involved a
wide body of students, and was keenly felt among the girls, but also among
some guys. Every student, when asked how Tom and Bob received their leadership authority, knew that it came from Mr. Lincoln. This caused jealousy
from those that did not have it and protectiveness and defensiveness from
those that did. Even Mr. Lincoln became defensive regarding his relationship with Tom, who "hangs out" at his house often. Although Mr. Lincoln felt
that his relationship with Tom was more like father–son, he failed to see that
many of the other students wanted the same relationship with him.

    Some of the girls accused Tom and Bob of playing a game with Mr.
Lincoln—of being a certain way in front of him, but then changing into less
"godly" men when away from him. Often in the informal conversations at
study hall and during free time, Tom and Bob were observed talking about
things with attitudes that would contradict what Mr. Lincoln promoted,
such as teasing girls in sexual overtones. At other times, Tom and Bob
would put people down for not thinking like they do, something Mr.
Lincoln considered "ungodly."

    The problem of Mr. Lincoln's favoritism was shown in an incident where
Mr. Lincoln left Tom in charge one day, over older female students who
had been at the school longer.[1] Harriet, a junior and the girl who has been
at the school the longest, and considered by most to be the school's most academically and spiritually stable person, reflected that some people re-
sented the fact that Tom and Bob were the spiritual leaders. She asserted
that at times they "push the boundaries and team up and almost attack people. I think this is why some people jump to find things that they've said or
done that are wrong."

    Mr. Lincoln openly admitted he plays favorites with some of the boys, es-
pecially Tom, because they were on a "spiritual" track and Mr. Lincoln felt
called to mentor them. He did not feel that he could mentor the girls because of the risk of anything looking improper. This concern of propriety is
felt throughout the evangelical community, and it is standard practice for
men and women not to be alone together, especially where one is in some
type of ministerial leadership.

    However, although the girls admitted they were jealous of Mr. Lincoln's
favoritism, they also had little interest in more than an academic relationship with him anyway. This left them feeling that they had no one whom

---

[1]The issue of students in charge while the principal is gone highlights other problems not
considered for this article.

they could trust. Their sense of isolation from an authority intensified their willingness to silence and submit themselves, because in Nancy's words, they "only have each other." Barbara, a junior and the principal's daughter, who is also Tom's best friend, was asked what it would be like without Tom and Bob:

Barbara: The girls would be more of the leaders. The guys would not be as persuaded to follow Jesus. They would follow the example of James and Stewart [the school's party-hearty rebels] more.

Researcher: Why are Tom and Bob so powerful?

Barbara: Their past involvements. They were very popular in their own areas before they came here. They're used to taking charge. They are just more aggressive, even though they are new to knowing God.

Barbara also made this comment concerning the girls and leadership: "The girls are scared. They've always been the leaders, but they weren't the leaders the right way. Now there's a push to grow toward God, but they don't know how. The girls were leading us toward the world, not God." The issue of girls being the wrong kind of leaders was a common thread in discussions. During an informal discussion concerning leadership in the school, the girls agreed that it was better to have boys in leadership positions who could do only a halfway job than for girls to be in leadership and do it 100%. To them, God wanted men in leadership regardless of actual skill. Women were allowed to take over only when there was no man available or willing. In their theology, this was the best way for God to bless them spiritually.

SUBMISSION THEOLOGY AND GENDERED RELATIONSHIPS

A female Christian, a lot of people think that they don't have as much authority and power as male Christians, like preachers, but God has given them the same authority as he's given men. If you have Jesus in your heart, you have the same power as a male. God's the same. God doesn't change. Even in the Bible there were women apostles and leaders everywhere.

—Louise, (senior)

Reviewing the issue of submission from a theological perspective, the main controversy regards a verse found in Ephesians 5:23 that states "the husband is the head of the wife." This verse is considered a "gray area" in the Bible. A gray area is any biblical passage or social-religious tradition that either loses significance outside its sociohistorical context, or in the case of Bible passages, may have multiple exegetical interpretations (Griffith, 1997).

Other examples would be the admonition by St. Paul for women to leave their hair long, which is no longer considered valid by most evangelicals, and three other gray areas: dancing, drinking, and cigarette smoking. Due to the fact that Charity had not written a doctrinal statement as part of the formal school policies, "gray area" issues were often sites where students negotiated between themselves. Louise, a senior, mentions this in her interview. She states:

> They [the school faculty] don't teach Christian principles. They may enforce them, but most of the kids that go here haven't been raised in Christian families, so they don't really know. Even in Bible class they talk about the Bible; but we're not "taught" the Bible, we just read the Bible. You have to be taught how to live a good life. They do, but they should show it more. A lot of kids here don't go to church, so this is their only example.

Mr. Lincoln, the principal who also teaches the Bible and a math class, mentioned that although almost the entire secondary school embraces some form of Pentecostalism, he still had to be careful not to step on anyone's denominational beliefs. This lack of clear absolutes became an issue when, without a clear distinction being made of the school's belief regarding the submission of women, the students were left to decide this important issue for themselves based on their views of each other and the example of the faculty.

Comments by Stan, a 16-year-old senior, helped to illustrate the multitude of ideas concerning submission present at Charity by putting the theology of submission that the students and faculty believe into three categories: (a) Women should totally submit and should follow the Bible's rules on the role of women entirely (he thought this is a twisting of the Bible, but that it does occur some at Charity) (b) women should be equal and in charge as equally as men; (c) women should not be made to submit, but are not equals; that men control the relationship; and whereas submission is only for her husband and only if no one can make a compromise, women can make decisions on her own. This surprisingly adheres to most Christian feminist teachings on the breadth of submission theology as well (e.g., Jacobs, 1998; Keyes, 1993; Storkey, 1985; Van Leeuwen, 1993).

Stan was also the only male to vocally oppose the present climate of submission. He did not believe Ephesians 5:22 applies only to husbands and wives, but also to men and women in certain situations, such as disagreement where no compromise is possible or matters of a spiritual nature. This idea of equality except in certain and specific respects, confusing as it is, was typical of the belief of most girls at Charity and of most conservative evangelicals as well (Gallagher & Smith, 1999). It was here, without the solidity of one belief, that confusion and interpretation work against the empowerment that the girls at Charity were seeking.

Among the girls at Charity, submission theology, and the nature of being a female Christian, ranged from senior Becky's "trying your best to get along with people and trying to not make mistakes" to senior Louise's "God has given women the same authority as he has given men." Susan, a junior, thought that being a female Christian meant having fewer obligations to society and the church as the men do. She said: "If something goes wrong, they are the ones to blame. We have to go and help them. We're there to help them and we have to understand that we are below them, but not less than them. So we go along them and we support them to do what's right as they lift us up for what we are doing." Harriet defined submission this way, "Submission means to me to come alongside, or to agree with and support. It is a mixture of respect, humility, equality, and love." Surprisingly, Darren, a 10th grader who was considered the "nicest guy at Charity," thought both "males and females need to submit to authority, but not to each other. Respecting each other doesn't mean obeying everything the guy says to the girls, or vice-versa." Permeating the students' dialogue concerning submission was the idea of authority and who was entitled to it. The idea of reciprocity in the relationship, even though it involved issues of power, was still evident. Interestingly, the missing piece of the students' discourse involved the distinction between husband–wife relationships and boy–girl relationships. Bible verses concerning submission speak only to the relationship between husbands and wives (Gallagher & Smith, 1999).

Beyond the problem of submission theology, two other factors helped to explain the gendered religious socialization of girls at Charity. The strong, overbearing nature of the few boys in power had a silencing effect on the girls, which in turn acted to keep hidden the girls' true feelings regarding their roles. The structural component allowing this "silent submission" to occur was the lack of absolutes in both doctrine and rules that the school allowed. Without clear doctrines, the girls felt powerless in the face of strong males to state their opinions on these issues. Even the rules of the school, which beyond a dress code were only to do as the Bible would have you to do, were ambiguous enough to allow attitudes and actions that foster the submission and silencing of the girls.

Submission was not only believed and discussed but also enacted. Female students exhibited it in obvious ways, such as not voicing opinions, to more specific and unassuming ways, such as giving up prime real estate (preferred seating) in the classroom seating pattern to the boys. One example of "putting them in their place" was that the boys gave the girls their prime real estate of chairs next to the wall only on chapel day when the girls had to wear dresses.

Mrs. Hunter, the English/Social Studies teacher, was aware that she also enacted submission and was frustrated that at times she felt Mr. Lincoln expected it of her. This passage from her interview shows not only the faculty role in submission, but the students' attitudes as well:

Researcher: Do you think women need to submit to men outside of marriage?

Hunter: No. Well, your authority [needs to be submitted to].

Researcher: Authority in general?

Hunter: I never looked at submitting as a joyful thing. I always looked at it as a pull my teeth out and I will if I have to.

Researcher: But it's funny that these girls, that's really a big deal for them, this submission thing.

Hunter: Really?

Researcher: Yeah, it's come up.

Hunter: See, I see them automatically submit. They might not realize it, but it's ingrained in them. In their little psyche, I see them do it automatically. And they also do the enjoying part of it. Like Louise will come down and say, "My battery's dead." And automatically she knows that one of the guys in the class is going to rescue her. And Becky stood up and, "Ooh, I can fix it" and Louise says, "No, no, no, let Darren do it." They enjoy knowing that those boys are going to take care of them, no matter what. And I enjoy knowing that I can go into the teacher's lounge and knowing that I can scream and bawl and Mr. Webster [another teacher] will pat me on the head and I can submit to him and I can lay it, it sounds really bad, but I can lay it at the foot of the cross and put it on his shoulders. I can put it on Mr. Webster's shoulders, and at the foot of the cross, and I can walk away and not worry about it. Now, they [the men] don't have that luxury. And I look at it as a big luxury.

Through such an example of submission, along with the obvious male favoritism, and their own discussion of the topic, the girls admitted they were increasingly being silenced, knowing that their voice would not be heard. Their voluntary and involuntary example of silencing was felt throughout the school.

Letting their voices be heard was the hardest thing for the girls to accomplish, according to Harriet. Angela, a sophomore, asserts, "If you voice your opinion too strongly, no one listens to what you actually say. They just hear the strongness of the words." Barbara, a junior and the principal's daughter, had perhaps the most telling report. She says, "Some girls are silenced toward God by the guys." Being "silenced toward God," not having the fullest possible relationship with Him, was the exact opposite purpose of Charity Christian School. This silencing of girls led to placing them in a liminal space where their thoughts and views were subordinate to others.

SUBMISSIVE TEASINGS AND BIBLE QUOTES

The primary mode of submission displayed at Charity was through "submissive teasings." These teasings ranged from reminding the girls of their presumed submissive position to forcing opinions on others through the use of Bible verses. These were both direct and indirect through a climate of gossip, argumentation, and silencing.

Teasing is an everyday occurrence on any school campus. Adolescent males use teasing to innocently show interest in a girl and/or to less innocently regulate her behavior by assigning the "bad girl" status (Taylor, Gilligan, & Sullivan, 1995). This was especially troublesome in a Christian school where chastity of the girls was expected and rewarded. Students at Charity used teasing in a more personal and deliberate way. Whereas the girls sometimes participated in teasing, usually over matters such as appearance and academics, the boys used teasing more frequently and more personally, eventually turning their teasing toward issues of submission.

Barbara, a junior, described the personal teasing directed at her as revolving around appearance issues as well as around being sheltered, whereas Louise, a senior, and Carla, a freshman, reported feeling that their self-esteem was lowered due to the teasing. Nellie, a freshman, casually related that she was teased constantly because she had attention deficit disorder and did not act "properly," which to her meant acting the way that is the most acceptable to the others. Susan, a junior, also shared a similar experience to Nellie in reference to teasing that involved her nonconformist attitudes and actions.

Both boys and girls were aware of the intimidating nature of teasing. Stan, the 16-year-old senior, was the only boy in the 11/12 grade section for 2 years. He felt like he knew the girls well and addressed the personal dynamic of teasing:

Researcher: Is there negative treatment at the school that puts the girls down?

Stan: There isn't any from the teachers or Mr. Lincoln, but some guys tease too much. They take it too far and it tears the girls up.

Researcher: Give me an example.

Stan: Once a guy called a girl a slut, but used different words and the girl was really hurt. The boy got in trouble and went to the

girl and they made up, but to me it shows that the boys are way
too personal in their teasing.

Researcher: How serious a problem is it?

Stan: People usually don't take it too seriously, but it can get out of
               hand. I think it's good though that it's usually resolved and
               isn't a huge problem.

Teasing that becomes too personal added to teasing that uses the Bible
was a lethal combination for those on the receiving end. Louise, Susan,
and Becky brought this up in their interviews. According to Becky, "You
hear a guy say: 'Well, I'm a guy and you need to listen to me' "; Susan said,
"They'll come right up to a girl and say, 'You must submit to me because
I'm a man.' "

Mrs. Hunter related that the boys will even tease her about submission although she does not go into details. She did mention though that her mood
will set the tone for the day, and if her mood was bad, she had on occasion
been teased by the boys as follows:

Mrs. Hunter: And they've also learned that it's OK to say; "You know, Mrs.
               Hunter's having a hormone time. She's in a bad mood today
               because she's having her time."

Researcher: Some of the girls I have interviewed have said that it's a con-
               stant, that the boys constantly use that submission thing, that
               "I'm the boy, you have to listen to me."

Hunter: Even to me [meaning they have said that she needs to submit
               to them].

Most of the teasing, including the "submissive teasings," was defended by
both boys and girls as being without meaning. Barbara, a junior, thought
the teasing was still better than it would be in the public schools, even
though she had never attended them. Other students, and even Mrs.
Hunter and Mr. Lincoln, thought the teasing was harmless and part of the
students' everyday lives, especially because they were adolescents.

Tom and Bob, as the recognized leaders of the school, were considered the main instigators of both "submissive teasings" and the more
personal teasing. When asked about this during an interview, Tom admitted his culpability whereas Bob defended himself and Tom, saying
the girls did it too:

Researcher: A number of girls have said that they have been teased "you
               must submit to me because you're a girl." It isn't just one or
               two; it's been across the board.

Bob: Yeah, I know what you're talking about. On the other hand,
              the girls tease us as well. What's that verse Louise brought up
              about how men and women will lead in discipleship ...

Tom: It goes both ways.

Bob: It's not like we do it hardly at all.

Tom: I have done it before, in the past.

Researcher: Does it teach you anything that almost every girl has brought
              it up as something they don't like?

Tom: I wish they would tell us. When we joke with them, they joke
              back and they throw things right back at us and so we joke
              back and than they joke back. It's kinda like a battle of the
              sexes thing. We don't really think anything about it, but then
              we hear this and it's like OK if you have a problem with it, you
              need to come to us and we would stop. It wouldn't bother me
              if they said something.

Tom and Bob's discussion highlighted their awareness of their actions. Mr.
Lincoln, the principal, mentioned after the study was finished that he felt
this area was dealt with at length earlier in the year and in his words, it was
"dead and buried." When the researcher indicated that it seemed to still be
present and in need of addressing, Mr. Lincoln still believed it was better
left alone.

Teasing was common at Charity, much like any school. According to
Taylor et al. (1995), teasing can be used to regulate behavior of girls. The
girls mentioned that the "submissive teasings" came into play after the
shift in power from female leadership to male leadership had occurred.
The boys were not fearful of losing their power because they were sure of
their position as "rightful leaders," so it was doubtful that the teasing
originates out of their feelings of vulnerability. Rather, it seemed that
they enjoy using their new power and the sense of domination that comes
with it.

When the girls lost their roles of leadership, they seem to also have lost
their voice. Barbara, a junior and the principal's daughter, had this understanding of the problem of the girls turning the leadership over to the boys
and the resulting loss of voice:

> The girls had prayer for the guys to be leaders. The guys wanted to start
> standing up, telling the girls to calm down and let them stand up. The
> teachers also did this. The problem came that the girls who were praying
> were not outgoing. The girls got scared of Tom and Bob and their view-
> point. You think, "They're the spiritual leaders," so I don't want to stand up
> and disagree. The guys will stop and ask what you think, but expect us to
> agree with them.

Barbara, along with most of the girls, reported that the boys, usually Tom and Bob, would quote Bible verses at the girls and the girls would often stop talking because it was easier than trying to fight with the boys over verses they felt they might not know well enough.

Tom and Bob received the brunt of the criticism because they were outgoing and forceful. They were sure of themselves and their Christianity and had a hard time understanding why anyone else would not feel that way. This then created an environment where only the strongest opinion was heard and learning the other's position was not necessary because, as Tom reports, "I'm so sure of my own opinion." Harriet supported this when she said, "If you don't agree [with the popular opinion], you are bashed for your beliefs. Others say things like 'you're wrong, you need to believe this way.' They [Tom and Bob] want agreement and when you don't, they say that you don't believe in God." Considering the insecurity of adolescents regarding the way they are perceived among their peers, especially in an environment that makes judgments based on Christian conduct, this type of silencing was very effective.

When asked how they let their voice be heard at Charity, girls responded in diverse ways. Becky, a senior, stated plainly that "only a few [girls] share their opinions while everyone else is too intimidated to share." Angela, a sophomore, reported that she tried to "word [my comments] to where they will not take it as an offense," whereas Nancy, a sophomore, did not voice her opinion sometimes because "I'm afraid of being proved wrong or screaming at someone."

Harriet explained that she usually agrees with the popular opinion, so everyone listens to her. Harriet did make this observation, however: "I've noticed that people who don't spend all their time spouting off opinions are more likely to be listened to." This contradicted the idea that those with the most forceful personalities were the ones listened to, but the influence of gender was not mentioned, but rather assumed. Louise, a junior, was able to shed a more positive, some might say even more Christian, light on the subject of letting one's opinions be heard. She stated, "I don't feel like my voice is heard, but I know that my actions and attitudes are being seen by everyone."

The very thing they are trying to be—strong, confident women of God—was the very thing that would inevitably get them in trouble with their peers, so they remained silenced in word, if not in deed. The silencing of girls at Charity was both intentional and involuntary. It was intentional on the girls' part so that their school experiences were more peaceful, if not enjoyable. It was involuntary when leadership was consistently bestowed on a gender that at times seemed less worthy. Again, this provided for liminal spaces in the girls' lives and school experiences; they were voiceless by default.

Throughout this study, the girls of Charity sought to find balance between themselves and their religious views. This is not much different than many people who seek to live betwixt and between secular and spiritual worlds. The girls in this study were influenced by the powerful force of evangelical Christianity and its oppressive views on the submission of women. Many religious women and girls in both private and public spheres of schooling still negotiate submission theology on a daily basis and it is here where the powerful lessons of educating the whole woman are found.

IN THE WORLD BUT NOT OF IT: GIRLS AND CHRISTIANITY

So what if I pray like a girl!
                                    —T-shirt worn by Nancy, (sophomore)

This chapter presented findings that point to one battleground largely ignored by academics, children's education outside the public schools, specifically education in religious schools. Furthermore, it provides a unique opportunity to see how gender and religion intersect in schools and in the construction of gendered identities. As evident in this chapter, how girls are being socialized as religious beings has profound implications for how they can live their lives as gendered beings.

As gender struggles to "come out of the closet" in many evangelical churches, it will struggle even harder to be heard at Christian schools, an area of fierce protectiveness among the churches (Bollar-Wagner, 1997). At Charity, the girls who fought hardest to be heard and not forced into submission were the ones who spent most of their lives in public school. The girls who willingly gave up their leadership roles and believed in the prevailing submission theology were the ones who had never gone, or had barely gone, to public schools. If Christian schools do not, as Bollar-Wagner has suggested, want their children raised in a bubble anymore, then issues such as race, gender, sexuality, and religion will have to be examined with more thought to "the other."

Girls at Charity felt powerless to change because they did not know where they stood, within the school and within the evangelical religion. The contradictions that existed between what even the boys felt about the girls, let alone what the girls felt about themselves in terms of their role in the church, acted as a powerful agent in their silence and their submission. Hence, they found themselves in a liminal state in the midst of a powerful tug of war that currently exists in the evangelical church regarding the submission of women and what the biblical interpretations of certain passages truly mean (Gallagher & Smith, 1999).

The girls at Charity were living what Mary Pipher (1994) describes as a "pressure to split into true and false selves" (p. 22). Their peace came in knowing that they had obeyed and done the right thing according to what they had been told by their main religious institution, the school, to feel was the truth. Their disquiet came in that, whereas they had been true to God and school, they felt that they had failed to be true to themselves.

DISCUSSION QUESTIONS

1. What influence does the education of girls in general have within the framework of this study?

2. How is religion both a participant and detractor from public schooling?

3. What lessons are learned from this study about understanding the education of conservative, evangelical Christians in both public and private settings?

REFERENCES

American Association of University Women. (1992). *How schools shortchange girls: Executive summary.* Washington, DC: AAUW Educational Foundation.

American Association of University Women. (1999). *Gender gaps: Where our schools still fail our children.* Washington, DC: AAUW Educational Foundation.

Associated Press Wire Service. (1999, June 11). Promise Keepers begin slide in numbers. *"Riverside" News-Press,* p. 18.

Balmer, R. (1994). American fundamentalism. In J. S. Hawley (Eds.), *Fundamentalism and gender* (pp. 48–59). New York: Oxford University Press.

Bly, R. (1990). *Iron John.* New York: Vintage Press.

Bollar-Wagner, M. (1990). *God's schools: Choice and compromise in American society.* New Brunswick, NJ: Rutgers University Press.

Bollar-Wagner, M. (1997). Generic conservative Christianity: The demise of denominationalism in Christian schools. *Journal for the Scientific Study of Religion, 36*(1), 13–24.

Eitzen, D. S., & Zinn, M. B. (1992). *Social problems.* Boston: Allyn & Bacon.

Gallagher, S. K., & Smith, C. (1999). Symbolic traditionalism and pragmatic egalitarianism: Contemporary evangelicals, families and gender. *Gender & Society, 13*(2), 211–233.

Griffith, A. M. (1997). *God's daughters.* Berkeley: University of California Press.

Heshusius, L. (1994). Freeing ourselves from objectivity: Managing subjectivity or turning toward a participatory mode of consciousness. *Educational Researcher, 23*(3), 15–21.

Jacobs, C. (1998). *Women of destiny.* Ventura, CA: Regal Books.

Keyes, M. (1993, Summer). Can Christianity and feminism agree? *Journal of Christian Nursing,* pp. 11–17.

Messner, M. (1997). *Politics of masculinities: Men in movements.* Thousand Oaks, CA: Sage.

Peshkin, A. (1986). *God's choice.* Chicago: University of Chicago Press.

Pipher, M. (1994). *Reviving Ophelia: Saving the selves of adolescent girls.* New York: Ballantine Books.

Sadker, D., & Sadker, M. (1994). *Failing at fairness: How our schools cheat girls.* New York: Simon & Schuster.

Stacey, J., & Gerard, S. E. (1990). We are not doormats: The influence of feminism on contemporary evangelicalism in the United States. In F. Ginsburg & A. Tsing (Eds.), *Uncertain terms: Negotiating gender in American culture* (pp. 98–117). Boston: Beacon Press.

Storkey, E. (1985). *What's right with feminism.* Grand Rapids, MI: Eerdmans.

Taylor, J. M., Gilligan, C., & Sullivan, A. M. (1995). *Between voice and silence: Woman and girls, race and relationship.* Cambridge, MA: Harvard University Press.

Van Leeuwen, M. S. (1993). *After Eden: Facing the challenge of gender reconciliation.* Grand Rapids, MI: Eerdmans.

Chapter 10

"We Ain't No Dogs": Teenage Mothers (Re)Define Themselves

Sandra Spickard Prettyman
University of Akron

> *Well I might be a teen mom now, but in a few years I won't be a teen
> and I'll just be a mom. So what will they call me then?*
>
> —Maria, 16

In the introductory chapter, Bettis and Adams delineate the liminality of
adolescence and femininity, both indeterminate spaces full of contradictions and shifting definitions. Adolescence is a time, a space, in our lives
when young people are expected, and allowed, to act in particular ways and
engage in particular experiences as they move toward adulthood and adult
responsibilities. How they negotiate this time and space will vary greatly depending on where they are located in the social, political, and economic
landscape of the time. In addition, adolescence is a historically contingent
category and definitions of what constitutes this period, this space, have
shifted and changed over time. However, one fact remains: Adolescence is a
temporary state, and although young people may move into it at different
times, in different ways, and for different reasons, they are always expected
to move out of it. Teen motherhood is a similar space, in that it is negotiated
differently depending on the social, political, and economic spaces inhabited by the girls who find themselves defined as such, as well as by the historical period in which they live. However, as Maria notes in the opening
quote, at some point teen moms move out of their teens and become just

155

mothers. Teen motherhood represents a liminal period in that these girls have moved out of what many would consider a "typical" teen lifestyle (free of worries and focused on the self) and into a more adult oriented social state (motherhood). They are still teens based on their age, but they are also adults now, having to take on adult responsibilities and care for not only themselves, but for a young child as well. They are neither teens nor adults, but both at the same time, the essence of liminality.

This new period in their lives brings many changes but also many possibilities, and it is important to understand how teen moms understand themselves as they enter and negotiate this new landscape so that their needs and interests can best be served. However, their definitions of self are constructed within and around community and cultural definitions that, more often than not, define them as deviant or delinquent. Media representations, important in constructing these larger community and cultural definitions, are often punitive and condemning. This chapter examines how one group of teen moms reacted to community definitions and media portrayals of teenage mothers that they felt were inappropriate and not representative of their lives, and how they used them to question their own definitions of self and teen motherhood. This identity work took place in various school spaces, and not just in the formal classroom, and offered these teen moms an opportunity to (re)define themselves and their place in the world. I argue that understanding how teenage mothers use media and community definitions to construct their own understandings of self must be taken into account as we formulate school and social policies and practices that will have an impact on their lives.

SITUATING THE STUDY

This particular project was part of a larger qualitative research study that took place during the 1996–1997 school year at Landview PREP Academy, an "alternative" secondary school for pregnant and parenting teens that services all 12 school districts in a southeastern Michigan county. This "alternative" school presents teen parents with an alternative to their "regular" school while they are pregnant and parenting. It is unique in this respect because most often these programs mandate that students return to their home districts once their babies are born. In addition, it provides students with diplomas that come directly from their home districts, as opposed to diplomas from an "alternative" school, which are often viewed as not as valuable. According to Carol Bryan, director of the school, PREP stands for People Reaching Educational Potential and represents "what we're really trying to do here." She describes the school as serving the needs of a population of students who "would probably otherwise have dropped out and weren't going anywhere," and also as providing services to the children of teenage parents, who had been designated as a potential "at-risk" group.

During the course of the school year I typically spent 4 days a week at the school, more than 500 hours during the course of the year. Most of this time was spent observing, helping, and hanging out with the students and staff, along with conducting formal interviews. In addition, I was able to attend, and often participate in, community presentations that students and the school presented, potlucks at the school for students, their families, and staff, and in the end, graduation. I also collected and analyzed documents, including examples of students' schoolwork, official school communications like newsletters and notices, and community documents related to the school and the issue(s) of teen mothers. The combination of participant observation, interviews, and document analysis gave me tremendous insight into the lives of these young mothers and students and the faculty and staff that work with them.

The analysis presented here is a piece of the larger project that sought to understand how teen moms construct themselves and are constructed by the world around them. The process of identity construction is a complex and dynamic process involving individual, institutional, and cultural influences. As Kenway, Willis, Blackmore, and Rennie (1994) have said, "girls are productions and producers of themselves and their times" (p. 201). This chapter examines how this production process unfolded at one moment in time for one group of teenage mothers, and the dissonance that resulted as they struggled to become producers rather than mere productions. It was a transformative process, not only for the teen moms, but for their school (and possibly the community) as well, highlighting the need for teachers, policy makers, and the media to take the voices of these young women into account as they write and think about how best to represent them and serve their needs.

POSITIONING AND DEFINING TEEN MOTHERS

> One of America's national myths has been that if teenage mothers simply postponed childbearing until they were more mature, their lives would improve substantially and the costs to society of early childbearing would decline dramatically. Such mothers would be more affluent, more likely to be married (and stably married), and more likely to bear healthy babies—babies who as adults would be well prepared to compete in the new global economy. But this myth is exactly that—a myth. (Luker, 1996, p. 41)

Adolescence is a time when many teens are trying out and trying on new ways of being as they move from the "carefree" world of childhood to the "responsibility-filled" world of adulthood. Through their adolescent exploration, however, teen mothers have taken on a new identity that is not temporary, and that they cannot "take off." Rather, they must now negotiate the tension between their own ongoing adolescence and their new adult role of motherhood. This tension, between childhood and adolescence on the one hand and adulthood on the other has led many to characterize teen mothers as "babies having babies" (Kelly, 2000; Luker, 1996). Teen mothers defy normative definitions of femininity that continue to revolve around the expectation that "normal" women will eventually marry men and have children. Teen mothers often have children without marrying men, and do not have them eventually, but have them at a time when most adults believe they are not ready to handle such pressures and responsibilities, either emotionally or financially. Thus, there are multiple components of their identity that help define teenage motherhood (and mothers) as problematic, including age, marital status, and economic status (Kelly, 2000; Luker, 1996). Many assume that these factors inhibit teenage mothers from being good parents, and thus that they will be unable to raise healthy babies who will grow into healthy, productive adults.

However, much of the current research paints a very different picture. It is true that greater numbers of young women who become mothers at an early age are not marrying today. However, about one in three teenage mothers in the United States does marry (Luker, 1996). In addition, the trend toward single motherhood is not only occurring with teens, but across the age spectrum, and only about 30% of the births to single mothers in the United States are to teenagers (Moore, 1995). Several decade-long studies of teenage mothers in the United States also refute the stereotype of teen mothers as long-term welfare recipients (Harris, 1997). Researchers have also found no correlation between teenage motherhood and high school graduation rates or subsequent economic earnings (Geronimus & Korenman, 1992). A mother's age has also been found to be less important than other factors in determining the potential abuse and neglect of her children (Buchholz & Korn-Bursztyn, 1993).

Yet, despite research to the contrary, public perceptions and media representations of teenage mothers continue to rely on negative and often deviant images of these young women and their futures, as well as those of their children. This is certainly highlighted by the initial conversation I had with Carol Bryan, director of Landview PREP, where she characterized these young mothers as students who "would probably otherwise have dropped out and weren't going anywhere" and their children as an "at-risk" group. Since the late 1960s and early 1970s, when teenage pregnancy became salient as a social "problem," the limited, and limiting, view of teenage pregnancy was that it represented a bleak future for both mother and child, a future that was now etched in stone. Campbell's 1968 statement highlights this sentiment: "When a 16 year old girl has a child ... 90 percent of her life's script is written for her" (p. 242). This assumption continues to represent the dominant discourse about teenage mothers and their children today. However, unlike the media, which paints a consistent portrait of negative images about teen mothers and their futures, the girls I observed and interviewed spoke in very different ways about themselves, their futures, and the futures of their children. They seemed to have a clearer understanding of how their identities as teen mothers were complicated by variables such as social class and race/ethnicity. They recognized both individual and collective definitions of teen motherhood, and how problematic it was to assume that all teen mothers and their futures were alike. Their understanding about the complexity of their lives and identities as teenage moms demonstrated how some of them might be more able than others to (re)write their life's script, despite the common cultural assumption that all of their lives were over.

WE AIN'T NO DOGS: STUDENT REACTIONS TO MEDIA REPRESENTATIONS

Landview is a conservative, rural county in southeastern Michigan, and images of teenage mothers here are not any different than in the rest of the country. Young mothers are most often defined as "bad," not only in terms of their parenting, but also for "choosing" to violate norms of femininity, for "choosing" to have sex as a teenager, and for making the wrong "choice" about keeping their child. These themes are vividly depicted in an editorial from the local daily newspaper from January 6th 1997. Below is an excerpt from the editorial:

> Our paper stopped doing regular feature stories and photographs on the first baby of the new year many years ago, mainly because the first baby born that year was to illegitimate parents. In the newsroom, many of us shake our heads in confusion when the news arrives: Another illegitimate mommy has given birth to the first baby of the year.... I think my reaction is always driven by a contrast of expectation and reality, Americans are expected to be born, be kids, grow up, get an education, start a career, settle down, get married and have kids to start the process over again. But the reality appears to be that more and more children are being born to young, unprepared mothers who don't have committed partners or a realistic plan for their lives, much less a satisfying career.

> The facts are clear: Illegitimate parents generally come from teen pregnancy, which tends to indicate that there's a problem with teens having sex ... Sex is still a taboo subject. Teach abstinence or teach nothing at all. Well, folks, it doesn't seem to be working. Oh, sure, maybe your babies aren't making babies. But I don't worry about kids who are not making babies. I worry about all the teen mothers giving birth this year to children who face slim

odds of success. Unless those moms' fairy tale dreams come true, they won't be able to help their children succeed at life. I worry because good people are having one or two kids while illegitimate parents are having litters of two or three or four or more kids.

That hits me in the tax return since I will be helping to cover medical bills for that family for years to come or to provide foster care when the state is forced to take the children away from bad parents. And I worry—I really worry—because my child will be going to school with children raised in a home by an illegitimate parent. I don't expect that the children of a single, under- or unemployed, 19-year-old mother of three will be prepared for school. And I expect to be paying the legal fees and trial expenses for one or more of those kids at some point when their soft moral background leads them to a life of crime. But maybe I'll get lucky, and I won't be the victim of their crimes.

Many of the cultural definitions of teenage pregnancy and motherhood as deviant and problematic coalesce in this editorial, and it is clear that it is not only about sex, but also about economics, education, morals, crime, and a plethora of other issues. Students, teachers, and staff at Landview PREP who had seen the editorial were outraged, and one of the teachers decided to use it as a learning tool in her classroom. Her goal was to encourage reading and writing by using an article that related to the girls' lives. Carla, the English and journalism teacher, wanted students to not only read the words, but also the world (Freire, 1971), and part of her goal was to "get them to see how these things affect their lives, but also that they can create change." Carla, a white, 40ish, middle-class woman, recognized that she came from a world very different than that of many of these young women, and she constantly strove to find ways to connect with them. She believed the editorial might help her do this since she could draw on broader media constructions of women in addition to the specifics addressed in the editorial.

When Carla first asked the students in her journalism class how many of them had seen the editorial, only a few students raised their hands. She passed out copies of the editorial and asked students to read it to themselves, underlining anything that upset them or that made them want to question the writer. As the students read, they got angrier and angrier, muttering obscenities and occasionally laughing at things they found entirely absurd. After a few minutes, Vicky, a tall, thin African American student, burst out: "He doesn't have the right to judge. Only one perfect person can judge another perfect person and he's not perfect." Carla asked how they would respond to him, and once again Vicky, throwing her hands up in the air, responded. "Where do we start?"

At first, the room was quiet. Where should they begin? No one said anything for several seconds, until Vicky almost exploded in indignation: "We ain't no dogs!" She burst out with several points in succession, her anger fueling her responses. Carla frantically wrote on the board, trying to keep up with her comments. Within seconds, several other girls joined in the discussion, their voices mingling, their ideas feeding off of each other. Their responses reflected their disappointment in a media that constructed them as deviant, when they saw themselves as taking responsibility for their lives.

> Like, hey, we made mistakes, but we're in school, you know, working hard so like, for like better life, for us but for our kids too. But he talks about us like our lives is over, like we're nothin', no better than dogs, irresponsible and like with no morals or values or nothin'. How does he know that? (Perla)

> I done some things wrong, but now I know that I gotta work hard and get a better life for me an my daughter and so I'm here, and who is he to say we got no morals and stuff. I'm turnin' my life around, around for the better. Does he see that? (Mona)

Perla and Mona, both young Hispanic mothers, present statements that are reminiscent of the confessional narratives young mothers tell in an effort to "recount their former 'wildnesses,' declare their new selves, and provide evidence of their maturity and responsibility" (Lesko, 1991, p. 45). The narratives are important vehicles by which to demonstrate their transformation from "problem" to "success." The theme of transformation was prevalent in the discussion that day, and students spoke often of how they had "changed since like we became parents" (Natasha). The students were disappointed that the editor had not spoken with teen parents—with them—because if he had he would have seen their transformation and been better able to accurately portray their lives. They clearly saw a different picture of themselves than the one he had painted in the editorial.

Carla wanted to use this idea of different perceptions of teenage mothers to help the girls recognize the complexity of the issues present in the editorial. She decided to split the class into two groups and asked one group to write down how they would represent teenage mothers and the other group to write down how the author had portrayed teenage mothers. Table 10.1 displays the lists that the two groups constructed.

Using the last question that students generated as a starting point (What's the real issue?), Carla and the students worked through the discrepancies between the two lists. She pushed them to recognize and name how definitions of teenage mothers were created and sustained by a variety of forces (the media, social service agencies, schools, the government, etc.), and how these definitions influenced their lives. A lively discussion ensued, with some students arguing "nobody defines me," and others arguing "you can't get around it, they got control."

Carla also pushed them to think about how multiple forms of oppression were intertwined, leading them to that last question: What's the real issue?

TABLE 10.1

Editor	Us
That we're like animals	We make mistakes like everybody else, but we're also taking responsibility
That we're all the same	We're back in school and working hard
That our pregnancy was our fault	We're supporting our children and want good futures for them
That our lives are over	We're all different and here for different reasons
That teenage mothers are no good	Many of us are very religious and faithful
That teenage mothers don't have morals	Some of us are married
That we have lots of kids and so called good people only have one or two	We are human beings and deserve to be treated respectfully
That we have no futures, we're losers	We want good jobs and good futures, we have dreams and goals
Most teenagers are having sex, so why is he more worried about us?	We don't want handouts, just opportunities to be successful
That our kids will be criminals and won't be prepared for school	We're good parents and good people
That we're unprepared and unrealistic (what parent isn't?)	We love our kids
What's the real issue? That we're poor, that we're single, or that we're teens?	

> Like bein' poor I think has more to do with our lives than bein' parents now, cuz we can grow up but we've all like seen how hard it is to get away from bein' poor, there's like no growin' out that. (Mona)

> OK, we all know it's like harder for a woman to get a good paying job than a guy, and when we get pregnant lots of guys leave us and so we have to support kids by ourselves. So like is it the jobs or because we're girls, or because we're poor, or what? (Lisa)

> Yeah, and he don't talk about it, but you know he's thinking, yeah like all those Black babies, or Hispanic babies, or whatever, like it's kind of racist, even though he doesn't say it. (Natasha)

These three young women, one Hispanic, one White, and one Black, recognized similar patterns and dynamics at play in the editorial. All three girls,

like most of the girls at the school, came from low-income families, and
struggled to provide for themselves and their children.

Carla and her students worked through the intersecting nature of oppression, in order to better understand how an editorial like this was possible, and why the editor might have conflated the various issues.

> Because like bein' a teenage mom means we're automatically poor, and
> probably Black or something, and so then we got no morals. It's like folks as-
> sume all those things are connected, but one thing don't mean another one,
> and bein' one thing don't mean bein' all of those. (Vicky)

> I think like he, like people have to believe that we're different than them so
> they don't have to think about how it might happen to them, or like he said,
> he's not worried about kids who aren't havin' kids, because they would have
> like other options and stuff, more support, or I don't know, maybe, they'd, it
> wouldn't be such an issue then. (Perla)

Students clearly saw that the editor was not only concerned about their age,
but also about their financial status, their morals, and their education,
which were all perceived to be problematic. Their status as teenage mothers
meant that they would be potential economic burdens in the future, and
that they would transmit their "soft" morals and values to their children
who would be unprepared for school because they had mothers who did not
succeed. Rather than accepting these dominant ideologies as "truth," Carla
asked her students to question and challenge them, naming their own values and beliefs about teenage motherhood. The result was that they were
able to define themselves in ways that made sense to them and that drew on
their experiences, rather than internalizing dominant ideologies that only
constructed them in one way—as deviant.

Another theme that emerged during their discussion was that of difference versus sameness. One of the major problems the girls saw with the editorial was that it assumed they were all alike, and that all teenage moms were
bad. The girls, on the other hand, articulated a tension between sameness
versus difference, and although they recognized that there were many differences in their lives, they also recognized that they were in some ways
bound by their common status as teenage mothers.

> He says we're all the same, and we is like all teenage moms, but all for differ-
> ent reasons and he can't know those. And so we are the same, but we're all
> different too. Some's poorer than others, some's Black, or White, or what-
> ever, some's smarter, some's, I don't know prettier. And those things can
> make a big difference in how people treat you, in how like you can be suc-
> cessful and stuff. (Mona)

> We's not all the same, even though people think so, even in this school. We all
> want different things outa life, and all do different kinds of things to get em,

but maybe we can like use our bein' the same to get those different things too. Like being here in school that's somethin' the same that we're usin' to get different things we want. (Natasha)

Both Mona and Natasha recognized that there were differences in their lives, they were individuals and to some extent their futures and their successes would be based on their individuality. Lesko (1991) argues that for teenage mothers: "given what is known about the economic plights of single mothers, and women of color, the training to be independent, autonomous, rational, and unique seems like a cruel joke" (p. 60). Instead, teenage mothers may need to develop a collective identity that would enable them to engage in collective action. Natasha began to recognize the possibilities that such a collective identity might bring. The girls articulated a tension between their commonalities and their individual differences, a tension that recognized they might be different and yet similar at the same time.

Toward the end of class, Carla asked students what they thought should be done with the ideas they had generated. The girls decided to write a letter to the editor inviting him to the school to see them and their children. "I think we should use the list to write him a letter and invite him to this school to see what we're all about. So's he can see that what he wrote isn't all true and how we're taking responsibility and can be good parents" (Vicky). Carla finished the lesson by having the girls begin a letter that would be sent to the news editor. She had gotten her students to read, to write, to think critically, and to engage in social action, events that did not happen every day in her class. In addition, themes that emerged here—transformation, interwoven forms of oppression, and difference versus sameness continued to surface, helping the girls question their own understanding of teenage motherhood and their connection to it. The lesson seemed to serve as a catalyst for subsequent conversations, interactions, and reflections, both in the classroom and outside of it, which helped many of the girls reconsider and (re)define what it meant to be a teenage mom.

When the girls left Carla's classroom that day, it was clear that her lesson had ignited a flame in many of them who were "tired of those stupid people pretending they know us and all." When they left her classroom, they could not leave the discussion, or their discomfort and disgust with what had been written about them. As they sauntered down the hall to get their children for lunch, many of them were still grumbling about "that stupid editor" and "the nerve of that paper." In the lunchroom, their chatter filled the air, along with the squeals, laughter, and cries of their children. Conversations about the editorial continued during lunch, and the themes that emerged during their lesson continued to form a backdrop for their reflections. Over the course of the next few weeks, the lunchroom served as a venue for exploring these themes in greater detail, and the girls debated them extensively. Although not a formal classroom, the lunchroom was certainly a space where learning occurred, and where much of the identity work of these young women took place. The lunchroom conversations that grew out of Carla's lesson, although not part of the formal curriculum, represented important learning for these young mothers.

LUNCHROOM LEARNING

Lunchtime at Landview PREP was a time for the girls and their children, and "adults" did not often spend time in the gym with them. Several staff and faculty served lunch items, but then typically left, unless there was a problem. When adults were present, they were perceived as violating the social and spatial boundaries of who belonged (McDowell, 1999). According to Nicolette, this time was for "you know social stuff, not schooly stuff," and Tracy added, "we can't like be ourselves if they're [school personnel] here." The administration believed this time to be valuable for helping the girls learn "how to relate to and fulfill the needs of their children" (Carol), and focused on the space as one that would help the girls develop their parenting skills. The girls most often talked about lunch as a time "when like we can be ourselves, not have to worry about teachers and classes and all that other stuff, or about like people judging us, like what we say" (Heather). The girls used this space as one that they could control, and for them it was more than just a place to learn parenting skills.

> It's like a time for being free, like kids, not like moms, even though our kids are here. We're still teenagers, you know, and so this is like time for us. We're supposed to be so many things, mothers, students, teenagers (she counted these off on her fingers) and sometimes we just need some down time I think. So lunch is kind of like for that, we get to talk about stuff that like we want, like clothes, and guys, and stuff that matters to us. You know, it's about like more who we are, not stuff we have to learn. (Vicky)

The girls perceived this time to be for them, about them, and not about "all that other stuff." It was a time when they could engage in the process of "becoming somebody" (Wexler, 1992), figuring out "who we are," whether that be as a mother, a student, or a teenager. The lunchroom was a space where these girls could "work" on their relationships and their futures, without the gaze and judgment of adults.

Although the girls most often talked about the lunchroom as a social space, it was also a political space, where teenage motherhood was complicated by other variables, such as social class, race/ethnicity, and learning (dis)ability, among others. These variables often defined who could sit where, who was included and who was excluded, and who controlled the space. This control of space denoted relations of power and privilege, and served as a visual reminder of social status and hierarchy within the school. Social status largely hinged on one's status as a "good" mother and on one's potential for future "success," as well as on traditional norms of femininity. For example, three students always sat off to the side with their children, apart from the other girls. Allison, Dawn, and Jennifer were all students with mild learning disabilities. All three were White and came from very poor families. Two of them were very overweight, and the other wore thick-framed glasses. Their clothing was often disheveled and occasionally dirty, but more importantly did not represent brand labels and the newest fashions. These girls did not epitomize traditional norms of beauty that young women, even teenage mothers, should try to emulate and attain. In addition, their parenting skills were often called into question by the other girls at the school, who believed that they were too "slow" to be "good" mothers (Jacki), which also called into question their ability to be successful in obtaining future education or employment. In spite of the school's attempt to include them and make them feel welcome, these girls were often marginalized by their peers. Seating arrangements in the lunchroom were a physical, and very visual, reminder of their exclusion.

Vicky, on the other hand, was one of the most popular girls in the school, with both the students and the staff. She was considered to be one of the girls who was most likely to "succeed" after she left Landview PREP, and had plans to attend a local 4-year university, perhaps going to law school afterward. She had good grades and was well respected by her teachers, who believed "she really does have the possibility to succeed" (Dan). Vicky was African American, tall and slender, and she and her son were always fashionably dressed. She was very articulate and one of the most outgoing and responsive students in the school, as evidenced by her participation in Carla's class depicted in the previous section. Her peers respected her, because "Vicky's like what we all wanna be: smart, funny, a knock out, guys love her, gets good grades, you know, all the stuff that makes you, I dunno, popular, or successful, or whatever. I just know we all wants to be like her" (Carrie). In the lunchroom, as in the classroom, her voice often dominated the conversation, and she was often instrumental in determining who got to sit where and with whom. This control of the lunchroom depicted the power relations that were often in play (or at work) in the space. The lunchroom, like the classroom, was a space where powerful lessons occurred, and where girls learned about themselves and their place in the world. For Allison, Dawn, and Jennifer, their place was off to the side, never at the center. For Vicky, center stage was the norm, along with the control that came along with it.

It was clear that although their status as teenage mothers bound them together, which was why they were all together at this alternative school, there were differences among them that the girls used to maintain boundaries and hierarchies. The lunchroom conversations on the day of the editorial lesson highlighted this. Vicky was sitting with several of her friends, Heather, Maria, and Sonia, along with their children. She pointed over to the table where Dawn, Allison, and Jennifer were sitting, and said: "That's why like people have those ideas about teenage mothers. Look at em, they don't know how to dress themselves, much less their kids, and they'll be like on welfare for like the rest of their lives." Her comment highlighted differences she perceived between herself and these "other" girls, indicating that the editor had a valid point about some teenage mothers. However, she clearly did not see herself as belonging to the category he described. "Like some of us are responsible," she went on to say. Maria, who was often very quiet, spoke up shyly: "But we weren't when we had our babies, or when we had sex maybe. Or, I don't know, for some of us it was out of our hands so maybe we were bein' responsible." Her comments reflected the tension between lumping all teenage mothers together and separating them based on perceived differences. Mona added: "Yeah, maybe you're too hard on them. At least they're here too, so's at least they wanna get an education. They might not like be as smart as you, but how smart was any of us to have kids now?" This tension between difference and sameness continued to surface in their conversations, causing some of the girls to reassess their relationships with other teenage mothers, like Dawn, Jennifer, and Allison, and to recognize how despite their differences they were bound by their status as teenage mothers.

> I don't know, like I never thought I'd be standin' up for them (nods her head over toward the table where Dawn, Jennifer, and Allison are sitting), but hell they're people too. Like I feel like I gotta stand up for all teenage mothers now because of what he wrote. He don't have the right to judge any of us. Like you [Vicky] said, we ain't no dogs so don't talk about us like that. Any of us. We might be different, and some might be on welfare, or not smart, or whatever, but we're all humans. You know what I mean? (Perla)

Perla's statement demonstrated a shift in her thinking and a recognition that despite their individual differences, they were all humans, and deserved to be treated as such.

Later in the lunch period, I went to sit with Dawn, Jennifer, and Allison, whose conversation also revolved around the tension between difference and sameness. Dawn pointed over to the table where Vicky was sitting: "They're just like us ya know. I know they think they're all better and stuff, but they still got babies just like us and they's still at this school, just like us." Jennifer agreed: "Well we sure all need the same kinds of things, like day care and jobs and school and stuff." Allison replied: "Yeah, but they got more, more I dunno, like possibilities, or like look at em, more money, more stuff, more brains, more ..." Dawn interrupted her, "Yeah, and sometimes more kids. So how smart does that make them?" They all laughed, looking over at Vicky and her friends, several of whom had more than one child. There was an understanding that the girls in this room were all the same, yet different, with similar problems and concerns, but different approaches and options for how to handle them.

For some of the girls, the tension between sameness and difference was also linked to the idea that multiple forms of oppression intersected, thus leading Vicky to articulate a difference between herself and learning disabled students. Dawn, Jennifer, and Allison were "like always gonna be poor and stupid" (Vicky) and therefore more likely to epitomize the multiple problems detailed in the editorial. Several days later this idea resurfaced, as Vicky once again denied Jennifer the opportunity to join their table. "Why you always so mean to her," asked Monique. "Cuz they're gross, I don't want them around my kid. Dirty and low class," Vicky replied. Some of the girls seemed disturbed by Vicky's response.

> Look around girlfriend, we's all poor here. Some of us might have a little more, but we're all in the same boat, else we wouldn't be here. You don't see no rich girls here, they're back at their home schools or whatever, but they ain't here. Just cuz those girls is slow ain't no reason to cut em out, they ain't no poorer than the rest of us. (Perla)

> And they ain't really no stupider either, none of us did real good at school, or we'd be back there, steada here. (Monique)

The girls challenged Vicky to think about how their status as poor women bound them together, whether they were learning disabled or not, and how their social class played into the perceptions of them as "problems." They recognized that teen moms who came from more affluent backgrounds might have different opportunities and different futures. "And even if they is slower, that don't mean we're better than them, just different is all" (Heather). Learning (dis)ability, social class, and teenage motherhood collided in this conversation as the girls grappled with how to make sense of the differences that did exist, as well as the similarities, and how these often connected to discrimination against them.

However, Vicky had a difficult time recognizing the collective identity that some of the girls articulated. Her own success in the school, which she and the school linked to the possibility for her future success, was based on her individuality and her acceptance of a "curriculum of individualization" (Lesko, 1991) where success or failure is determined individually. "The process of becoming schooled is a process of seeing oneself as an individual who is separate from others, whose interests are distinctive, whose person is unique" (p. 56).

Vicky bought into the meritocratic myth because that was how the school and society defined success and achievement, which she desperately wanted. This led her to assert several weeks later that:

> I am different than them, and better too. This [teenage motherhood] ain't holdin' me back, I'm turnin' my life around. Maybe I was wild and didn't care before, but now, it's different like. Just look at my grades. And I'm goin' to college, I'll make it. But not them. They don't have what it takes, you know what I mean.

Vicky noted her transformation (from wild teen to good student, from not caring to going to college), a transformation that was individually achieved, and clearly linked to her possibility for success, in school and in her future. However, this focus on the individual is problematic. It placed all the responsibility for success or failure (and transformation) on the individual and assumed that if teenage mothers bought into middle-class values of rationality and independence they would be successful, discounting the continuing significance of race and class in such success (Lesko, 1991). What Vicky failed to take into account was that despite her achievement at Landview PREP, she would continue to face difficulties entering college and the work force because of her social class and her race. Some of the other girls spoke about how difficult it would be for her to succeed, despite her transformation.

> You wanna go to college, but how you gonna pay for it all girl? There ain't no such thing as a free ride, and they might give you some money, but nobody's gonna give it all to you, and then you got daycare and all. What you gonna do then? At least here we got some stuff, but out there, it's a different kinda reality. (Perla)

> I ain't seen nobody really make it. Like that one girl she went to school for a while and she's a prison guard now. Not that that's all bad, but that ain't a lawyer, you know what I mean? (Heather)

> Let's face it, you a Black girl. People look at you and like that guy who wrote that stuff they think things bout you, and you can't stop that. And stuff they think, they write, that stuff makes a difference. Look at him callin' us dogs and stuff, people buy that and then where you? (Jacki)

Social class, race, and teenage motherhood were woven together to create a tightly knit fabric of oppression that would make it difficult for Vicky to achieve her goals based only on her individual status and success.

Several days later the theme of transformation resurfaced, as several of the girls spoke about the upcoming trip to a local middle school to participate in the Postponing Sexual Involvement (PSI) program. PSI was a program designed to expose middle school students to the dangers of engaging in sexual activity, and took an abstinence based approach. The program, overseen by middle school counselors and health teachers, relied on the use of high school students who came in during the course of 1 week to discuss issues with the younger middle school students. High school mentors came from the local high school and represented students who had been identified as high achievers and good role models by their teachers and administrators. Different than these teenage role models, teenage mothers were brought in for a day to talk about their experiences, giving middle school students a "real view of the real dangers of sexual activity" (Maureen—middle school counselor). Landview PREP students did not serve as mentors and positive examples, but as examples of what could go wrong when you engaged in sexual activity.

Participation in PSI was not mandatory for PREP students, rather students were identified by the school as being good candidates for participation. Once chosen, it was difficult for girls to turn down the invitation to participate, because it was a means by which to demonstrate their reform and their acquiescence to school and cultural norms of success.

> Here we go again, we gotta pretend like we're all changed and stuff, tell everyone how sex is bad and we won't do it no more. Like anybody believes it. (Perla)

> Yeah, well speak for yourself. I don't plan on bein' in this place forever. I plan on makin' somethin' outa my life and I don't want no more babies, not now anyway. So not having sex is ok with me. (Monique)

> Let's face it, our lives have like changed, maybe better, maybe worse, but they is different. And lots of us want different things now, because of our babies. We like matured, our thinking, the ways we act, we're more responsible, even if other folks don't think so. So maybe it's good we get to tell other kids this stuff, maybe it will keep them from bein' here. We need to talk about how hard it is, you know, how we're still students and how hard it is to do that and have a kid at the same time. (Vicky)

The PSI panels the girls participated in "function as rites of social redemption" (Lesko, 1991, p. 52) where they could recount their former wildness and then detail how they had changed as a result of becoming mothers as teenagers. Responsibility and maturity dominated the discussion, here and in the panels, as did the importance of using birth control and not becoming pregnant, because "why would you want your life to be harder, like this?" (Mona). Lesko's (1991) analysis of similar "success stories" and the functions they served for teenage mothers highlights the problematic nature of such confessionals that are often based on norms of individualism, rationality, and mothering. However, some students rejected the individualistic nature of the stories and panels, and argued that perhaps they needed to talk about their collective identity.

> Yeah, we're all talkin' about how I did this and I did that, but why don't we talk about like how that editor talked about US (emphasized), as if we was all the same. Why don't we talk about how like bein' poor means more than bein' a teen mom? Or how hard it is whenever you're poor to make it, whether you got a kid or not? (Perla)

> Cuz they want us to say certain stuff, and we gotta make ourselves look good. We can't go in and talk about how good sex is or how our problems are cuz we're poor. Our problems is cuz we were wild, we had sex, we dropped outa school, whatever. They don't wanna hear nothin' else. (Heather)

Perla and Heather articulated their discomfort with the panels and the emphasis on individual transformation, but they recognized the necessity for it. Without it, the school and society would not believe they were worthy of what little support they did get, and would not only continue to portray them, but treat them, in a negative way.

Sameness versus difference, transformation, and the interlocking nature of oppression all originally surfaced as themes in a classroom lesson. However, these themes continued to resurface and influence the girls well beyond the classroom walls. The lunchroom served as another space where they could engage with these themes in order to better understand who they were, individually and collectively, and where they could engage in the ongoing work of identity construction. The process provided them with a means by which to (re)assess who they were in a world that continued to construct them and their futures in particular ways. The girls, who were most often pushed to adopt an identity based on individual attributes, occasionally had insights about the importance of developing a collective approach to their lives and their identities, at the same time that they recognized problems with such a collective approach. This tension played out in their relationships with each other and in the social and political spaces they inhabited, but it also served to challenge their thinking about themselves, the school, the media, and the world.

CONCLUSION: ALTERNATIVE UNDERSTANDINGS

The lives of these young women did not lend themselves to neat generalizations; their identities were complex and often contradictory. They struggled with questions of sameness and difference, questions about the interrelatedness of race, class, and gender, and questions about how their future success depended on their transformation, from "wild" and irresponsible teen to "good" and responsible adult. Their responses in the classroom and the lunchroom indicated that although they recognized the individual nature of their experiences and circumstances, there was still a collective nature to their identity. Many of them worried about what would happen if they just focused on their individual differences, and not on their similarities, whereas others, like Vicky, worried about what would happen when they were individually associated with a collective identity that they did not embrace. Their conversations and interactions represented attempts to dislodge and complicate dominant discourses about teenage mothers. They highlighted the contradictions within the dominant discourse, at the same time recognizing the contradictions in their own. Kelly (2000) details how teen mothers in her study used both dominant discourse and a reaction against it in their constructions of self.

> ... the teen mothers used both strategies: they used one discourse against another, and they took advantage of the contradictions within the dominant discourse in an effort to forge a positive identity for themselves. They began to represent themselves, but the ultimate success of their effort would depend on others taking up their way of speaking, too. (p. 163)

Teenage mothers in this study used multiple ways of positioning themselves within the school and within the culture, often relying on both connections and divisions to construct who they were, and who they should be.

In an effort to forge positive identities for themselves, these young women sometimes relied on demarcating themselves from others and painting an individual portrait rather than a collective one. Helping them recognize the collective nature of their oppression might move them toward greater individual agency, as well as collective empowerment (Kelly, 2000; Luker, 1996). However, what seemed most important was their insistence on being producers of their own identities rather than mere productions. Lessons like those Carla constructed helped these young women engage not only in the acquisition of language skills, but also in the development of identity work. How can lessons like this, and programs like those at Landview PREP, help young mothers engage in the important identity work that goes on in schools in positive ways? How can we help them recognize their collective voices and power, as well as their individual agency? The voices and understandings of the young women in this study can serve as important tools for educators, policy makers, and the media as we explore how to help them produce positive identities for themselves, hopefully shifting community and cultural understandings of teenage mothers at the same time so that in the future, these young women no longer have to assert: "We ain't no dogs."

DISCUSSION QUESTIONS

1. Did you know anyone in your own schooling experiences who became pregnant? How was this person talked about and perceived by other students? By teachers and school personnel?

2. Why do you think most of the students in this school came from poor families? Perla mentioned that their middle class peers would not be found at the school. Why do you think this is? What options are available to girls with more money?

3. Given what these students said about themselves, do you think their identities were based more on individual or collective positions? What evidence from the study would you use to support your argument? In your own life, can you recognize ways that your own identity is based on individual or collective positions?

REFERENCES

Buchholz, E. S., & Korn-Bursztyn, C. (1993). Children of adolescent mothers: Are they at risk for abuse? *Adolescence, 28*(110), 361–382.

Campbell, A. (1968). The role of family planning in the reduction of poverty. *Journal of Marriage and the Family, 30*(2), 236–245.

Freire, P. (1971). *Pedagogy of the Oppressed*. New York: Harper & Row.

Geronimus, A. T., & Korenman, S. (1992). The socioeconomic consequences of teen childbearing reconsidered. *Quarterly Journal of Economics, 107*, 1187–1214.

Harris, K. M. (1997). *Teen mothers and the revolving welfare door*. Philadelphia: Temple University Press.

Kelly, D. (2000). *Pregnant with meaning: Teen mothers and the politics of inclusive schooling*. New York: Peter Lang.

Kenway, J., Willis, S., Blackmore, J., & Rennie, L. (1994). Making "Hope Practical" rather than "Despair Convincing": Feminist post-structuralism, gender reform and educational change. *British Journal of Sociology of Education 15*(2), 187–210.

Lesko, N. (1991). Implausible endings: Teenage mothers and fictions of school success. In N. Wyner (Ed.), *Current perspectives on the culture of schools* (pp. 45–63). Cambridge, MA: Brookline Books.

Luker, K. (1996). *Dubious Conceptions: The Politics of Teenage Pregnancy*. Cambridge, MA: Harvard University Press.

McDowell, L. (1999). *Gender, identity, and place: Understanding feminist geographies*. Minneapolis: University of Minnesota Press.

Moore, K. A. (1995). Executive summary: Nonmarital childbearing in the United States. In *Report to Congress on out-of-wedlock childbearing* (pp. v–xxii). Washington, DC: U.S. Department of Health and Human Services.

Wexler, P. (1992). *Becoming somebody: Towards a social psychology of school*. Washington, DC: Falmer Press.

Part III

AFTER SCHOOL

Chapter 11

Black Girls/White Spaces: Managing Identity Through Memories of Schooling

Cerri A. Banks
Syracuse University

> *I always thought that there ought to be two separate venues you can go to. Like one you can go to for the actual education and then another you can go to for the whole growing up and being a teen thing. If there was someway they could separate that, it would be so much easier.*
> —Ashley Michaels (graduate student, 11/21/01)

At the time of her interview Ashley Michaels, quoted in the opening was a master's student studying public relations at Upstate University in Central New York. Here, in response to the question, "How would you rewrite your middle and high school experience?" Ashley alluded to the need for adolescents to negotiate their academic work and their work of "growing" and "being" in schooling places. Implicit in her response is the idea that both academic work and the work of identity are necessary components for success.

For Ashley, having two separate places to conduct this task would make it much easier. Of course, the education system in the United States does not have such separate venues, and most youth are forced to navigate their way in the physical surroundings we label school and school grounds. A close look at the practices of adolescents in schools reveals that even in the most

177

restricted educational systems students find and claim adult-free spaces and discourses, "in-between spaces" (Bettis, 2001) where they set about the work of being, the work of identity (Ferguson, 2000).

Ashley was one participant in an ongoing research project with graduate women from a wide range of academic disciplines at Upstate University. The participants all attended predominantly White elementary, middle, and high schools. The term "predominantly White schools" refers to schools whose student, faculty, staff, and administrative bodies, as described by the women, were made up of mostly Euro-American White people and where students of color are a numeric and curricular minority. The schools are located in both suburban and urban settings and the women interviewed identify in whole or in part as African American. Each participant completed multiple, in-depth qualitative interviews designed to unearth how they narrate their schooling experience in relation to identity.

Because these adult women are narrating from memory, *how* they remember becomes important. Rosenwald and Ochberg (1992) write that "how individuals recount their histories, what they emphasize and omit, their stance as protagonists or victims ... all shape what individuals can claim of their own lives. Personal stories are not merely a way of telling someone (or oneself) about one's life; they are the means by which identities may be fashioned" (p. 1). Also important is how the women made and make meaning of the significant events and discourses that occurred during those adolescent years in both their academic and social experiences, particularly those events and ideals that rule literal, physical spaces outside of the classroom.

This chapter examines schooling memories as recounted by Black women who attended predominantly White schools as adolescent girls. It focuses on their social experiences on school playgrounds and in school hallways, utilizing the intersectionality of race, class, and gender as an analytical framework with which to conceptualize their experiences. This discussion exposes some of the challenges Black girls face in identified school settings and gives a glimpse into the identity work that occurs as a result.

READINGS AND REPRESENTATIONS

There is a barrage of literature that focuses on African American youth and schooling. The texts are varied and the themes include but are not limited to: ways to educate Black youth (hooks, 1994; Ladson-Billings, 1994; Majors, 2001), life stories and conversations about race and racism in schools (Fox, 2001; Garrod, Ward, Robinson, & Kilkenny, 1999), urban schooling and Ebonics (Anyon, 1997; Perry & Delpit, 1998), and issues of identity including school achievement and self-segregation (Ferguson, 2000; Fordham, 1996; Leadbeater & Way, 1996; Tatum, 1997). Examination of this plethora of literature reveals that Black youth, in all schooling practices and spaces, are always negotiating race, gender, and class[1] and fighting essentialized notions of who they are as people and as students. What Loury (2002) describes as the "embodied social signification" (who society thinks one is), the stigma attached to "bodily marks" (including skin color), and socioeconomic status (social class), all have a direct impact on what happens in schools (p. 58). This battle against essentialized notions then is significant for Black girls because their identity is often homogenized by stereotyped ideas and dialogues about their race, class, and gender. For example, conversations surrounding Black adolescent girls are often limited to topics of teen pregnancy, drug abuse, welfare reform, sexuality, promiscuity, school failure, poverty, and violence (Lamb, 2001; Leadbeater & Way, 1996). These limited conversations make it easier to exclude adolescent Black girls from countless, significant conversations both in and out of schools. Disarming stereotypes and broadening the discussion requires creating space where their individual voices can be heard. It calls for placing the narrative itself at the center not stereotypes or theory (Rosenwald & Ochberg, 1992; White, 1980).

Intersectionality and the Lives of Black Girls

Black adolescent girls face exclusion from academic discourses similar to the historical exclusion that Black women faced in the feminist movement and the academy, forcing them to adopt analytical tools and methods, as part of a Black feminist movement that put their complicated narratives at the center (hooks, 1984). Collins (2000) explains that one such tool, intersectionality, specifically the "simultaneous and multiplicative convergence of race, class, gender, ability and sexuality" (p. 18) as interlocking systems of oppression must be recognized and heavily weighed into any discussion of women and girls of color. Using a Black feminist, intersectional lens places the women interviewed and their narrative about adolescent life in school at the center of this discussion and analysis. As Collins writes, this method "not only returns subjectivity to Black women (and girls) by treating them as agents of knowledge, they simultaneously demonstrate that race, class and gender intersectional is not merely an approach one should adopt but an approach having conceptual and methodological merit" (p. 117).

Intersectional analysis explains that "there is no singular experience representing all women" or in this instance all Black adolescent girls (Zerai & Banks, 2002, p. 12). It further explains that it is not enough to say that each adolescent girl has a different life experience. Rather, accurate analysis in-

---

[1]In this chapter I use "race, class, and gender" in the discussion of intersectionality. Though only three categories are mentioned, the analysis includes all systems of oppression.

volves examining and critiquing a system that privileges and assigns normalcy to particular social locations—that is, particular bodies and their place in society. In the United States these advantaged bodies are usually White, male, heterosexual, free of disability, and wealthy. The lives of those not holding these privileged positions are impacted by inequalities that result from a lack of social, political, and economic power. The fewer privileged locations occupied the less power an individual has and thus is more vulnerable to the stigma and oppressions that affect social life including racism and discrimination, poverty, stereotyped representations, and in schools, exclusions and accusations. (Collins, 1998; Wildman & Davis, 2002).

For example, Jane, who is studying at Upstate University, is a biracial woman, who self-identifies as African American. Jane's mother is White and her father is Black. She has light skin, which she proudly claims "tans easily," and she wears her hair in a natural twisted style called dreadlocks. Jane tells the story of being accused of stealing by her teacher in elementary school, where she was the "only Black person" most of the time and one of "only two or three" other times:

> One time there was a kid who was stealing food out of people's lunches and she blamed me. I think she blamed me because one day I had traded cookies with another girl, who had a broken arm, and so she saw me putting her cookie in my bag but she hadn't seen me put my stuff in her bag first so she thought that meant I was stealing them. I remember being livid and crying and I was like "I did not do this, I don't know why you're accusing me." ... It turned out it was a White boy in our class who had been stealing it. She tried to apologize afterward. I just kept my mouth shut but my face always betrayed me so I had really a disgusted face. I just wouldn't look at her. I could not look at her and she kept saying, "Will you look at me," and I was like "I can't." I was uncomfortable with the whole thing. I couldn't believe that she had accused me of that. I would not sit near the lunches anymore. I would not leave my lunch over there. I kept it in my desk and I think that's when I told my mom I wanted to start paying for lunch 'cause then there would be no switching or swapping and if my friend with the broken arm wanted to switch cookies with me anymore we would have to do it at lunch.

> This was in third grade. So I was like I don't know, maybe seven or eight or nine? I don't know at the time if I had known it to be racism but I knew something wasn't right. I'm like "What would make her accuse me over another kid, why? Why would she say it was me?" So right then I knew that something wasn't right and I think that's why I couldn't look at her. Even though I couldn't say that's racist because I didn't know that word. It was immobilizing for me. But I think it wasn't just a feeling of her being racist towards me that made me immobile; it was my anger towards her for how could she do this to me? You know, the only grade in her class I remember doing not as well in was cursive, which improved immediately, and all my other grades were A[s] and I can prove that because I have my report cards still. I did well in school

at that age and I thought that meant I would deserve to be treated nice by a teacher and I wouldn't be accused of things like that. I was friendly. So ... it just was a shock. It was really a blow to me.

At first glance it would appear Jane was the victim of an innocent mistake. Her mere physical presence near the lunches and the practice of switching cookies with another student in the class could make her suspect. As Jane recounted her story, she admitted that in the third grade she did not have a name for what she was feeling about the accusation, but she remembered being a victim of something that just "wasn't right." She had a physical reaction of shock and immobilization in the face of her accuser in the aftermath. Jane exhausted the reasons she felt she should not be accused including the fact that she was a good student and friendly and further belied the long-term impact of the accusation and the work to combat it by stating, at the time of the interview, that she could *prove* her good grades by showing her report card. Jane took it upon herself to change her surroundings, to buy rather than bring her lunch and to confine any sharing to the school lunchroom in order to remove all possible circumstances that could lead to her being suspect. As Jane continued her story, it became evident that something more than circumstances and surroundings was at play. Despite her work to safeguard her reputation and her psyche, due to her social location Jane was always a suspect. She continued:

So that reminds me of another thing that happen. It was during my school years. I think I was in fourth grade and I went to this church camp and again I was one of the only Black kids there and that summer there was a thief and I was one of the suspects. Someone was going into the cabins at night or during the day and stealing people's money. Money never was stolen out of my cabin, it was the other cabins. We're not always accounted for by the, the staff or whatever because they'll send two of us to go get wood or whatever. I don't know why I was even a suspect and I think at that age I knew, I *expected it* 'cause I had already gone through this experience with my third-grade teacher *so I knew I was a suspect.* And I remember all the kids started to shun me and I was alone by myself for a few weeks that summer. I remember there were these two twins who didn't believe it because they were with me all the time. And they said, "We know it wasn't you." So I remember I was getting upset and I, I'm not a quitter and I was getting to the point where I was ready to go home. I remember they took me and a couple of the other kids aside and they brought us into this one lodge one at a time and were questioning us. And I was like, "I don't know what you're talking about, I didn't steal anything." Turned out again it was a White boy. So that summer I just was so upset about the whole situation and I remember they tried to apologize to me and I was like "Don't apologize. Just don't let it happen again." It just left such a bitter taste in my mouth. It's one thing to be accused of a crime if I did it, but since I didn't that's what bothers me, and there's no way for me to—how could I like defend myself against that? They were only accusing me 'cause I'm Black. I know that and at that time I think I knew that too but I just, I couldn't verbalize it because again I still didn't know racism, like the word. Instead of being sad and feeling like "How could this happen to me?" it wasn't a surprise so I was just mad. For the rest of the summer I was quiet. I would not speak to people. I would sit there and people would try to talk to me and play games, I would just be like "I don't want to." And I would sit there and look in the grass.

After a second accusation Jane again exhausted the reasons she should not be accused of stealing, even citing the opinion of two twin friends, as witnesses to her innocence. Again she realized, "something is not right." For Jane, being a suspect was not just about access or her physical location, near the cabins or the lunches. Even though she did not have the words to describe the source of her feelings the first time, by the second accusation Jane connects the feeling to race and makes the statement "They're only accusing me 'cause I am Black." With this statement Jane recognized that it was not just the color of her skin that caused the accusations but rather what "being Black" signified in these settings where she was the only Black girl in groups of all White people, namely the likelihood of low socioeconomic status creating a need and a propensity to steal to fill it—or differently stated, the convergence of her race and class and the societal ideals about criminals that the accusing teacher and counselor associated with her social location. Even though she was a "good girl" in school and had two good friends to vouch for her at camp, who these adults "thought she was," informed by essentialized beliefs about the lives of individuals occupying this particular social location outweighed the privilege of "not being accused" that Jane thought she deserved.

Collins (1998) explains that "not race, nor gender nor economic class alone can adequately explain the Black woman's (or girls) experience but rather that these are intersecting systems that converge and collide and operate simultaneously and often oppressively in their experience" (p.116). Jane was not just a good girl at camp or at school. She was a Black girl, one who may take cookies and give nothing in return, and she was subject to all the stereotypes about Black youth and crime that her White counterparts, even the guilty parties who turned out to be White and male were not.

Zerai and Banks (2002) make it clear that it is not enough to say about Black adolescent girls that their race makes their experience different from the White girls and boys they attend school with: rather, it is more accurate to say that each girl's experience, like Jane's, is always conditioned by race, class, gender, and other social positionings all at once or simultaneously. Tatum (1997) argues that identity work for Black youth involves thinking of themselves in racial terms. Intersectional analysis adds that Black adolescent girls can never claim that only Blackness informs their existence. They must consider that they are Black and female and wealthy or poor and so on and that these locations come with particular discourses and consequences. It is the material consequences of the interlocking of race, class, and gender as systems of oppression that render Black girls almost invisible in many conversations and supports stereotypes in others. Jane was physically immobilized and silenced by this youthful trauma and identified it as "one of the worst memories about elementary school."

BLACK GIRLS/WHITE SCHOOLING PLACES

Examining the lives of Black female adolescents as individual and whole humans and not a homogenous group will provide proof that the experiences of Black girls in schools cover a wide continuum and reflect the need for discourses around identity that do also. As the girls navigate their subject locations and work on "being teens" in places other than the classroom, *where* they are has as great an impact on their identity work as *who* they are and *who* they are shifts and changes as they move "betwixt and between" material spaces (Adams & Bettis, chap. 1, this volume, p. 6). The women interviewed talk about their identity work as adolescent Black girls in predominantly White schools in places outside of the classroom, like the playground and in school hallways. Their adolescent stories give insight into the complexity of the identity work Black girls do in schools.

If You Can't Beat 'Em, Join 'Em …

Ashley Michaels is African American. Her father is Jamaican and was born in the United States. Her mother was born in the Bahamas. Ashley explains that her parents always wanted to be a part of mainstream American culture and saw academic, social, and economic success as a way to fulfill that goal:

> That is the mentality in my family of first-generation immigrants. I think that has done a lot to shape who I am that my parents have always been really focused on me making it in America as an American and doing what you're suppose to do to be successful here, which is going to the best schools, getting an education, acting a certain way, speaking a certain way … getting a good job. (11/7/01)

Ashley grew up in an upper-class suburban neighborhood in California. She describes her neighborhood as "mostly White, upscale" and one where "children can run out in the street and be safe." She further explained that her neighborhood social group consisted of "White kids." To facilitate their goal of assimilation Ashley's parents forbade her from "speaking in slang or broken English" and hanging out with Black kids they felt would "corrupt her" and introduce her to drugs and gangs. Ashley explains that her parents' values were not meant to show disrespect for their culture: "If you don't [act a certain way] they're [White people and educated Blacks] gonna think you're a little ghetto Black person. There's definitely that mentality in my family but in no way a lack of respect for our culture and our past. There are definitely still ties to the African American culture and the Caribbean culture" (11/07/01).

As an adolescent Ashley attended a predominantly White middle and high school for gifted students that focused on science and math. In Ashley's case the school was physically located in an urban setting and shared space with another school for minority students:

> It was like having two totally different schools that physically were in the same place. In California most of the schools are outside and they have separate buildings. They are not really connected physically like they are on the East Coast. The way the school was set up there were two programs. The school was called Williams-Tech Institute; Williams was the base school and Tech Institute was the magnet part of the school and our [gifted students] rooms at Tech Institute were the nice rooms on main campus. The Williams classes were in bungalows that were built afterwards. (11/07/01)

Ashley rode the bus from her home in the suburbs to the school in the city:

> My school was a magnet school centered physically in the "Black" area of town. Instead of doing what most magnet schools do in being in the White part of town and busing in the Black kids, it was in the Black side of town and bused in White kids. So what happened was that kids who were bused in who were mostly White and a couple of Asians were taking a whole separate set of classes than the other kids in the school. Honors classes were only open to Tech Institute kids. (11/07/01)

Socially Ashley explained she faced many challenges as a Black female at her predominantly White school. She described herself as "Queen Oreo," like the cookie, Black on the outside and White on the inside, and explained that she endured taunting from both White students who called her "nigger" and Black students who called her "Uncle Tom." Because her social circle consisted of White students, Ashley admitted she initially had little interaction with Black girls near her campus and the interactions she had at times caused discomfort:

> I think I was getting my first exposure to Black students who hadn't been raised in White world like I had. And that was eye opening and rough. I was really confused not always feeling comfortable around other Black students ... simple things like walking through the halls and seeing a group of Black

girls and just not feeling comfortable physically being around them. I just I wouldn't know what to say or how to act. I wondered how they looked at me. If they looked at me as one of them or one of the other and more than anything just feeling out of place. (11/21/01)

For Ashley, her physical locations informed by social class—that is, living in the suburbs, riding the bus into the city, and attending classes in the nice classrooms instead of the bungalows—separated her from other Black students materially and socially:

I talked funny, I dressed like the White kids, you know. I had hair down my back. I had money for clothes that a lot of them didn't have and teachers really liked me. They knew my parents from the community and we were an "upstanding Black family." They were concerned with me falling in with the wrong crowd with the bad Black kids. (11/21/01)

Ashley had to negotiate her parents' and teachers' ideas of how she should not be "a little ghetto Black person" with her own social experience and the interactions she had with the Black students at Williams. She credited one critical incident that occurred in the schoolyard with changing her whole outlook on who she was and facilitating her taking charge of who she was to become:

Black girls hated me something fierce. I got jumped at least twice one time in which they cut off my hair, which is why I don't have hair down my back anymore. That's why I look over there so I don't cry when I have to look you in the eye. There were a bunch of girls after school and I was walking across campus 'cause on one side of campus was the standard building of campus and the bungalows were in another area and my speech class was in the bungalows. So I was walking back from the bungalows to go over to the main campus to catch a bus or something. And three or four Black girls came out of nowhere and started yelling at me. I was used to getting scared so I kept walking. One of them came and pushed me over and another came and like grabbed my hands. The next thing I knew, I still don't know if it was like scissors or knife or whatever, but they grabbed my hair, pulled it back, chopped it off, laughed, and ran off. I didn't know who they were. I couldn't pick 'em out. I wasn't about to go and bring more attention. I mean they always talk about kids getting beat up and they don't want to tell anybody 'cause they get more. My mom, I told her that I decided I wanted to cut my hair and so I had a friend cut my hair. Of course I was in a year's worth of trouble for that but I wasn't about to tell her and have her come to school and cause a ruckus and bring more attention to me. Nothing ever happened and I mean to this day I bet if I went back home and walked through the area and saw one of them they probably wouldn't even realize who I was. So I mean I don't think it was a big thing to them.

In this instance Ashley was literally moving between her two worlds at school. She was walking between the physical buildings that separated her from other Black girls on campus. Ashley was also losing the fight to navigate her social world and falling victim to a violent assault. *Where* she was became as significant as *who* she was as her race, class, and gender converged in this schooling space.

Cutting Ashley's hair was a raced and gendered attack. In the United States, Black hair has always carried political, social, and economic implications. It has been the site of resistance against dominant White societal ideals of feminine beauty. It has also been a site of contention among Black people. According to Byrd and Tharps (2001) "the European standard of straight, long hair as a signifier of beauty led to historical accounts of slave holders shaving the 'wooly' heads of slave women in attempts to dehumanize. After Emancipation 'straight hair translated to economic opportunity and social advantage' since those possessing it were more aesthetically acceptable to the European eye" (pp. 14–17). In modern times the inventions of chemical treatments to straighten and lengthen Black hair have sparked heated debate over the authenticity of chemically straightened hair styles verse natural kinky hairstyles versus the proverbial "good hair" attributed to Black people whose hair is wavy or straight without chemical alteration. In the United States, hair that is straight and long has social advantage to this day. As Byrd and Tharps explain, "In this country it is impossible to ignore the fact that pop culture paradigms of beautiful Black women are coifed with long straight hair" (p. 155).

Ashley's hair had waves but it was not kinky, and it hung down her back. To her attackers this signified a powerful social location associated with Eurocentric ideals of beauty that render Black girls with short, kinky hair undesirable. To Ashley's attackers, this combination of factors—the hair down her back, the money to buy clothes, the attendance at the school for the gifted, and the acceptance by White teachers—signified a position of privilege and power to which they did not have access, and their act of violence was an aggressive attempt to dominate her physically because they could not do so socially (Lamb, 2001; Simmons, 2002).

Ashley never told her mother or teachers about the attack, fearing adult interference and confrontation would provoke the girls to continue persecuting her. Implicit in this response is the idea that there are spaces at school like the school yard that adults cannot control and students must negotiate. The impact of this experience is evident not only in the fact that evoking the memory as an adult brings tears to Ashley's eyes but also in the identity work it prompted: "More than anything else that precipitated my determination that I was not going to be on the outside of this group because if I was on the outside of this group I was not going to make it through school—*that I needed to join 'em 'cause I was definitely not going to be able to beat 'em."* Ashley felt she had to start associating with the Black kids at Williams in order to survive in her educational setting. She joined a Black student union, became deeply interested in Black history and Black women writers, and for the first time in her life went to a Black church. She explains that she began "dating Black boys on campus" and hanging around groups of Black students, "sometimes just standing near where they gathered." Ashley recognizes that all of her experiences were part of her identity work. The incident that occurred in the school yard prompted a period of exploration and discovery and to some extent rebellion against her parents' wishes in places outside of the classroom, as she sought out students at Williams school between classes and after school. What started out as a survival technique became a critical path to self-discovery. Ashley created a venue at school where she could do her identity work. She concluded the interviews by saying:

> I think I have decided that regardless of whether or not I've always socially been in groups with Black people I still feel like I experienced Blackness on some level. I finally realized that experiencing Blackness can be the kind of experiences I have had. It can be being raised in a White culture as a Black girl. I mean that is part of being Black and so when I finally got that through my head I was like. "Ok. Well yeah." That was a big thing for me.

For Ashley and other Black female adolescents in predominantly White schools, "experiencing Blackness" and defining that experience individually is the work of identity. This work of defining is challenged by raced, gendered, and classed interactions that occur in spaces like school corridors. In these spaces where students must pass and often roam and where adults attempt to enforce constraints, Black adolescent girls face challenges related to popularity, inequitable regulation of bodies, and covert racism.

Hallway Hierarchies

In schools, hallways are more than corridors through which students pass enroute to classes and other activities. This schooling space is a dynamic social site where power struggles occur, hierarchies are established, and identity-informing interactions take place, both when the hallways are bustling with bodies and when they are almost empty. In school hallways, "social relations intersect with social structures and give the space meaning" (Mitchell, 2000, p. 294). Students actively use this space to tout one identity as superior to another. For example, discourses regarding coolness and popularity are often played out in busy school hallways, with those deemed popular getting the most greetings and laughs, and engaging in conversations with classmates. Conversely, not being popular is also identified and solidified through interactions in busy hallways. Kate explained: "I don't remember speaking to many people in the hallway. One of the cool kids had their locker next to mine so I would try to talk to her when we were at our lockers and she wouldn't give me the time of day. None of my friends were any of the cool people." Hallway lockers are a primary structure where students store academic and personal belongings at school, and they are a large part of public and private hallway life. For the cool girl with a locker near Kate's, keeping her distance from a self-proclaimed uncool adolescent helped her publicly maintain the social power that comes with standing on the top rung of the hierarchical hallway ladder, the rung labeled *popular*. For Kate, attempting to gain *access* to the popular crowd through the cool girl while at her locker and being rejected was a private, identity-informing interaction. She explains: "I guess I made an attempt to be cool but every time I did I was shot down so after awhile I just said there was no point. I had my friends those are the ones I talked to the most. I didn't care anymore what snotty people thought." Kate decided after that school year that she was happy with herself and her group of friends. She found the "snottiness" of the popular crowd annoying and decided that their opinion of her was no longer important.

In predominantly White schools, White students use the hallways as a place to engage in covert racist behavior, hurling derogatory racial slurs that insult and degrade Black adolescent girls, sensing that in this space their words are less likely to be heard by teachers and staff. Van Ausdale and Feagin (2001) explained that "language is embedded in relations of power and influence and that children use racial references to control others, to establish who belongs and who does not and to assert a White status and identity with its privileges and a Black status and identity that is marked by lesser privileges" (pp. 106–107). Consider Jane's experience, which she identified as her worst memory as a new Black adolescent girl at her predominantly White middle school:

> I think my worst memory was probably the situation in the first or second week of school. I was walking down the hall with one of my newly made friends and this boy was like "nice nigger" and ran away. That just sort of set the tone of what I expected from that school district and its people from that point on. I wanted to go find out who he was 'cause I really wanted to do something to him … confront him, say something back just as mean to hurt him too. I don't know that I would have been violent. I never have been in a fight before but I wanted to say something to let him know that it just wasn't OK and that I could say something just as mean to him too. I remember being angry. I remember just crying because I felt like I couldn't do anything. (5/22/02)

This racial slur coming from a White male student influenced Jane's expectations of others around her. It set her apart from the larger school population and asserted that she was different and did not belong. This male established his position of social power and the privileges associated with his Whiteness by speaking to Jane in a way that identified her Blackness as inferior. The hallway provided a space where he could run away and Jane could not retaliate. She was left crying and feeling helpless. For Jane, this hallway experience and its aftermath informed her identity work:

> I told my mom about it and she really didn't do anything. I was demanding to go to the school and I wanted all these changes to be made and I was like "I don't want to deal with racism and I'm not going to be everybody's lesson." She just hugged me and said, "It's going to be OK and they are a lot of ignorant people." I was like "telling me that doesn't change anything." That was definitely my worst feeling of futility 'cause I couldn't do anything about the kid and the people who I thought would help me didn't in the way that I wanted help.

As an adolescent Jane recognized that she did not want to be in a position to "teach" others about racism, or be anyone's lesson. She realized that one cannot always rely on support from expected sources. Jane explains that the memory of this experience still stirs up a desire for revenge and informs how she handles situations today:

> I mean at this point, whatever encounters I have I can deal with them on my own and if I want to take action I can do it and not have to rely on anyone else to do the things that I think are necessary. I think I still wish I could have caught that boy. I would have liked to have done something to him. I still feel that way [laughing]. I still feel that way.

Hallway hierarchies regarding race, gender, class, and other ideological positions, which forcefully inform the lives of Black girls, are also created by school rules and policies. For students, roaming almost-empty school hallways, especially during class time, provides a break from "boring classes," a chance to spy on boyfriends, girlfriends, or crushes, the opportunity to indulge in "nosy behaviors" like peering in other classrooms, the occasion to meet up with friends to make after-school plans or to complain about teachers during class periods, and a time to pass notes. Roaming provides "a sense of freedom" in an otherwise highly regulated space: "I liked to walk in the hall when it was empty. I think it was just neat. I liked the break from the class and it was just kind of cool to snoop around and peek in other classrooms and you know make a long trip to the bathroom and then come back" (5/22/02). Many students acquired this type of private "hallway time" by asking to go to their lockers where they exchanged, collected, and connected with personal items.

Adults in schools utilize hallway space, but adolescent discourses about race, class, and gender, and the resulting identity work are usually out of their domain of consciousness and control. Recognizing this, adults, teachers, and staff attempt to regulate hallway space in several ways. Schools often require teachers and staff to sit or stand as hallway monitors, managing students as they pass through. They establish rules and policies about when, where, and how students can be in the hallways and create material regulators like security cameras that record student hallway activity, metal detectors to prevent students from bringing weapons to school, and hall passes that students must obtain to move through the space during times other than changing classes and that they must produce on demand when questioned regarding their presence in the space (Ferguson, 2000; Trump, 1998).

When problems in schools arise hallway restrictions are often the first attempt to curb an atmosphere for trouble even if the trouble doesn't occur in the hallway. Ashley explains:

> I was standing by the corner of the stage in the cafeteria and I looked over and there was this young White boy and there was a group of Black guys standing around him. They were trying to take his hat and were pushing him and he was crying. I went over and tapped one of the guys on the shoulder and said, "Why don't you leave him alone." He started yelling at me. I turned to walk away from him and my backpack hit him in the stomach. He got up and shoved me to the ground and the lunchroom aides rush over to aid me.

After the incident, Ashley got a 1-day suspension from the school and the Black male, who had been in trouble before, was expelled. It wasn't only these two students who were penalized; the entire student body felt the effects of the incident. Ashley continued, "Right after that the school as a whole started the policy about how many students can hang out at once. Only three students could hang out in the hall together at once." School administration exercised power by using the incident in the cafeteria that occurred between Ashley and the male student as the catalyst for an attempt at studentwide containment. "Hallway time" was restricted by rules regarding how many could interact or "stand in a group" and thus adults attempted to gain control over a space students owned. For many students, this ruling touched a nerve. As a Black adolescent female, Ashley's sense of justice was violated: "Most students thought the rule was ridiculous. The biggest problem is that it wasn't enforced across the board. If eight White students stood in a group, it was fine. If five Black students stood in a group, it was a problem. So I think that was the big problem." Facilitating inequality through injustice supports hallway hierarchies where some students are deemed worthy of privileges and others are not. Ashley was aware that certain rules were enforced only when Black bodies, bodies perceived to cause trouble, were involved. In these hallways, from Ashley's perspective, White students held a place on the hallway hierarchical ladder labeled *nontroublemaker*.

This place of privilege was solidified by their being allowed to stand together in groups of more than three to converse without being penalized, in spite of the school rule.

For Black adolescent girls at predominantly White schools, the hallway is not just a space they pass through en route to other activities; rather, it is a place where race, class, and gender intersect. Identities are informed by negative material consequences stationed at this intersection. These consequences include limited inclusion or complete exclusion from social discourses and practices of popularity and coolness, physical restrictions, and racist verbal violence. All of these are the result of ideological hierarchies often reinforced by school rules and policies and played out in student interactions in school hallways.

IMPLICATIONS AND CONCLUSIONS

The Black graduate women interviewed described the process of recalling and retelling adolescent stories based on their experiences at predominantly White schools as both "freeing" and "painful." Many of the recollections brought laughs. Many brought tears. All of the experiences recounted have informed the identity work these women did as Black adolescent girls and inform who they are today.

Allowing these narratives to be told broadens the understanding of where education takes place. For women informants and adolescent girls who share similar social locations and school settings, education involves not only the reading, writing, and arithmetic taught in school classrooms but also the social lessons learned in spaces outside of the classroom. This knowledge challenges the assumption that an abundance of classroom teachers and resources creates the best schooling experience. It facilitates the argument that the work of being is just as important as academic work and when the spaces students use for this identity work are made hostile by oppression the school experience becomes oppressive.

For Black adolescent girls, the merging of race, gender, and class as structures of oppression played out in school interactions require unique navigation skills. They face challenges to their being and questions about who and where they are as students from parents, Black students, White students, teachers, unfair school policies, and social discourses. They often find themselves plotting their course all alone, trapped in the hallways between these spaces. Making space for their narratives expands the discussions about Black adolescent girls, enabling girls like Ashley to see that their experience is a Black experience and a valued experience. It provides insight into the ways school systems can support these girls by examining the prejudices, biases, and stereotypes that inform schooling ideals and practices and then infusing diversity education into every aspect of school life to change these ideals. Black adolescent girls cannot physically carry out "the work of being" separate from school places. Equitable education requires that we use their stories to support and scaffold this work, creating safe spaces conducive for all learning.

DISCUSSION QUESTIONS

1. Discuss intersectionality as an ideological tool for analysis. How does this tool help conceptualize the experiences of Black adolescent girls, like Ashley, Jane, and Kate, in predominantly White school settings? How does this tool inform the lives of White students at school?

2. Make a list of five policies that schools implement to regulate student use of schooling spaces outside of the classroom. Evaluate these policies and their enforcement. Do they support hallway hierarchies? Who benefits and who suffers? In what ways?

3. Define identity work. How is the identity work of students informed by school interactions in spaces outside of the classroom?

REFERENCES

Anyon, J. (1997). *Ghetto schooling: A political economy of urban educational reform*. New York: Teachers College Press

Byrd, A., & Tharps, L. (2001). *Hair story: Untangling the roots of Black hair in America*. New York: St. Martin's Press.

Collins, P. H. (1998). *Fighting words: Black women and the search for justice*. Minneapolis: University of Minnesota Press.

Ferguson, A. (2000). *Bad boys: Public schools in the making of Black masculinity*. Michigan: University of Michigan Press.

Fordham, S. (1996). *Blacked out: Dilemmas of race identity and success at Capital High*. Chicago: University of Chicago Press.

Fox, H. (2001). *When race breaks out: Conversations about race and racism in college classrooms*. New York: Peter Lang Press.

Garrod, A., Ward, J. V., Robinson, T. L., & Kilkenny, R. (1999). *Souls looking back: Life stories of growing up Black*. New York: Routledge.

hooks, b. (1984). *Feminist theory from margin to center*. Boston: South End Press.

hooks, b. (1994). *Teaching to transgress: Education as the practice of freedom*. New York: Routledge.

Ladson-Billings, G. (1994). *The dreamkeepers: Successful teachers of African American children*. San Francisco: Jossey-Bass.

Lamb, S. (2001). *The secret lives of girls: What good girls really do—Sex play, aggression, and their guilt*. New York: The Free Press.

Leadbetter, B. J. R., & Way, N. (1996). *Urban girls: Resisting stereotypes, creating identities*. New York: Basic Books.

Loury, G. (2002). *The anatomy of racial inequality*. Cambridge, MA: Harvard University Press.

Majors, R. (2001). *Educating our Black children: New directions and radical approaches.* New York: Routledge.

Mitchell, D. (2000) *Cultural geography: A critical introduction.* Malden, MA: Blackwell.

Perry, T., & Delpit, L. (1998). *The real Ebonics debate: Power, language and the education of African American children.* Boston: Beacon Press.

Rosenwald, G. C., & Ochberg, R. L. (1992). *Storied lives: The cultural politics of self-understanding.* New Haven, CT: Yale University Press.

Simmons, R. (2002). *Odd girl out: The hidden culture of aggression in girls.* New York: Harcourt.

Tatum, B. (1997). *Why are all the Black kids sitting together in the cafeteria?* New York: Basic Books.

Trump, K. S. (1998). *Practical school security: Basic guidelines for safe and secure schools.* Thousand Oaks, CA: Corwin Press.

Van Ausdale, D., & Feagin, J. (2001). *The first R: How children learn race and racism.* New York: Rowman & Littlefield.

Wildman, S., & Davis, A. (2002). Making systems of privilege visible. In P. S. Rothenberg (Ed.), *White privilege: Essential readings on the other side of racism* (pp. 89–95). New York: Worth.

White, H. (1980). The value of narrativity in the representation of reality. *Critical Inquiry, 7,* 5–27.

Zerai, A., & Banks, R. (2002). *Dehumanizing discourse, anti-drug law and policy in America: A "crack mother's" nightmare.* Burlington, VT: Ashgate.

Chapter 12

Unstraightening the Ideal Girl: Lesbians, High School, and Spaces to Be

John E. Petrovic
Rebecca M. Ballard
The University of Alabama

> *It's a big world. High school doesn't last. And it's definitely a better*
> *world. People don't have time to follow you around kicking you in the*
> *back of the foot and call you a lesbian. Stick it out. You will be OK.*
> —Advice of a participant in this study to other high school girls

The opening quotation makes starkly clear the school climate in which many lesbian, gay, bisexual, transgender, and questioning (LGBTQ) youth find themselves. Schools become places where LGBTQ youth are forced to adopt a "stick it out" attitude and hope that there is indeed "a better world." This is because heterosexism pervades society and institutions, especially schools. Heterosexism is a form of discursive subjugation. It is a form of oppression that both assumes and presumes the superiority of heterosexuality, suggesting that heterosexuality is required while (and by) casting non-heterosexuality as abnormal, deviant, or immoral. As with all forms of oppression, heterosexism creates and supports certain privileges for those in power (Petrovic & Rosiek, 2003). An intimately related construct, and a term that is also employed in this chapter, is heteronormativity. As Petrovic and Rosiek argue:

If heterosexism is the form of oppression, then heteronormativity is the tool that perpetuates it. Heteronormativity is the normalization of hetero-sexuality and those practices that promote and perpetuate that normaliza-tion. This involves, often explicitly but more frequently implicitly, the abnormalization of non-heterosexuality. It is the nonquestioning of heter-osexuality and heterosexual images and the fear of naming all things non-heterosexual. There is a strong interrelation between these two constructs given that heterosexism makes heteronormativity practicable while hetero-normativity serves to perpetuate heterosexism. (p. 161)

Many statistics and narratives have been gathered that demonstrate the ex-tent and force of heterosexism, heteronormativity, and the resultant marginalization, in both schools and society, of LGBQT youth. The effects of verbal, physical, and emotional abuse (O'Conor, 1994; Uribe & Harbeck, 1992) are reflected in students' stories of self-mutilation, both in the physi-cal sense of cutting, alcoholism, drug use, and poor academic performance and in the emotional sense of lowered self-esteem and internalized homo-phobia (Bass & Kaufmann, 1996; Chandler, 1995; Strong, 1998) as well as in increased suicidal tendencies among LGBTQ youth (Center for Popula-tion Options, 1992; Remafedi, 1994).[1]

Because of these stresses and the silence that tends to surround the entire issue of same-sex orientation, students report that one coping strategy is to construct straight identities in order to fit in (Due, 1995; Elze, 1992). After all, the ideal girl fits into the social construction of a straight identity, ac-cording to the participants of this study. This leads us to the question of how the ideal girl is depicted and how young, self-identified lesbians handle the double identities bound upon them by the constructions of gender and sex-ual identity (Probyn, 1995). These constructions form the boundaries of the places and spaces available to nonheterosexual women to *be*. Thus, in this chapter we ask, Where can young lesbians explore and *be* themselves?

Identity has been conceptualized in the context of "Who am I?" The often-overlooked question around identity is "Where am I?" (Hall, Coffey, & Williamson, 1999). Thus, as Bettis (2001) points out, it is necessary to explore how social context and discursive practices in and out of school in-fluence how girls construct their identities. More specific to our purposes, the concept of the ideal girl and the geographies of that girlhood must be problematized and interrogated from the perspective of lesbians con-strained to occupy this space, a space in whose construction they have had no voice. Where are lesbians in their youth and where can they *be*? In short, our concern is with the myriad ways the identities of ideal girls or lesbians overlap, where and why they are separate identities, and how they influ-ence each other.

---

[1]This is not to say that LGBTQ youth do not find healthier coping strategies.

The specific research questions that guided this study were:

1. Where can high school girls be lesbian or explore their sexual identity? Again, this goes beyond mere physical places to a broader notion of "spaces," which includes both physical places (e.g., a bedroom or school) and more ethereal (e.g., virtual or mental) spaces.
2. How do high school lesbian students define, view themselves within, and negotiate the space of "ideal girl?"
3. What are the discursive practices that limit or expand the options available to them as to how to be a girl and how to be a lesbian?

We approach this chapter with the assumption that the relationship among language, social institutions, and power creates a discursive field within which one constructs her identity or subjectivity. To reiterate, our focus is on the myriad ways in which notions of gender are constructed. Here, we employ feminist poststructuralist theory to examine this relationship as it affects social constructions of gender, especially the specific constructions of "ideal girl" and "lesbian."

It is through feminist poststructuralist theory that we can see the discursive field of heteronormativity and received views of femininity that are reinscribed every day. In other words, feminist poststructuralists hold that femininity or the markers of ideal girlhood are constantly contested and reformed. For example, girl power has rejected passivity, quietness, and acquiescence as primary markers for signifying normative girlhood in favor of participation in sports, self-assertiveness, and self-confidence (Adams, 2001). So what is it that young lesbians see in the contested space of normative girlhood? *All* young women are told by MTV and the girl power–soaked media that they have more choices to live their life as they see fit. Despite these messages, the only images that young lesbians see pertain exclusively to heterosexual women who have desires for men, makeup, and size zero bodies: basically the marketed, unattainable perfection, which is produced by and for the gaze of the patriarchy. Thus, the geography of girlhood with respect to nonheterosexuality is the examination of the way that a lesbian shapes her sense of an ideal girlhood, the ways in which being a lesbian reforms or sustains femininity, and the spaces in which this reformation takes place.

To uncover these spaces, we conducted interviews with participants ranging in age from 18 to 22. This age range reflected our desire to have participants who were temporally as close as possible to their high school experience because they would be responding to questions that reflected on their high school experiences and not their present (university or other) experiences. All of the participants were White and all arrived at the university after leaving their rural or small hometowns. The interviews followed a protocol, which included potential probes for each primary question, designed to elicit data to address the primary research questions.

Given the sensitive nature of the topic and the difficulty in identifying a sufficient number of high school–age participants, the sample was one of convenience. One of the researchers petitioned college students that openly identified as lesbian or queer; however, other participants self-selected into the study in response to a solicitation on a university Listserv administered by the Queer–Straight Alliance. As has been pointed out, "unless they disclose their identity … gay and lesbian students are an invisible minority" (Lopez & Chism, 1993, p. 1).

The participants reflected on their personas in high school and identified themselves as the captain of the cheerleading squad who didn't know why she was cheering because she hated it; the smart girl who used sex to gain the attention of boys; the nerdy girl who felt utterly unnoticed by the student body; the confused girl who was caught in the middle of being and knowing what was ideal and what was not; the funny girl who was also clinically depressed and teased by others because she was overweight; the tough girl who had fun in high school mostly because "she doesn't let crap get to her"; and the strange girl who was invited to parties because she would have a new color hair each time. The one thing they all had in common was that they knew they were lesbians.

The tape-recorded interviews were transcribed for analysis. Using traditional qualitative research methods, the data were coded and subjected to several rounds of domain analyses. This helped to ensure that the investigators did not miss "hearing" reflections, comments, or discussions that inform the research questions other than the one that was intended to guide responses at a particular moment in the interview process.

Initial coding, analyses, and categorizations of the data were conducted individually by each author. The interview protocol itself provided the authors with initial domains, such as "ideal girl" and "sexual orientation." Specific items in the protocol also served as early categories under which to sort the data from each of the interviews, pulling all of the data together. Relying on the protocol in this way also permitted the authors to relocate and keep in mind throughout the analyses the original research questions (LeCompte & Preissle, 1993). Moving from these gross categorizations, each author created more refined domains.

The authors then compared their individual categorizations of the data, collapsing some data into overlapping domains and creating new domains as necessary. This followed Spradley's (1979) taxanomic sorting of the data. Thus, the gross domain of "sexual orientation" led to the subdomain of "spaces to be lesbian." This, in turn, led us to identify each such space. The core properties of each of these "spaces" were used to develop a definition of the category. Finally, the authors worked together to choose participant quotes or observations that best illustrated each category.

Given differences in the authors' experiences and backgrounds, the goals of this strategy were to assure that the authors (a) were categorizing the data in similar ways, (b) were not systematically missing data, and (c) were not systematically inserting or force fitting data.

In this chapter, we first present the various spaces that the participants identified and described as they reflected on where they could or could not explore their sexual orientation, where they could or could not be lesbian. We then move to a discussion of how these girls negotiated these spaces, and we introduce the necessarily simultaneous process of negotiating identities. Here we focus on lesbian identity and the straight identity required to negotiate traditional notions of femininity.

SPACES TO BE OR NOT TO BE

There were essentially four categories of spaces that our participants identified as spaces that formed the boundaries within which the construction of their identities took place. In this section we define and illustrate the following: geographical, physical, virtual, and temporal spaces.

Geographical Spaces

The initial hurdle for girls who are lesbians is geographical space. Here we use geographical space quite straightforwardly to refer to the communities in which the girls were raised. All of the girls in this study were from rural areas or small towns. As Inness (1997) argues:

> Scholars should not lose sight of the fact that the majority of lesbians and gay men in the US are not in the vanguard of the movement and do not live in the cradles of gay civilization. Many gays and lesbians live in areas with small gay communities or no discernible gay presence; they are trying to survive in what are often inhospitable, conservative environments. (p. 135)

The participants' communities were generally politically and religiously conservative. In short, these girls were locked into locations that limited their level of comfort to be a lesbian. For example, Beth, who grew up in a rural community, pointed to the silence surrounding gay and lesbian issues in "a really small town": "We had a Hardee's and a McDonald's when I was in high school. We were out in the middle of nowhere so most of the people were very close-minded. And we really don't hear the word gay and lesbian. It's not really talked about. It's just not in the universe. You know, it's kind of not there."

The limitations of locale had a tremendous impact on just being a lesbian. As Inness (1997) observes, "Standard geographical descriptions of the United States typically fail to allow a space for lives and experiences of gays and lesbians" (p. 133). Thus, a typical scenario required for exploring sexual identity for these participants involved getting away from home. As Jenny pointed out, "when I am away from my hometown ... that's when I really started to come out really." Such geographical isolation is one reason that "Lesbian youth are particularly vulnerable to 'non-existence' as they are frequently not acknowledged during their adolescence and instead, seem to appear as adults" (Black & Underwood, 1998, p. 15).

In thinking about getting away from home, the ideal of college became a particularly important coping mechanism. For example, to deal with the confines of the closet while desperate to come out, Catherine frequently told herself, "I will just wait until I move away and go to college and I will come out there because I won't know any of these people ... and that was like one of the main reasons that I went out of state for school."

These experiences within geographical spaces are consistent with Inness' (1997) observation that:

> Lesbian/gay cultures, and hence lesbians and gays coming out within them, are tremendously influenced by the external "straight" geography. Further, queer geography contains unique elements that do not occur within straight geography; for instance, queer geography is plagued by gaps and holes in places where gays find life so unbearable that they never come out to themselves at all or, if they do, they flee at the earliest opportunity to more accepting locales. (p. 150)

These geographical spaces served to lock the girls in this study into adopting heterosexual identities. Escape became a prerequisite to being.

Physical Spaces

Physical spaces simply refer to specific places within the geographical space such as one's school, house, bedroom, a park, or even, as we discovered, a dirt road. Among these, school offered the least sanctuary for the exploration of sexual identity. For these girls "school" evoked primarily negative associations: "depressed," "afraid," "hurtful." As reflections of society, schools replicate a primary source of such associations: silence. Here all of the girls' experiences were similar to Katie's: "[Nonheterosexuality] was never addressed by teachers.... It wasn't in any of the sex ed classes or the health classes or the parenting classes or anything like that."

Perhaps it was this kind of silence that gave license to the voices that did not remain silent. These voices of course included those of other students, those who, as Katie continued in her observations, yelled "faggot at any male that was in the chess club with me ... and basically anyone who was disliked was a faggot and anything that was stupid was gay." Even more important, these voices occasionally included those of teachers or administrators. For example, Jana recalled the principal's response to her tale of verbal .abuse: "Well, stop acting gay and people will stop making fun of you."

Though school was generally neither a safe nor comfortable place for these girls to explore their sexual identity, a few managed to find school-related spaces in which to do so. For example, football games and the bus during school trips were two of those spaces. Jana pointed out how she and her girlfriend, with whom she never communicated in school except by secret note, could finally on such occasions sit by each other and talk and, once in a while, hold hands while hidden under a blanket.

Outside the school setting, participants cited the bedroom as a place for them to grow into their "ideal" girlhood, the girlhood of lesbianism. Though being in the bedroom often had nothing to do with sexual activities, it was here that girls learned about lesbians and sometimes about sex. And still, the bedroom was private and silent at the same time. Wendy recalled:

> Me and my girlfriends spent time hanging out in my room, but we weren't having sex. But it was different. It wasn't like being in a bedroom with just a friend. It was like we knew about each other, but didn't know how to talk about it. Later on in high school, some of us finally just asked each other. But that felt like it took forever.

Physical spaces "to be" had to be actively sought out or created, usually within other physical spaces. For example, the school as a physical space was not safe. These girls had to find or create safe, or at least safer, spaces within that larger space. However, the silence around nonheterosexuality permeates even available physical spaces. Thus, another type of space, which Wendy hinted at earlier, is necessary. This we call the "intuitive space."

Intuitive and Virtual Spaces

In reaction to the silence created around the topic of sexual identity, Wendy and her friends created an intuitive space: a vague understanding of each other that allowed them to feel more comfortable. It is a space of privacy, intuition, and subtle revelations—through joking or other banter—that creates a comfort level unavailable, and perhaps not creatable, in other physical spaces. It is a space neither completely here nor there, pulled out by intuition but pushed back by the silence of heteronormativity.

"Gaydar"—the inherent ability to detect the sexual orientation of another person—is one source of the intuitive space that Wendy and her friends created. "Gaydar" is based on the construction of norms in the queer and nonqueer world. Because gender and sexual identity are constructed, one way these girls found each other despite the silence of homosexuality was through intuition or rather through other lesbians' subtle revelations. A subtle revelation is an attempt to maintain the safe silence around nonheterosexuality while reinforcing the intuitive space. Such revelations might include the subtle hints or clues as to one's sexual identity.

This "intuitive space to be," though comforting, is quite a small space and many could not find it. Lisa, for example, spoke about a friend with gaydar: "Because she grew up in a bigger town and apparently there were lots of lesbians there. I don't know. I guess it was in the water. And so, you know, she could pick up on it. You know, I am like blind. I don't have the gaydar. Seeing myself was hard enough." Lacking gaydar, intuitive spaces, or physical spaces, the Internet offered a "virtual space" that was an important one in the liminality of lesbianism. There are increasing numbers of chat rooms and Internet sites aimed at a lesbian audience. Jenny, for example, had ongoing conversations with another girl on the Indigo Girls chat board. (Note that the Indigo Girls represent another kind of lesbian "indicator." There are also chat rooms that are more direct in their appeal to lesbian girls. For example, Yahoo! includes a group of rooms for "Lesbians, gays, and bisexuals." This group includes specific rooms such as "Just the Girls" or "Lesbian, gay, and bisexual teens.") Thus, gaydar or intuition was not required. As a virtual space providing both anonymity and invisibility, the Internet provided a safe space to explore one's identity with others in similar situations, with similar issues.[2]

Through this medium, the girls in this study were able to talk to other girls and to express themselves through writings of curiosity, anger, poetry, fiction, journals, and storytelling. Some participants even called themselves TechnoDykes because they were Web savvy or Web builders themselves.

Another virtual space was the television. Three of the girls specifically mentioned "Ellen," Ellen Degeneres' situation comedy. Catherine explained: "That was the only thing I had … anything on television was the only thing I had contact with anything gay." But Catherine went on to recall how paranoid she felt watching "Ellen" with her mother there. Catherine's fear was that her mother would think she watched the show because she was gay. She worried whether she gave anything away while she was watching it that would make her mother think that. Did she laugh at the wrong time?

---

[2]Our use of *safe* here should be read within the context of this chapter. It is not meant to downplay other safety concerns outside the scope of the chapter, such as the fact that Yahoo! has no real mechanism to ensure that adult predators do not enter teen rooms.

Did she seem too sympathetic? Did she laugh at just lesbian stuff or "normal" funny stuff? Did her mom laugh? Thus, even this virtual space did not feel safe. It required a private, safe, physical space.

Temporal (Sometimes Vicarious) Spaces

Temporal spaces are similar to intuitive spaces to the extent that they occur within one's inner consciousness. As such, they clearly represented the most private and safe places for these girls to explore and create their identities. Specifically, we define temporal spaces as those spaces that exist only in the subject's own consciousness as reflections of her past or future re-presentations as a girl and/or lesbian.

Such reflections are often triggered by others' outward actions. For example, Catherine commented, "When I would see gay women or men around town and I would just stare at them ... I felt like I was just rude to them, but I was just like wow that is really cool, you know? Like I am going to be like that someday, being able to walk around with my girlfriend holding hands." Here Catherine creates a future space to explore her sexual identity: "I am going to be like that someday."

Although they need not be, temporal spaces are also vicarious spaces. Catherine's temporal space was induced by the real experiences of others. Similarly, Jenny recalled the only girl known to be gay in high school: "I remember thinking how she was more open... she could be more tomboyish or basically do whatever she wanted and she kind of didn't care I guess." As we explore in a subsequent section, these girls characterized the ideal girl as "stable," "wearing what they want," "being comfortable with who they are," and "not caring what people thought of them." Extrapolating from this, it is not inappropriate to conclude that Jenny's reflections about this other girl included the creation of a temporal space.

In sum, temporal spaces allowed these girls to act on and explore lesbianism in a way unavailable to them in any other space in their present. In other words, if our identities are indeed discursive productions, then discourse, in its broadest sense, must certainly include soliloquies, internal conversations, or what we might more quickly call daydreams.

The internal conversations that the girls in this study engaged in were driven not only by the pull of temporal spaces set in their futures—"when I am away from my hometown" or when "I move away and go to college"— but also by the push of temporal spaces set in their pasts and presents. Most frequently the push came from negative associations and the severe constriction of past and present spaces. For example, Amanda's vicarious experience came through a gay girl on the basketball team as Amanda sought "to see how everybody else was responding to her." If Amanda's school was fairly typical, probably the response was, as Jenny recalled about the gay girl in her high school, "horrible for her ... and she did it by herself." This is precisely why lesbians in high school must constantly negotiate different spaces and identities for themselves.

NEGOTIATING SPACES AND IDENTITIES

Conceived as a nonphysical place, "straightness" as an identity offers lesbians a space to exist. As made clear in this section, it certainly does not provide them a place to *be*. The difference, as we see it, is that "existing" should be equated to survival and "being" to flourishing. Thus, in this section, we explore the effects of compulsory heterosexuality on the ways that these girls negotiated their identities.

Beautifully, Dutifully Straight

A prerequisite to negotiating spaces was the skill of negotiating identities. Given that they face emotional and physical hostility at school, as the participants in this study often did, "it is not surprising that many lesbians conceal their sexual identity in specific environments ... and at specific times by negotiating asexual or heterosexual identities" (Valentine, 1994, p. 8). For these girls this usually meant fitting into some notion of the "ideal girl." The most common characteristics of the ideal girl were "active," "smart," "attractive," and "fit." Girls who tended to have these characteristics were cheerleaders. They also probably had a boyfriend or slept with the right boys for, as Amanda observed, "who [a girl] had slept with the most" seemed to be an important measure. In other words, the ideal girl was straight.

Fitting into this notion of the ideal girl required lesbians to develop straight identities (Valentine, 1994). After recalling how she and her girlfriends would hang out in her room "knowing about each other" but not broaching the subject, Wendy lamented, "In the meantime, we went on dates with boys and ... well, I know that I was looking at other girls, and not my date. But, we had to date, you know?"

Again, the "in the meantime" space that Wendy mentions here was a heterosexual one. What is presented to these girls daily as the ideal girl often does not look like them, feel like them, love like them, or play like them. Creating the straight girl identity required more than dating. Katrina elaborated: "Well, in high school, I was comfortable with who I was, but then, I was being straight and dressing the part, you know. It is easy to feel OK when you are the same as everyone else, but really, I know that I was not. I just did what I had to do at school. And at home, I could be myself even though I wasn't always sure what that was." Similarly, Catherine pointed out how she "would wear a dress so that they would still think 'oh yeah, she's a girl.' So, and then I would talk about guys a lot." Being straight and dressing the part were common strategies used by these girls in trying to traverse "girl" and "lesbian" spaces. These strategies developed from the sense that this is part and parcel of the "ideal girl."

Of course, being straight required many other negotiation skills or sacrifices beyond dating or talking a lot about guys. One of these skills was to completely repress the self. In Jenny's case, for example, she simply "convinced [her]self not to act on being gay ... because [she] was afraid of what everybody would think and was also afraid what [her] parents would do." Instead, Jenny just "blocked it [thinking about her sexual orientation/identity] out."

For those who had decided to "act on being gay," secrecy became an important skill. After describing how she and her girlfriend felt somewhat safe to be with each other on the bus during trips or at football games, Jana made clear just how tight the "straight" jacket was while in school: "We would never communicate ... like talk and stuff unless it was through notes. We had lockers right next to each other. We wouldn't even look at each other. We would like slip each other notes when nobody was looking in between classes." Jamie similarly illuminates how different spaces mandated certain behaviors congruent with either a straight or gay identity: "We would be in certain places and Katie [Jamie's girlfriend] would be all over me and then we would get in other places and she would walk 10 feet away or something. We never held hands or anything like that so I guess it was changing who I was." Here we see the extreme infringement of compulsory heterosexuality in daily interactions: friends who dare not even look at each other or who walk 10 feet apart. This is because girls who engaged in certain behaviors or activities could be labeled gay, a label that came with fairly dire social consequences. (Recall Amanda's claim of how "horrible" it was for the one gay girl at her school. Or consider Katie's recollection of one girl who was "outed at school then completely ostracized.")

Girls who "hung out together" were gay. Girls who dressed the wrong way were gay. Girls who played certain sports, "like a lot of softball players or the basketball team," were gay. Girls who "never dated guys" were gay. Buff girls, short-haired girls, and girls who "weren't all prissy" were gay.

Privilege and Straight Girls

One way that heterosexism gets reproduced is through the construction of privilege. Thus, the obligatory negotiation of identities that nonheterosexual girls face can also be a way of tapping into privilege. More frequently, however, the privilege that comes with straightness is a source of frustration for the nonprivileged. Notice how Sandra connected the ideal (straight) girl with privilege: "Real girls are part of the A crowd, the popular crowd. You know, she hangs out with boys who are athletes. She goes to all the parties and dances and has the perfect dress. Clothing is really important. It seems like whatever the current trend is … that is what she wears. She has a million friends and teachers love her." The girls in this study tended to take a "live and let live" attitude toward those "real" girls discussed in Sandra's comments. Again, what frustrated them was the privilege that accompanied it. As Catherine argued: "If girls wanna dress up and all that stuff, it is fine. I guess … it is just when you don't do that … I mean I dress like this [signals to her outfit of jeans and hooded sweatshirt] and you are like definitely not treated the same. You may have other talents and stuff, but they don't really get you anywhere." Here Catherine gets directly at some of the discursive practices, mainly of those with power and privilege, that help to maintain the characteristics of a particular space: ideal girl. In the end, Catherine conceded, "You just have to know that high school only lasts 4 years."

SUMMARY: OPENING SPACE FOR THE *LESBIAN* IDEAL GIRL

It is important to study lesbian space in school because "queer people inhabit and create a different kind of space than do heterosexuals, and the terrain of queer space needs to be explored and mapped to understand more fully its multivalent nature" (Inness, 1997, p. 145). Upon coming to understand the discursive production of heterosexuality, educators must also recognize the effect that compulsory heterosexuality has on lesbians in school. Educators have a responsibility to understand the geography of lesbian space in order to provide a more conducive learning environment, an environment that challenges privileged notions of "girl."

As we discovered, lesbians view schools as heterosexist institutions that do not recognize their girlhood. Thus, they are much more comfortable exploring their sexual identity in places that are frequently outside the school setting, such as the bus, football games, the Internet, television, and the bedroom. These spaces were quite varied, representing geographical, physical, intuitive, and temporal spaces. Though varied, these spaces were also quite restrictive. Because of this, the girls in this study were required to negotiate their identities in less than ideal ways. They were forced to fit themselves into a particular discursive production of femininity as that of smart, attractive, and cheerleader-like; but most important here was the requirement of fitting into a straight identity. As we saw, taking on this heterosexual identity required the girls to wear certain clothes, to engage or not engage in certain sports, and to date boys, among other things, for these were the primary discursive practices explicit in the dominant discourse of normative adolescent femininity. Boxed in by these practices, the girls became reluctant participants in the sustenance of heteronormativity and dominant notions of femininity.

The girls experienced tensions between trying to live up to the image of the ideal girl and trying to construct an identity as lesbian. Certainly these two goals were not always oppositional. For example, recall Catherine who wore dresses to fit in, but who also remarked that if girls want to dress up "and stuff," "it is fine." In other words, the characteristics of the typical ideal girl and lesbian could certainly overlap. As we have noted, one problem was the privilege that accompanied the former. Having talents, looks, or dress that did not fit the dominant notion of girlhood "don't really get you anywhere." Another problem was that fitting in or passing undermined the girls' desire for resistance and limited, at least in certain contexts, their ability to explore their lesbian identities. Thus, although they could overlap, there was necessarily a separation of and a moving between their identities of girl and lesbian.

Moving between two identities necessitated seeking out and creating spaces of reformation in which to explore their other identity as lesbian. Although available on only a restricted basis, it was within these spaces that they could resist typical productions of the ideal girl and identify alternative understandings of ideal girlhood robust enough to accommodate their sexual identity. For them, the ideal girl could play any sport; she did not have to date guys; and she could be buff and short-haired. Furthermore, the ideal girl was stable, had a good personality, had common sense, and, most important, was comfortable with who she was.

Although we have primarily considered the question "where to *be*," a question for further discussion is, *how* do these girls find spaces to *be*? Lesbians find hope in their own definition of the ideal girl, in the comfort of being themselves, and in their desire to be. In this sense, and related to the temporal and intuitive spaces described earlier, lesbians in high school *are* their own space. For these girls, time is the fluid space that changes, by their own perseverance, the definition of the ideal girl for themselves. As Munt (1999) argues:

> Desire pushes a space for identities to form: we want to become. These identities are not complete, but pass from here to there, in a process of constitution. Desire, expressed through motion, can produce a multivalent self resonant with the specification of its past, expectant for the effects of the future and only momentarily embodies in the ephemeral, temporal, flash of the present. (p. 26)

And not only does desire produce space, but shame, although being a negative emotion, can produce space as well. Shame, or fear, kept many of these girls silenced. Munt describes this shame as:

> [It is about] what one is, or is made to be; but it can also be a transformative experience. At the moment one is cast out, one enters a new space of defini-

tion and individuation, thus at the moment of othering this split forces a new self to rise and form. (Or fall and die.) The space of development is already substantially predetermined, but like the self, it is constantly in motion, and amenable to flux. (p. 123)

Geographically, the space to become the lesbian ideal girl is a transitional, temporal space—it is the borderlands of sexuality and gender and girl-hood—in which one must unstraighten the ideal girl as defined by hetero-normativity and position oneself into a nonheterosexual space of how the geographies of lesbian girlhood are negotiated, endured, and surpassed.

DISCUSSION QUESTIONS

1. Drawing on the examples provided by the participants in this chapter, explain how heterosexism and heteronormativity function. Can you provide other examples of heteronormativity and heterosexism in schools and society?

2. What are some ways you as an educator might challenge hege-monic notions of "ideal girl" and heteronormativity? What "spaces" could you help to provide or make safe?

3. The participants in the study expressed frustration with "straight privilege." What does it mean to have "privilege" in this sense? What is "straight privilege"? Can you provide examples beyond those expressed by the participants in this study?

REFERENCES

Adams, N. (2001, April). *Girl power: The discursive practices of female fighters and female cheerleaders*. Paper presented at the annual meeting of the American Educational Research Association, Seattle, WA.

Bass, E., & Kaufman, K. (1996). *Free your mind: The book for gay, lesbian, and bisexual youth—and their allies*. New York: HarperPerennial.

Bettis, P. J. (2001, April). *Introduction to Symposium: Geographies of girlhood: Identity in-between*. Paper presented at the annual meeting of the American Education Research Association, Seattle, WA.

Black, J., & Underwood, J. (1998). Young, female, and gay: Lesbian students and the school environment. *Professional School Counseling, 1*(3), 15–20. (Retrieved November 2, 2001, from Academic Search Elite database)

The Center for Population Options. (1992). *Lesbian, gay and bisexual youth: At risk and underserved* [Fact sheet]. Washington, DC: Author.

Chandler, K. (1995). *Passages of pride: Lesbian and gay youth come of age*. New York: Random House.

Due, L. (1995). *Joining the tribe: Growing up gay & lesbian in the 90s*. New York: 1st Anchor Books.

Elze, D. (1992). It has nothing to do with me. In J. Blumenfeld (Ed.), *Homophobia: How we all pay the price* (pp. 95–113). Boston: Beacon Press.

Hall, T., Coffey, A., & Williamson, H. (1999). Self, space, and place: Youth identities and citizenship. *British Journal of Sociology of Education, 20*(4), 501–514.

Inness, S. (1997). *The lesbian menace: Ideology, identity, and representation of lesbian life.* Amherst: University of Massachusetts Press.

LeCompte, M. D., & Preissle, J. (1993). *Ethnography and qualitative design in educational research* (2nd ed.). New York: Academic Press.

Lopez, G., & Chism, N. (1993). Classroom concerns of gay and lesbian students. *College Teaching, 41*(3), 97–93. (Retrieved November 2, 2001, from the Academic Search Elite database)

O'Conor, A. (1994). Who gets called queer in school?: Lesbian, gay, and bisexual teenagers, homophobia and high school. *The High School Journal, 77*(1 & 2), 7–12.

Munt, S. R. (1998). *Heroic desire: Lesbian identity and cultural space.* New York: New York University Press.

Petrovic, J. E., & Rosiek, J. (2003). Disrupting the heteronormative subjectivities of Christian pre-service teachers: A Deweyan prolegomenon. *Journal of Equity and Excellence in Education, 36*(2), 162–169.

Probyn, E. (1995). Lesbians in space: Gender, sex, and the structure of missing. *Gender, Place, and Culture, 2*(1), 77–85.

Remafedi, G. (1994). *Death by denial: Studies of gay and lesbian suicide.* Boston: Alyson.

Spradley, J. P. (1979). *The ethnographic interview.* New York: Holt, Rhinehart & Winston.

Strong, M. (1998). *A bright red scream: Self-mutilation and the language of pain.* New York: Viking Press.

Uribe, V., & Harbeck, M. (1992). Addressing the needs of lesbian, gay, and bisexual youth: The origins of PROJECT 10 and school-based intervention. In M. Harbeck (Ed.), *Coming out of the classroom closet* (pp. 9–28). New York: Haworth Press.

Valentine, G. (1994). Toward a geography of the lesbian community. *Women & Environments, 14*(1), 8–11. (Retrieved May 27, 2003, form the EBSCOhost database)

Chapter 13

Disputation of a Bad Reputation: Adverse Sexual Labels and the Lives of 12 Southern Women

Delores D. Liston
Regina E. Moore-Rahimi
Georgia Southern University

> *It hurts because we are sensitive and emotional. We scar easy and we might play it off but deep down inside that we listen to it, it would take root and we are beginning to think … we start thinking that's all we are worth.*
>
> —Pepsi (interview transcript, 2001)

This chapter is derived from a larger feminist inquiry research project that presents an analysis of the life stories of 12 Southern women who were labeled as promiscuous in high school.[1] By examining their stories and experiences, this study describes how the reputation of teenage promiscuity shaped their lives. The women who participated in this study all lived with the reputation of a "slut" at some point during their high school experience. However, this fact does not mean that their experiences were uniform

---

[1]This chapter is based on Regina Moore-Rahimi's dissertation study at Georgia Southern University defended in spring 2002. For a more in-depth presentation of the stories of the women who participated in this study, see *Costs of Desire: How Sexual Labeling in School Influences Life Choices of Women*.

211

and invariant.[2] As Tanenbaum (2000) writes, "There is no general consensus about what qualifies a girl as a 'slut.' Instead there are multiple, shifting distinctions between 'good' and 'slutty' " (p. 88). Thus, the stories gathered from these women reveal the multiple ways that they were, and sometimes continue to be, marginalized by a culture that holds different standards and ideals for men and women (Edwards, 1981; Garcia, 1982; Ore, 2000). Indeed, based on our research, we are convinced that shifting and oftentimes mutually contradictory criteria form a double standard that perpetuates the marginalization of women in our contemporary landscapes and holds women in condemnation almost regardless of what they do or say.

In academic research studies (Daniluk, 1991; Duncan, 1999; Fausto-Sterling, 2000; Hillier, Harrison, & Warr, 1998; Holland, Ramazanoglu, Sharpe, & Thomson, 1994; Irvine, 1994; Kitzinger, 1995; Lees, 1993; Tolman, 1991), as well as in popular-culture studies (Mann, 1994; Pipher, 1994; Tanenbaum, 2000; Wolf, 1997), the message is clear: There is a sexual double standard for males and females. Katz and Farrow (2000) have written that although women may be experiencing greater freedom to participate in sex than in the past, they are "still constrained by a more covert but powerful double standard about morality" (p. 802).

As Capp (1999) has written, the double standard is considered to be the "cultural thesis that female sexuality is regarded as a male possession so that sexual *immorality* by women has been regarded as a heinous fault while male lapses might be regarded as relatively trivial" (p. 70). Butler (1990) suggests that the double standard of sexuality has been perpetuated by the assumption that the "libido is masculine and is the source from which all possible sexuality is presumed to come" (p. 53). This patriarchal script of sexuality has very tightly constrained a narrow to nonexistent range of "acceptable" *female sexuality* (sexual desire). Women and girls are taught that acceptable sexuality exists in terms of male sexuality (Daniluk, 1991; Hillier et al., 1998; Kane & Schippers, 1996; Regan & Berscheid, 1995; Van Roosmalen, 2000). Male needs and desires permeate any cultural discussion of sexual desire, whereas females are taught to silence their needs and desires. Females who do not conform to that standard are labeled and punished, often by an adverse sexual reputation and resultant social ostracism.

The concern of this project is to uncover the painful practice of labeling and stigmatizing females for sexual behaviors for which males get rewarded

---

[2]Certainly, not all women experience life in the same manner, yet to use this point to argue that one cannot write about the "experience of women," as in the case of sexually adverse labeling, would only encourage the same silencing that prevents many from having their voices count. Our work is based on the theoretical perspectives of feminist standpoint theory (Harding, 1991; Harstock, 1999) and postpositivist realism (Moya & Hames-Garcia, 2000), which recognize the necessity to write of identity categories while understanding these categories as socially constructed.

(Garcia, 1982; Hillier et al., 1998; Lees, 1999; Stanley, 1977). This labeling and stigmatizing occurs through the cultural regulation of female sexuality. Reputation, although only one means of regulating female sexuality, is a powerful social act that offers deeply embedded messages for girls constructing their self-concepts (Lees, 1993). Moreover, the labeling of girls as "sluts" or any other word connoting negative sexual images, can occur for a variety of reasons not limited to sexual behavior (Sheeran, Spears, Abraham, & Abrams 1996; Stewart, 1999; Tanenbaum, 2000). Sexual labeling of females is a serious form of harassment that serves to limit the self-development (Hamachek, 1985; Josephs, Markus, & Tafarodi, 1992) of not only the girls who have been labeled, but of all girls, as this phenomenon perpetuates a sexual inequality.

This study emphasizes personal dimensions of women's lives as they negotiated the treacherous terrain of sexuality and coming of age between 1985 and 1995. The high school experiences of these women came long after the Women's Liberation Movement and during the height of the social conservatism of the Reagan/Bush presidencies. Furthermore, they were among the first generation of women to enter adulthood with a full recognition of the scope of the AIDS epidemic. These larger cultural and historical facts can be understood as framing the participants' lives within a generalized antisexuality discourse that accentuated the negativity of the label "slut." Adverse sexual labeling is a form of sexual harassment that is as prevalent now as it was 20, 50, or even 100 years ago (Duncan, 1999; White, 2002; Wolf, 1997). The current discourses of abstinence and character education that have emerged in the wake of the Reagan/Bush presidencies and the AIDS crisis have served to perpetuate the traditionally hostile environment for young women coming of age in the United States.

WHO IS A SLUT?

The common cultural understanding of slut is a woman who engages in promiscuous heterosexual intercourse, usually with a number of male partners. Slut and labels similar to it ("whore," "tramp," "easy lay," "sleeze," "skank," etc.) generally assert that the referent seeks sexual encounters and engages readily and frequently in sexual intercourse, activities that set her apart from the "good girls." However, there are a number of other possible implications of these labels, for example, girls who participate in sex outside of a monogamous relationship and girls who participate in sex before marriage. Tanenbaum (2000) points out, "in today's climate 'slut' refers to any girl who appears open and carefree about her sexuality" (p. 88). Indeed, even mere affiliation with others who have been labeled slut can taint a young adolescent's reputation.

A young woman can develop a "bad reputation" through a variety of means: the way she dresses, the way she talks, the friends she has, her performance in school, her sexual proclivity or refusal to have sex, and uninformed suppositions by peers about any of these. Most tragically, rape or sexual abuse often leads to the acquisition of the label slut by an already victimized young woman (Tanenbaum, 2000; Tolman, 1991).

However attained, once such a stigma has been applied to a young woman it is extremely difficult to rid herself of that label (Stewart, 1999; Tanenbaum, 2000; Wolf, 1997). Labeling a young woman as a slut serves to control her developing sexuality and dramatically limit the range of her experiences and possible identities (Phillips, 2000; Tanenbaum, 2000). As Tanenbaum writes, "because 'good' girls can become 'bad' girls in an instant, slut-bashing controls all girls" (p. 87).

All girls share the potential risk of being labeled "slut." These words apply only to females (Stanley, 1977) and as such underscore the gender inequality in notions of sexuality. Using reputation as a form of marginalization *is* sexual harassment and serves as a cultural reminder to young and adult women that sexual power exists within a male-dominated world (Kalof, 1995). Often, students and even the staff of a school marginalize, mistreat, abuse, and disregard a labeled girl (Epstein & Johnson, 1998; Orenstein, 2000). Such experiences in school, particularly at a time when adolescents are developing their self-identities, can leave girls with feelings of worthlessness that can influence the development of their adult lives and detrimentally affect their growth potentials (Whitbeck, Yoder, Hoyt, & Conger, 1999).

Acknowledgment of the struggles of adolescent females with their emerging sexuality in a hostile and oppressive environment formed the grounding assumption of this study. Feminist classics of women's moral (Gilligan, 1982), intellectual (Belenky, Clinchy, Goldberger, & Tarule, 1986), and sexual development (Irvine, 1990, 1994) set the theoretical stage for our work. More recent developments in feminist theories have also informed this research project. Emerging perspectives on the social construction of sexuality (Daniluk, 1993; Holland, Ramazanoglu, Sharpe, & Thomson, 1996), as well as recent challenges to (Butler, 1990) and elaboration of identity politics (Moya & Hames-Garcia, 2000) have also influenced the interpretation of our research findings. Furthermore, this study has benefited from recent studies of female adolescent development, especially studies of emergent sexuality (Katz & Farrow, 2000; Lees, 1993; Phillips, 2000; Tolman, 1991). Finally, the recent and popularized studies of Tanenbaum (2000), Wolf (1997), Pipher (1994), and White (2002) have provided useful insights on which this study has been modeled.

Unlike these other studies, our research project maintained a more narrow focus in terms of geography and context. Conducting the study in the southern United States steeped the participants in discourses of Christianity and expectations peculiar to Southern femininity. Moreover, because findings from the literature indicated that much of the labeling of "sluts" occurs at school, many of the interview questions revolved around school experiences and the responses of classmates, teachers, and other school staff.

MODES OF INQUIRY AND PARTICIPANTS

At the time of this study, the participants were between 25 and 35 years of age. The women interviewed revisited their experiences as young women who were given adverse sexual labels. Participants in this study were found in a selected region of a southern U.S. state comprising rural, urban, and suburban communities.[3]

Interested volunteers who contacted the researchers were then asked to complete a brief questionnaire providing a demographic profile and general background information. The researchers selected 12 women from among these volunteers for in-depth interviews.[4] Prior to the interviews, the participants were asked to complete a demographic profile sheet. On these sheets the women identified themselves in terms of race,[5] sexual orientation,[6] religious preference,[7] socioeconomic status (SES) while growing up,[8] and educational level at the time of the interview.[9]

As noted earlier, the studies of Wolf (1997), Tanenbaum (2000), and Phillips (2000) provided useful models on which our methodology was based. Following the recommendations of Spradley (1979) in-depth interviews based on, but not constrained by, open-ended questions were conducted with each of the 12 participants. The interviews focused on each woman's reflections on the circumstances surrounding her acquisition of the label slut; the response of her peers, teachers, school counselors, and administrators; the perceived impact of sexual double standards on her sexual and psychosocial development; and her response to the adverse sexual label. Following the interviews, transcripts were provided to the participants for "member checking" (Bloor, 1997). The transcripts were then analyzed for

---

[3]Their interest was secured through a combination of "word of mouth" advertising and flyers distributed to a wide variety of formal and informal women's organizations and groups. As flyers were distributed to a group, members were encouraged to pass along the flyers to other groups of women.

[4]These 12 participants were selected for racial/ethnic as well as socioeconomic diversity.

[5]Five self-identified as White, five as Black, one as Hispanic, and one claimed no racial label.

[6]All but one claimed the label heterosexual. One self-identified as bisexual.

[7]Ten self-identified as being raised Christian, one self-identified no religious affiliation, and one self-identified a Jewish heritage.

[8]All five Blacks, the one Hispanic, and the one who refused a racial label self-identified as "poor" or "lower middle class," and all five Whites identified as "middle class."

[9]Eight graduated from high school, whereas four dropped out.

common themes as well as "unique" circumstances and compared with the current available literature noted earlier.

THE STORIES OF 12 SOUTHERN WOMEN

Twelve women participated in this study. As Table 13.1 illustrates, the labeling of young women in this study ran the gamut between extremes of sexual activity, race, and class. The women in this study were labeled whether they were willfully sexually active or not; whether they were White, Black, or Hispanic; whether they were relatively rich, middle class, or poor.

In the pages that follow, we provide a thematic overview of the experiences of the women we interviewed. We start with the struggles these women endured as they negotiated the pervasive double standard of contemporary U.S. culture. We then show the variety of conditions under which these women came to be labeled, as well as the sense they tried to make of their lives as they found themselves constrained within this double bind. Finally, we make a plea for educators to participate in constructing a new discourse of sexuality in an effort to help loosen this double bind.

SOCIOCULTURAL CONTEXT OF DOUBLE STANDARDS: THE IMPOSSIBLY NARROW IMAGES OF FEMININITY

Most of the interviews began with a discussion of the participants' memories of popular-culture presentations of femininity and sexuality from their childhoods. The participants' reflections on the images of women constructed a very narrow band of acceptable behavior. In popular culture, "good women" were presented as "attractive and alluring" and yet "not slutty." Furthermore, these fictional "good women" walked this tightrope without becoming "a tease." Walking this line may be accomplished in the realm of fantasy, but the real women in this study found the route much too flimsy to traverse.

Unsurprisingly, given the tight constraints of these presentations of femininity, the behaviors and images of popular culture were often outside the experience of the participants in this study. Heather reflected on *Seventeen*: "The girls were all very perky and very attractive. That's not the experience I had. It was totally foreign" (Heather, 2001, interview transcript, p. 1). Disaffection with the popularly approved image of the American female was not limited to White girls; African American participants echoed similar sentiments. Shayanne noted: "The whole Barbie doll image. You had to be very feminine and like the whole aura of smelling like flowers and just soft stuff. I was nothing like it. Everywhere I saw it; I was nothing like it" (Shayanne, 2001, interview transcript, p. 1). Camille recalled reading Danielle Steele novels:

TABLE 13.1

The Breakdown of Participants in the Study of 12 Southern Women

Pseudonym	Age	Race/ Ethnicity	Childhood SES	Education	How Was Reputation Attained
Camille	26	Black	Lower middle	H.S. diploma	Sexually promiscuous
Deanne	26	White	Middle	H.S. diploma	Not having sex with popular boy
Heather	32	White	Middle	H.S. diploma	"After having sex a couple of times"
Joanne	30	Black	Poor	H.S. dropout	"Dressing provocatively, and having few female friends"—many male friendships
Jocelyn	25	White	Lower middle	H.S. diploma	"Had sex with boyfriend"
Kathryn	25	White	Middle	H.S. diploma	Confidence and being flirtatious
Kesha	25	Black	Poor	H.S. dropout	"Had sex with boyfriend"
Lee	27	None accepted	Poor	H.S. diploma	"Hung out" with "metal heads"
Pepsi	35	Black	Poor	H.S. dropout	Unclear, but finds sex with men is route to power
Shayanne	25	Hispanic	Poor	H.S. dropout	Became pregnant
Tammy	35	Black	Poor	H.S. diploma	"Not having sex with boyfriend"
Tonya	27	White	Upper middle	H.S. diploma	Rape victim, became pregnant as result

I think I remember the thing I got from them more than anything was that beauty was extremely important ... eventually beauty would get you a man and you would be happy in some way, shape, or form. Through romance, but you had to make yourself accessible. I'm African American so beauty for us was always White, blond. So to translate that over to African American it would be light skin, long hair, good hair. As close to looking as White as possible and maybe, yeah, I think that would be the definition for a Black person. (Camille, 2001, interview transcript, p. 1)

Much has been written elsewhere regarding the toll of such expectations upon African American women (Edut, 1998; Leadbeater & Way, 1996); nonetheless, Kesha's story helps remind us that the consequences are more than mental:

> Mainly I would say I read a lot of *Jet* and stuff and they had a lot to do with you know Black women have to be successful and, you know, the images, and they had like the beauty of the week and it's always been the perfect woman, perfect shape, where they were so called clean and everything, and I always been thick, so I used to always not eat as much or whatever so I stayed thin.... I mean at first I was like, when I was in school, I was like one of the popular persons because I was like real slim, but I stayed sick because I didn't hardly use to eat. (Kesha, 2001, interview transcript, p. 1)

Thus, the participants understood that they were expected to strive for feminine ideals that were at best difficult and oftentimes impossible. This was particularly true with regard to sexuality. Deanne recalled reading *Vogue* and *Seventeen* magazines and watching television and the confusing messages that these media presented:

> Well, one you had to be beautiful, a certain size or big-breasted or whatever. You had to be seductive. Not so seductive that you were just throwing yourself out there ... not slutty looking, but approachable ... The shows I remember are like "90210" or, that was basically all I watched was that when it came on. The guys wanted the easy girls and if you didn't show it, then you were called a slut or whore or whatever because you didn't produce it. But they wanted somebody that wasn't slutty acting or whatever. They wanted you but yet they didn't want someone that was so easy and gave it up. (Deanne, 2001, interview transcript, pp. 1–2)

Jocelyn offered a parallel understanding of the internal contradictions presented by television:

> Women were much more polite, less sexual. The women that were sexual were considered sluts. The women that were overtly sexual, like if you think about "Dallas" or one of those terrible soap opera shows, there were always like the slutty women that were inappropriate and unacceptable ... It was always the way she dressed, which was always much more revealing, generally much more makeup; she didn't really have a lot of female friends, because the women hated her in general ... The men that were promiscuous or had multiple partners weren't ever looked down upon by their peers and the women always were. Women had the stigma and they didn't have a lot of girl-friends. But the guys ... (Jocelyn, 2001, interview transcript, pp. 1–2)

Lee was able to succinctly articulate the confusion regarding female sexuality in popular culture:

My idea of real women's sexuality in the mid- to late '80s was that there was a gross double standard at play. That the men could go out and party and do whatever they wanted and pick up as many women as possible with as little as a shrug. If a woman were to go out and do the same with even one or two men and it were to get out, that you would probably be living it down for the rest of your life. (Lee, 2001, interview transcript, pp. 1–2)

Lee later connected these mixed messages with the broader context for women in our society:

I think that women are expected to be less-sexual creatures than men. I think this is bullshit and I don't know whoever came up with this theory. Yes, the gender that has the capacity for unlimited orgasms is the one that is going to sit there and not be interested in them. That's just brilliant. But I think a lot of the men that I've been involved with, just through lack of knowledge, expect women not to be as sexual. If you're aggressive, I think that it makes a lot of men uncomfortable. (Lee, 2001, interview transcript, p. 10)

Most of the participants provided memories that showed how this gendered double standard played out, often quite explicitly, in their personal lives.

My mother didn't talk to me about, you know, she wasn't open; I'll put it like that. The only thing she would say is that a woman can't do what a man can do. Because a woman's name will become mud, where a man get up, he can walk away and he still holds his dignity. I also probably learned from church, maybe a few sermons may have touched base about what they would call loose women; they classified them as like prostitutes. If you're not married, you're just the same, but it's not really true if you think about it. (Tammy, 2001, interview transcript, pp. 1–2)

Tammy was not the only participant to connect the slut label with "sermons from church." As noted earlier, 10 of the 12 women interviewed self-identified as Christian growing up. Nearly all of these women recalled stories of the "fallen women" that were prevalent in their churches; stories of Eve, Jezebel, Delilah, and Mary Magdalene as opposed to Ruth, Esther, and the Virgin Mary. Unlike studies with a national perspective such as Tanenbaum's or White's, our study uncovered a more explicit connection between "good girl" images and biblical prescriptions regulating female sexuality: "It's cool for the guys to have a reputation of being a player, but if a woman has that title, she is frowned upon—a whore or a slut … When you are labeled that, you feel cheap—just looked upon like a prostitute or whore. Even if you haven't done anything to prompt the name calling" (Deanne, 2001, interview transcript, p. 10). This double standard for boys and girls in high school was particularly apparent regarding the AIDS crisis and the resultant push for safe sex and/or abstinence. Tonya explained that for a young woman to carry a condom, "was just not cool. It was cool for a guy to have a little condom ring in their wallet; it was like stature. For girls, it was like 'what are they going to think?' You know it was just like a label. 'Oh, she's expecting it, she's going to get it.' She must be a slut. Sex was okay if you were a guy, not okay if you were a girl" (Tonya, 2001, interview transcript, p. 5). The participants noted that girls were placed in a "lose-lose" situation. If they carried a condom, they would confirm their label, but if they didn't they risked exposure to AIDS. Tellingly, most girls risked exposure to AIDS rather than validate the slut label in the minds of their peers.

Getting Labeled

Given this nest of powerful and yet mutually contradictory images of feminine sexuality, it was tragically easy for a young woman to run afoul of the expectations of her peers and acquire the label of a slut. Tonya reflected upon the arbitrary and unsubstantiated reasons that a young woman could be labeled: "You know it was just so stupid; it was like 'she wears a shorter skirt than the general population, so she must be a slut.' 'She developed faster than the rest of us; she must be a slut.' 'She wore the makeup' or 'she had the money where she could wear the really nice clothes, so she's a slut' " (Tonya, 2001 interview transcript, p. 3). Thus, although 3 of the 12 participants admitted to being promiscuous as teenagers, most did not. In fact, there were just as many women who had never had sex when they acquired the label.

Intriguingly, even Kathryn, who described herself as a "perky blue-eyed, blond-haired cheerleader" closely matching the popular culture feminine ideal, was labeled a slut without having had sex. Kathryn said that she believes she acquired the label because she was confident and was friendly with everyone, including boys:

> I remember having hard times with friends as far as girls—I remember in 10th grade I was called a "slut" by some friends and I was thinking "how can you call me a slut because sluts are girls who sleep with a whole bunch of different guys and I've never even kissed a guy?" … I think some of the girls were jealous, because I mean I did have a lot of confidence, I still do have a lot of confidence. I don't think everyone was jealous; no I think some girls were just literally outraged. (Kathryn, 2001, interview transcript, pp. 3, 5)

Two other participants acquired the label when they refused to have sex:

> It happened around my junior year it started and it carried on into my senior year. I mean even though you don't do the act or whatever, you still fool around and you're known as a slut or a whore or whatever, a tease. Basically I mean just experimenting with guys, if you don't give it up they are going to

call you that and that's what I experienced. They called me a whore and all that because I didn't give them what they wanted ... The teachers, they hear, but I mean, it's just kids. They don't believe. The teachers I had, they didn't say anything about it. Because I kept my grades or whatever, so it's not like they really paid attention to it. (Deanne, 2001, interview transcript, p. 4)

He [my boyfriend] wanted to have sex with me and I wouldn't. So what he did, he started spreading rumors that I did this and I did that and none of it was true. Because I didn't do it. But, because some people knew that I had in the past, that I wasn't a virgin, they believed it and it seemed like it just spread and everybody believed it. (Tammy, 2001, interview transcript, p. 3)

In all of these stories we see how the impossibly narrow range of acceptable behaviors for women made them vulnerable to negative sexual labeling despite the fact that they had not had sex. Simply being a woman meant that the label could be applied by anyone and would likely stick. The sociocultural context steeped in Christianity served to reinforce the dichotomy that girls were either "pure" virgins or "whores." Thus, if the girl was unable to firmly claim her innocence as entirely virginal, the dominant discourse of "fallen women" would apply.

Three other participants acquired the label of slut immediately after their first sexual experience when their male partners advertised their conquests. Jocelyn said that "her first true love" tried for 6 months to have sex with her, and finally she "caved in" (Jocelyn, 2001, interview transcript, p. 5). The friends of her boyfriend, hearing of this, started making up stories about her, calling her names like "slut" and "whore" and ridiculing her throughout her school days. Kesha's life took a similar turn when her long-time boyfriend decided to lift his status by lowering hers:

When I first had sex, I was 17 and I never had sex with nobody else—just him—and he went back and told everybody that me and him had sex and stuff. Then it started—that's when everybody started labeling me—I hadn't been with nobody but one guy and everybody started labeling me and stuff and calling me a slut and talking about I'm a whore, all this you know what I'm saying, and they was always whispering and everything. I had been with him for a long time and I didn't understand it—you know what I'm saying. It wasn't like I was running around with the whole school. (Kesha, 2001, interview transcript, p. 2)

Simply not fitting in with mainstream social expectations and having sex once led to the labeling of Lee. Lee said her interests during high school were in hard-rock music and science fiction, so her friends were mostly male:

I hung out with a crowd of metal heads, everybody called them burnouts. What my friends didn't know and I'm kind of proud that I kept from them is that I managed to keep a few of my friends and not let on that I graduated

18th out of a class of about 400 and kept a 3.9 GPA. While I was hanging out with those guys, just by association, I'd walk by and people would mutter under their breath a variety of unsavory comments. A lot of judging a book by its cover. I would walk by wearing skintight acid-washed jeans and somebody goes "slut" or "whore" or whatever. Honestly it was kind of preferable to walking by and hearing somebody say "nerd" or "geek" at the time. (Lee, 2001, interview transcript, p. 3)

Lee had sex for the first time at 17 with a boy that attended her school. He came back and told the "entire school" about the experience. After that, her experience with name-calling and being ridiculed only worsened and the label slut stuck with her.

The two tragic and ironic labelings occurred after physical harassment and rape. Joanne recounted perhaps her most painful experience in school and the decisive point in her educational experience:

I got in a fight with a guy ... he was a real real big guy, he played football. One particular evening we was at the lockers and he came up and he felt me. At first I was like ah this is a big boy you know and my brothers ain't around and I didn't do anything. He did it again and we got in this real big fight and he was like "oh, you're nothing but a whore anyway, why you trippin'?" There was a big old commotion and I got put out for 10 days. Ten days and I couldn't come back to school. ... When we went to the office all that [football player] would say was that "she hit me with her locker." They didn't ask me "did he feel you?" And I was like "he felt me!" and they was like "no big deal." They didn't really care. Because I hit him with my locker means that I assaulted him or whatever. He didn't get put out, he didn't get reprimanded: He didn't get anything. He went to play with some school in Canada or something—I didn't go back to school. I ain't never gone back to school ever again in my life—never, ever went back.... He got a high school diploma. I had to get my GED [general equivalency diploma]. But I never ever told anybody ever and I work with a lot of people—I never told nobody because I just feel like I would get another label. (Joanne, 2001, interview transcript, pp. 2–3)

Most tragically, after she was raped, became pregnant, had an abortion, and was raped again, Tonya became known as a "slut": "I started dating a guy my junior year. We dated most of my junior year and couple of weeks into the summer and we broke up. We were at a party of a whole bunch of mutual friends of ours and he raped me that summer, and I got pregnant" (Tonya, 2001, interview transcript, p. 6). Tonya did not tell anyone she was raped or pregnant except for her older sister, who took her to get an abortion. Later, at a party where she had had too much to drink, she was raped again by the same boy. She became pregnant a second time, and the other girls started to notice. Her changing figure and frequent trips to the bathroom led them to speculate about her pregnancy, calling her "slut" and "whore." After her second abortion, Tonya's peers mocked her by saying "at least we don't go out and get knocked up and go out and have an abortion— you baby killer" (Tonya, 2001, interview transcript, p. 4).

However, aborting a pregnancy was not even necessary for one to be called a slut. Shayanne's label was acquired when she became pregnant and gave birth while still in high school. In fact, the birth of her child only reinforced the label:

> When I got pregnant, I heard it all the time [slut, etc.] and it was always little things like people would walk by talking about "only tramps get pregnant" and saying that the "only girls that were sluts and tramps are the ones that were pregnant." It didn't make any sense because they are all out there doing it; it just happened to be me that got unlucky that time. After she [Shayanne's daughter] was born, I would get tons and tons of "can I have your number, here's my number, give me a call." (Shayanne, 2001, interview transcript, p. 5)

The process of getting labeled denied these women control of their own sexuality and desires. Some were labeled for being sexually active by their own choice, some were labeled for not being sexually active, and still others were labeled after being raped. Whatever the path to the label, their sexual desires became regulated into patterns that made them feel "dirty" and "worthless." This, in turn, generated a cycle of increasing social isolation.

A Self-Fulfilling Label

The social isolation and alienation that resulted from the label of slut often started a spiral in the women's lives that made the label much more apt than it was when it was first applied to them. For example, Jocelyn says that she became promiscuous after her peers began calling her names. Once labeled a slut, she had "several partners," which added fuel to the fire and gave her peers more "reason" to emphasize her adverse sexual label. Crucially, Jocelyn said that her promiscuity came not out of any sexual desire, but the "need for attention." Thus, Jocelyn found that only by living out the label that she acquired could she find the social support that the label itself denied her.

Tonya was similarly entrapped by her experience as a rape victim and her label. She decided: "It was like I had a choice of telling them what really happened to me or letting them think that I'm just a slut and a baby killer. So I took that because it's not anybody's business what happened ... An abortion will go away, rape doesn't" (Tonya, 2001, interview transcript, p. 5). So she did not respond to her tormentors and instead lived in silence and shame. She withdrew from all of the people in her school, participated in no school activities, but she was able to graduate. Like Jocelyn, Heather, and Deanne, Tonya describes herself as becoming extremely promiscuous immediately following high school: "I have slept with over 200 men, which I'm not proud of and it's not something to brag about, but that was where I was at. I was going to get back at him [the rapist]" (Tonya, 2001, interview transcript, p. 9). Also like Jocelyn, Tonya admits that her sexual activity[10] was not out of desire; in fact, despite her numerous sexual encounters, she said she can't recall ever having a sexual desire of her own. Many of the participants noted that when they participated willingly in sex they did so for reasons other than sexual desire, such as trying to "live up to" or move beyond the label.

As these stories of adverse labeling as a self-fulfilling event suggest, after being called sluts in high school, nearly all of the participants have struggled with issues of self-esteem, sexuality, and intimacy as adults. Many have never gained confidence in their ability to be perceived by peers as an acceptable or normal person. Most have wandered in and out of unhealthy and abusive relationships. These unhealthy patterns of low self-esteem led many of the participants to date and often marry young, often to verbally and physically abusive partners.

CONCLUSIONS

Important to this study is an exploration into the development of sexual self. Our view of ourselves as sexual "beings" is a necessary component for a concept of who we are. Katz and Farrow (2000) have termed this dynamic of self "sexual self-schemata" (p. 782). They have contrasted positive/negative sexual self-view by positing that a positive sexual schema involves viewing oneself as "passionate, romantic, and open to sexual experiences," whereas a negative sexual schema was characterized by "embarrassment or inhibition" (p. 782).

Reputation is acquired and maintained through the discursive practices of a girl's peers, often perpetuated by both male and female adolescents (Tanenbaum, 2000). Both girls and boys participate in regulating a girl's sexuality by employing the use of reputation. However, girls' and boys' reasons behind participating in marginalizing the stigmatized girl may be altogether different (Tanenbaum, 2000). Many young women participate in the name-calling and ostracizing of the labeled girl, because association with "the slut" may cause damage to their own reputation (Tanenbaum, 2000). Treating the labeled girl as "other" helps assure other girls "not-I"

---

[10]One way that women attempt to recover following rape is to engage in sexual activity with multiple male partners. Once the inability to enforce a "no" is highlighted through rape, women feel the only way to reclaim control over their own sexuality is to say "yes" (Daly, 1984).

status. In other words, in order for some girls to be "good," others must be "bad" (Lees, 1993). Ussher (1989) has termed this the Madonna/whore dichotomy whereby an "individual woman cannot be good and bad so she must be placed in one or the other of the categories" (p. 14). This is the dichotomous nature surrounding women's sexual existence that has been constructed and maintained through patriarchal design. Our study highlights the particularization of this constraint in the South as Christian and "southern belle" images of proper femininity conflate to tighten the reins on the range of acceptable behaviors for women.

The prevalence of the male-centered sexuality forms this sexual double standard that has set up particular gendered scripts for sexuality (Carpenter, 1998; Sheeran et al., 1996; Van Roosmalen, 2000). Those scripts have led to the view that women's worth comes not from a desire of their own, but as a result of their desirability to men (Kalof, 1995). Such a construction of sexuality not only leads to a muted development of female sexual development, but also presents a dangerous terrain through which women have to negotiate their sexuality (Hillier et al., 1998; Tolman & Debold, 1993).

Although their interpretations of the early messages they received through culture vary, the variety of their interpretations only serves to highlight the notion that girls have a barrage of contradictory messages through which they must discern meaning for their lives. Their interpretations also point out that images in culture offer little solace to girls struggling with issues of sexuality. Yet, there is some consistency found in the male-centered nature of the social construction of sexuality, in the denigration of female desire. As women we are to be desirable to men, regulating with constant maintenance our physical bodies, yet we are to possess no desire ourselves. The existence of reputation persists because of the differing levels of acceptance of sexual behaviors for men and women.

Role of Schools in Making Change

Educators can and should play a vital role in helping reconstruct a positive discourse of emergent female sexuality. Currently, most educators stifle the discourse of female sexual desire by chanting slogans that deny the desires of young women. Educators remain silent about female sexual desire and thereby force the next generation to find their own way through to adulthood through hostile terrain. Educators can and should construct a discourse of sexuality that eliminates the sexual double standard and acknowledges that the desires of young women are as strong as the desires of young men, while recognizing that AIDS is a very real threat to the lives of adolescents. In this way, educators can begin to build a viable path through sexual and psychosocial development for all their students. The participants offer insight into what happens when sexuality is stifled, when ridicule is permitted in schools, and when the full development of girls is prevented. This study represents a move toward the reconstruction of discourse, the move toward change.

Such an alteration requires thorough cultural change. The suggestions provided next are by no means "the answers." Rather, they address some of the behaviors contributing to stifled female sexual development. The school alone cannot alter the kind of change that needs to take place regarding the view of sexuality. However, because much of the harassment of these young women occurs at school, schools clearly need to play a large role in eliminating this harassment. These suggestions offer a beginning, a place from which educators can begin to see the role we play in maintaining the cultural inequality of sexual education:

- Educators must not tolerate the use of a sexual reputation to harass female students. Name-calling must be viewed as a form of sexual harassment and must not be tolerated by the school staff.
- There must be an atmosphere provided where girls feel free to talk openly about their sexuality. Young women should be allowed to express and discuss their own sexual desires in an atmosphere free of violence and denigration. Counselors and others should be sympathetic to their plight.
- There should be courses offered to address the cultural practices of sexual discrimination and the sexual double standard.
- There should be courses offered to curtail the sexual activity of teens and warn of STDs (sexually transmitted diseases) must also address other issues of concern to young women: the pressure to have sex within certain monogamous heterosexual relationships; the lack of acceptance of girls carrying condoms; rape, date rape, and incest.

More research is needed to further explore the role of the school in the development of female sexuality. Just as recent studies highlighting the impact of bullying on school violence have given teachers cause to step in and stop this harassment, more studies like this can raise awareness of teachers of the need to step in and stop the harassment and social ostracism of adolescent women. The aim of this project has been to explore the marginalization of women labeled slut in order to understand how the cultural aspects of female sexuality lead to oppression in the form of harassment and how such social labeling ultimately affects women's self-development and their life choices.

Although feminists, as well as other scholars, have made strides in helping to change the perceptions of gender and sexuality (Carpenter, 1998; Christian-Smith, 1988; Conboy, Stanbury, & Medina, 1997), little has actually changed to prevent girls from receiving such harmful stigmas and becoming victims of sexual harassment through the attainment of perceived negative sexual reputations as the women in this study had to endure.

DISCUSSION QUESTIONS

1. The authors of this chapter claim that there is a different standard of sexual behavior for males than for females. Do you agree? Why or Why not? Do you think there *should be* different ways of expressing sexual desire for males than for females? Why or why not?

2. How is sexual desire regulated by the possibility of adverse sexual labels? That is, how are the young girls who are adversely labeled affected by this harassment? Are young girls who are not labeled in this way also adversely affected by this labeling? Is the sexual desire of young males also regulated by the process of labeling young women?

3. A few ways that educators might work to disrupt the dominant sexual discourses are highlighted in this chapter. Can you think of other ways that educators might work to ameliorate the struggle for healthy expressions of sexual desire among today's youth?

REFERENCES

Belenky, M. F., Clinchy, B. M., Goldberger, N. R., & Tarule, J. M. (1986). *Women's ways of knowing*. New York: Basic Books.

Bloor, M. (1997). Techniques of validation in qualitative research: A critical commentary. In G. Miller & R. Dingwall (Eds.), *Context and method in qualitative research* (pp. 37–50). London: Sage.

Butler, J. (1990). *Gender trouble: Feminism and the subversion of identity*. New York: Routledge.

Capp, B. (1999). The double standard revisited: Plebian women and male sexual reputation in early modern England. *Past & Present, 62*, 70–101.

Carpenter, L. (1998). From girls into women: Scripts for sexuality and romance in *Seventeen* magazine: 1974–1994. *The Journal of Sex Research, 35*(2), 158–168.

Christian-Smith, L. (1988). Romancing the girl: Adolescent romance novels and the construction of femininity. In L. Roman & L. Christian-Smith (Eds.), *Becoming feminine* (pp. 75–98). Philadelphia: Falmer Press.

Conboy, K., Stanbury, S., & Medina, N. (1997). *Writing on the body: Female embodiment and feminist theory*. New York: Columbia University Press.

Daly, M. (1984). *Pure lust: Elemental feminist philosophy*. Boston: Beacon Press.

Daniluk, J. C. (1991). Female sexuality: An enigma. *Canadian Journal of Counseling, 25*(4), 433–446.

Daniluk, J. C. (1993). The meaning and experience of female sexuality: A phenomenological analysis. *Psychology of Women Quarterly, 17*, 53–69.

Duncan, N. (1999). *Sexual bullying: Gender conflict and pupil culture in secondary schools*. New York: Routledge.

Edwards, S. (1981). *Female sexuality and the law: A study of constructs of female sexuality as they inform statute and legal procedure.* Oxford, England: Martin Roberson.

Edut, O. (1998). *Adios, Barbie: Young women write about body image and identity.* Seattle, WA: Seal Press.

Epstein, D., & Johnson, R. (1998). *Schooling sexualities.* Buckingham, England: Open University Press.

Fausto-Sterling, A. (2000). *Sexing the body: Gender politics and the construction of sexuality.* New York: Perseus Books.

Garcia, L. (1982). Sex-role orientation and stereotypes about male–female sexuality. *Sex Roles, 8*(8), 863–876.

Gilligan, C. (1982). *In a different voice: Psychological theory and women's development.* Cambridge, MA: Harvard University Press.

Hamachek, D. (1985). The self's development and ego growth: Conceptual analysis and implications for counselors. *Journal of Counseling and Development, 64*(4), 136–142.

Harding, S. (1991). *Whose science, whose knowledge?* Ithaca, NY: Cornell University Press.

Hartsock, N. (1999). *Feminist standpoint revisited, and other essays.* Scranton, PA: Westview Press.

Hillier, L., Harrison, L., & Warr, D. (1998). "When you carry condoms all the boys think you want it": Negotiating competing discourses about safe sex. *Journal of Adolescence, 21*(1), 15–29.

Holland, J., Ramazanoglu, C., Sharpe, S., & Thomson, R. (1994). Power and desire: The embodiment of female sexuality. *Feminist Review, 46*(2), 21–38.

Holland, J., Ramazanoglu, C., Sharpe, S., & Thomson, R. (1996). Reputations: Journeying into gendered power relations. In J. Weeks & J. Holland (Eds.), *Sexual cultures* (pp. 239–260). New York: St. Martin's Press.

Irvine, J. (1990). *Disorders of desire: Sex and gender in modern American sexology.* Philadelphia: Temple University Press.

Irvine, J. (Ed.). (1994). *Sexual cultures and the construction of adolescent identities.* Philadelphia: Temple University Press.

Josephs, R. A., Markus, H. R., & Tafarodi, R. W. (1992). Gender and self-esteem. *Journal of Personality and Social Psychology, 63*, 391–403.

Kalof, L. (1995). Sex, power and dependency: The politics of adolescent sexuality. *Journal of Youth and Adolescence, 24*(2), 229–249.

Kane, E. W., & Shippers, S. (1996). Men's and women's beliefs about gender and sexuality. *Gender & Education, 10*(5), 650–671.

Katz, J., & Farrow, S. (2000). Discrepant self-views and young women's sexual and emotional adjustment. *Sex Roles, 42*(9–10), 781–805.

Kitzinger, J. (1995). "I'm sexually attractive, but I'm powerful": Young women negotiating sexual reputation. *Women's Studies International Forum, 18*(2), 187–196.

Leadbeater, B., & Way, N. (1996). *Urban girls: Resisting stereotypes, creating identities.* New York: New York University Press.

Lees, S. (1993). *Sugar and spice: Sexuality and adolescent girls.* London: Penguin Books.

Lees, S. (1999). *Losing out.* London: Unwin.

Mann, J. (1994). *Growing up female in America.* New York: Warner Brothers.

Moya, P., & Hames-Garcia, M. (2000). *Reclaiming identity: Realist theory and the predicament of postmodernism.* Berkeley: University of California Press.

Ore, T. (2000). *The social construction of difference and inequality: Race, class, gender, and sexuality.* Mountain View, CA: Mayfield.

Orenstein, P. (2000). *Flux: Women on sex, work, love, kids and life in a half-changed world.* New York: Doubleday.

Phillips, L. M. (2000). *Flirting with danger: Young women's reflections on sexuality and domination.* New York: New York University Press.

Pipher, M. (1994). *Reviving Ophelia: Saving the selves of adolescent girls.* New York: Random House.

Regan, P., & Berscheid, E. (1995). Gender differences in beliefs about the causes of male and female sexual desire. *Personal Relationships, 2*(4), 345–358.

Sheeran, P., Spears, R., Abraham, C., & Abrams, D. (1996). Religiosity, gender and the double standard. *Journal of Psychology, 130,* 23–33.

Spradley, J. P. (1979). *The ethnographic interview.* New York: Holt, Rinehart & Winston.

Stanley, J. (1977). Paradigmatic woman: The prostitute. In D. L. Shores & C. P. Hines (Eds.), *Papers in language variation* (pp. 303–321). Alabama: University of Alabama Press.

Stewart, F. (1999). "Once you get a reputation, your life's like ... 'wrecked' ": The implication of reputation for young women's sexual health and well-being. *Women's Studies International Forum, 2*(3), 373–383.

Tanenbaum, L. (2000). *Slut: Growing up female with a bad reputation.* New York: HarperCollins.

Tolman, D. L. (1991). *Adolescent girls, women, and sexuality: Discerning dilemmas of desire.* New York: Haworth Press.

Tolman, D. L., & Debold, E. (1993). Conflicts of body and image: Female adolescents, desire, and the no-body body. In P. Fallon, M. Katzman, & S. Wooley (Eds.), *Feminist perspectives on eating disorders* (pp. 301–317). New York: Guilford Press.

Ussher, J. M. (1989). *The psychology of the female body.* New York: Routledge.

Van Roosmalen, E. (2000). Forces of patriarchy: Adolescent experiences of sexuality and conceptions of relationships. *Youth and Society, 32*(2), 202–227.

Whitbeck, L., Yoder, K., Hoyt, D., & Conger, R. (1999). Early adolescent sexual activity: A study of eighth, ninth, and tenth graders in two-parent and single-mother families. *Journal of Marriage and the Family, 61*(4), 934–946.

White, E. (2002). *Fast girls: Teenage tribes and the myth of the slut.* New York: Scribner's.

Wolf, N. (1997). *Promiscuities: The secret struggle for womanhood.* New York: Fawcett Columbine.

Chapter 14

Border Crossing—Border Patrolling: Race, Gender, and the Politics of Sisterhood

Lyn Mikel Brown
Colby College

Sandy Marie Grande
Connecticut College

> *If women want a feminist revolution—ours is a world that is crying out for feminist revolution—then we must assume responsibility for drawing women together in political solidarity. That means we must assume responsibility for eliminating all the forces that divide women. Racism is one such force.*
>
> —bell hooks (1981, p. 157)

We sat on couches, chairs, the floor, eating popcorn and candy, laughing, whispering, and chatting. We were a racially diverse group of women—two professors and nine students[1]—eagerly gathered in Sandy's apartment to

---

[1]Specifically, the group consisted of two professors of Education and Human Development, Sandy Grande (Native American) and Lyn Mikel-Brown (White), both heterosexual, from working-class backgrounds; five students of color: three African-Americans (two working class, one middle class), two Latinas (both working class), all heterosexual; four white women: two lesbian, two Jewish, three upper middle class, and one working class. The students were all undergraduate juniors and seniors, ages 20–22. All names used in this chapter are pseudonyms.

231

watch the film *Girls Town*, the first in a series of films we planned to watch to-gether. In addition to providing a social space to come together, our hope was that the movies would also serve as beginning places for real conversa-tion, as a space to interrogate race/ethnicity, class, sexual identity, and gen-der as interlocking systems that shape not only understandings of ourselves but also our relationships with one another.

After the films we crowded around microphones placed in the center of a coffee table, our bodies positioned in a horseshoe with a video camera framing us, and talked. We anticipated that in these conversations we would confront the familiar barriers to developing alliances across color lines and move beyond feminist analyses that privilege voice and desire (what Teresa Ebert refers to as a "ludic feminism") toward a critical exami-nation of power relations, and social and material location, that enables coalition building. We thought that by deliberately organizing such an in-formal yet purposeful space, we could create an opportunity for these young women to experience communitas—a community of equals, able and willing to disrupt and question the usual order of things, especially the ways they have come to experience what is central and marginal here at the college and in the wider society. This seemed especially important given that undergraduate colleges like ours, which serve as institutionally sanctioned rites of passage, designed to give substance and meaning to the "betwixt and between" of late- adolescent identity development, so of-ten reproduce the status quo. We felt that such a "purposeful space" would enable these young women to try out new conceptual and analytic tools learned in their formal coursework in ways not possible in their classes, hoping these conversations would lead them to an altered perspective on power and privilege and a sense of new possibilities.

We also know that, with few exceptions (e.g., Fine & Macpherson, 1992; Pheterson, 1990; Taylor, Gilligan, & Sullivan, 1996; Weis & Carbonell-Me-dina, 2000), there has been little effort to bring girls/women of color and White girls/women together to examine the tensions and struggles that dis-tance them from one another in particular contexts and circumstances. And this would seem a most important conversation to have among college-age women, given the lengthy critique of White feminism by women of color and given the common goals for social justice feminists and womanists share. Certainly, the women students in our group were excited and hope-ful; they wanted to have this conversation even though they had quite dif-ferent experiences, desires, and expectations for its outcome.

Given the inherent complexities, we chose the cohort of nine women deliberately, ensuring a predominance of women of color to counteract assumptions of "normalcy" that prevail at the college and that generally privilege White women in conversations around gender oppression (see Pheterson, 1990). In all but one case (one of the White women recommended a friend), we asked students we knew to join this group, either because they had taken courses that interrogated power and privilege or because they were viewed (and viewed themselves) as women who had been doing the work of race. Specifically, Sandy selected five women of color with whom she had either a social or working relationship, and Lyn chose three White women who had taken an advanced course she taught on girls' development and education. Generally speaking, the White women had done their "work" around race in this and other academic courses. In addition to courses, the women of color also did their work in institutionally supported, student-controlled spaces that they had either instituted or developed.[2] Our hope was to create in this liminal place between public and private what Lois Weis and Doris Carbonell-Medina (2000) call a "recuperative space"— a place "for breathing, relaxing ... without the constant arrows of stereotypes and social hatred" (p. 627).

As it turned out, it took only two films and two conversations before it became clear to the women of color that our exercise was not working. They asked to meet in racially segregated groups because, in their words, "it wasn't going anywhere." They needed to meet alone and figure out what was going on. The White women resisted this idea. They felt things were just reaching a "comfort level," and that the group was poised to cross "the boundary from formal discussion into informal discussion." They reluctantly agreed, however, to meet as a separate group.

This chapter focuses on the tensions within the first two conversations, why they didn't work for the women of color and why the White women didn't notice or didn't understand. We then explore what the subsequent segregated discussions tell us about the space we created and the tensions and the barriers to communication. Finally we reflect on what this means for attempts at coalition building or creating alliances between White women and women of color. Because the initial large-group conversation dramatically differs in content, tone, and rhythm from both of the ensuing segregated conversations, we write this chapter in four voices: Voice 1 reports the conversations of the entire group of nine women, Voice 2 reports the reactions of the White women to the large-group conversation, and Voice 3 reports the reactions of the women of color. Although our interpretations weave throughout the chapter, Voice 4 speaks the feelings and thoughts we, as group facilitators and participants, experienced. We also consider the broader implications of these conversations for our students' shifting identities and for antiracist education.

---

[2]We refer to ongoing student groups such as SOAR (Society Organized Against Racism), SOBHU (Students Organized for Black and Hispanic Unity), and Bridge, a queer/straight alliance group. One of the White women was involved in both the Women's Group and Bridge.

VOICE 1: WOMEN OF COLOR AND WHITE WOMEN— PATROLLING THE BORDERS

Prior to the initial meeting, both groups of women knew only that they were coming together to watch a series of films about women and girls and to discuss them in an informal atmosphere with a diverse group of women. They knew this was a rare opportunity to discuss issues of gender and race in a relaxed, safe space. Playfully dubbed "Chick Flicks" by Marianne, African American, they were excited about the promise of community and of crossing borders in a campus climate sharply divided by race. There was an air of insurgency, of coalition, and of possibility. Despite the promise, it was not long before we realized that even in this very first meeting, there were racialized assumptions that deeply affected the way the group moved together. For example, the White women assumed that the women of color already knew one another and that, unlike themselves, they were already a group, an alliance. In reality, a few of the women of color knew each other or had taken classes together, but there was no preformed "groupness."[3] The White women also immediately racialized the overall group identity as White and Black—Black being the absorption of all color into one identity, which of course erased the experiences of the Latina women and Sandy.

In relation to the perceived homogeneity of the women of color, the White women experienced themselves as separate and individualized, without common ground and without support, a group only by virtue of their exclusion. "I remember the first time, when we met for lunch," Katie, White and middle class said, "We felt like it was really uncomfortable. I kind of felt like maybe, like you guys were sort of talking privately, and then you turned to us, and then you went back to each other … it felt like we got off to a weird start." The White women felt alone and insecure going into the meetings, and these feelings were based, in part, on racialized assumptions. They neither asked about the range of feelings the women of color might have had nor considered the comfort and pleasure the women of color might enjoy in this unusual experience of being in the racial majority—both (in)actions were indicative of the operations of White privilege.

There were, in addition, very different assumptions about what the exercise was to be all about, not unexpected given the general nature of the invitation. The women of color expected conversations primarily about race in which "we just were gonna say it." They wanted to move beyond the usual silent discomfort they experienced in their predominantly White classrooms; they expected to address difference and they expected conflict: As Anita,

---

[3]Within this assemblage of five women of color there were differences in race, ethnicity, and class that had yet to be addressed and tensions among the women that were never fully aired.

African American, says "I thought when we knew we were gonna be there we weren't going to be scared of conflicts." Trish explains the White women's expectations:

> I felt like the reason we were having this discussion was to talk about gender. But then it was turned into, like, race, and like, you're saying it's good that you guys are feeling your Whiteness, but that doesn't have anything to do with being a woman, so I just don't see, I mean all this discussion about race here ... wasn't the focus supposed to be about commonalities among women?

The White women hoped to find such commonalities, places of understanding and connection and comfort and they assumed everyone would: Anna, White and middle class, explains, "We all try to find sameness, differences are difficult." One can imagine the tensions induced by these very different expectations.

In the first group conversation, the women of color attacked the issues of race brought up in *Girls Town* and moved quickly to illustrate the range of microaggressions and institutional racism they experienced at school, at work, in relationships. Energized by this opportunity, they jumped in, took enormous risks, told detailed childhood stories, and talked about their painful experiences of racism and sexism at the college. The White women were shell-shocked; they listened intently but said little. The watershed moment in this first conversation arrived when Maritza, Puerto Rican and raised in the United States, told a deeply moving story of abuse, neglect, and childhood survival. The women of color reacted to Maritza's story with compassion and also used it as a springboard to introduce their similar and different experiences. The White women fell mute. They listened in silence because, as they later explained, "I really felt that I couldn't relate at all ... to her uniqueness, difference" or because "I couldn't add to that ... I almost couldn't invade that space" or because "I wanted to respect her experience" or I would be "asking her to be a teacher again, to educate me" or I was afraid of further "oppressing" her. They could see no place to enter the conversation that didn't add to the pain or point to their racial difference, to their privilege, to their conflictual perceptions and experiences. They rationalized and intellectualized. Maritza was deeply offended by the White women's silence.

This experience was a turning point because it spoke volumes, to both the White women and the women of color, about the cavernous space between them. The White women were not prepared for the intensity of the interactions or the personal nature of the stories of racism and survival. The women of color were perplexed and then angered by the lack of response from the White women. The collective space, so wide open initially, became in this moment untrustworthy to the women of color—an all too familiar ex-

perience of fetishism (Fine, 1997) and liberal intellectualism enacted by
White folks.

This first gathering broke up soon afterward and the second and final
full meeting took place a week later. The relational dynamics shifted dramatically in the second meeting. The women of color were more reticent
and cautious. They were aware going into this meeting, they said later, that
they felt as if their stories were "interruptions" to the White women's experiences of reality and that their expressions of anger and frustration made
the White women uncomfortable. They became more suspicious and quiet.
The White women perceived their silence as an opening.

The second conversation began with a confession by Anna and with a series of apologies by the other White women for their professed ignorance of
issues connected to race. This less than auspicious beginning shifted the conversation toward the fears and uncertainties of the White women, who began
to introduce themselves and their anxieties individually. "OK, I'll start,"
Anna begins. "I'm from a very White WASPY background, I'm Jewish actually, but anyway I've read some about inner-city life, and I guess what I've
been exposed to in terms of my reading is the African American situation."

Anna's reference to "inner city" marks difference and also her assumptions about people of color. As she frames the issue of race in a Black–White
binary, as "like the two extremes; there's no gray in the middle," the women
of color move quickly to complicate this construction. They invoke geography, the historical tensions within and between racial groups, the invisibility
of those not on the national radar screen—Puerto Ricans, Chicanas, Cuban
Americans, Asian Americans, Native Americans.

The difference between this and the first meeting is stark—the conversation has moved from the willingness of the women of color to share their experiences to a more distanced, intellectual effort to educate the White
women about race. The White women are confused—wasn't the last conversation an invitation to speak personally? They begin to search for a connection. They invite assurances that they sometimes feel equally as different
and oppressed as the women of color. The women of color will have none of
it. Anita, African American, is firm in her view: "I really think it is about
White refusal to acknowledge real difference." Whites, she explains, find it
easy to "lump everyone into one big group of minority ... assuming we all
have the same experience" and this means a lot gets effaced.

At this point, Anna enters and connects this erasure with her experience
as a lesbian. "It comes with heterosexuality too," she says. "There's no space
for difference ... it's just interesting how many of us are excluded." Anna's
attempt to connect through shared experiences of difference again feels
like an erasure to the women of color, which of course is not her intention. It
is the true postmodern moment—difference is difference regardless of any
particular social reality or political history. The White women repeatedly

use the generalized "us" and "we" to feel connected to the women of color, not recognizing how this is an assertion of racial privilege. They do not hear Anita's claim that it's Whites that are doing the lumping; it's Whites that find it "easier to say Black and White together." The White women don't hear, in part because they do not identify with the Whites to whom Anita is referring. Trish, in fact, finds in Anita's words an opportunity to bond with the women of color and distance herself from those other Whites: "Like I've heard nothing but one side. I was the blond-haired, blue-eyed White girl.... I don't want to be like that blond-haired blue-eyed White girl."

It seems that the White women want two things from the women of color and from this conversation: They want to connect psychologically—to feel included and to be seen as the same in their frustration with most White people—and they want understanding and absolution for their Whiteness. They want to decrease their differences or disagreements with the women of color through shared victimhood. Searching for such lines of connection they render the history and structure of racial experiences invisible. They explain away differences that make a difference and in so doing, ironically, underscore their privileged positions as constructors of reality. For example, Katie, White and middle class, speaks from a privileged position when she includes herself in the "we" who talks about everything that's wrong and who wonders what to do with all this racial difference: "We talk about everything that's wrong, but what can you say? What can we say to change it you know? Because you can't, even if you do address individual groups, you can't ... because you can't lump even in a little group and so how do we expect it to change? You know, how do we expect to address everyone's issues?"

The White women then try to connect with the women of color by disconnecting from or apologizing for their experiences of growing up White and uneducated around race. Trish explains:

> I don't want to offend anybody but at the same time watching [the film *Mi Vida Loca*] is like such another world for me and I recognize that I'm such, like, a sheltered little White girl. I know I am. It's really hard for me to talk about these things ... and like I'm sorry. I don't have any experience or like even exposure to like other cultures.... Like it's really hard for me to sit here and ... I don't know.... It's hard to talk about it when you feel so ignorant. It's something, you know, you want to be other than I am. And it comes up, but I don't know, it's just so hard to jump in and say something from my heart.

Over and over the White women bring the conversation back to themselves, their pain, their ignorance, their embarrassment. They want to "say something from the heart," but they can't until the women of color make them feel safe, let go of their realities and privilege the White women's personal pain, take care of them and erase differences that make the White

women feel vulnerable. Indeed, the White women's "comfort zone" is the
place of deepest alienation for the women of color. When Sandy explicitly
names Whiteness and pushes the women to consider that "any feeling of superiority is always about being or wanting the solution to be learning about
other people's experiences," the White women respond emotionally. "I'm
having problems with my Whiteness," Trish laments, but it's the personal
angst, the psychology of it—the sense of exclusion and fear of hurting others, the sadness and the fear—that the White women experience as the
problem, not the structured privilege.

Throughout the conversation, the dialogue of the White women remains
heavily centered on the psychological and the women of color make several
attempts to rescue the conversation from its exile to public confessionals and
personal testimonies. As the White women address their feelings and the psychology of difference, the women of color reframe the issue as one of institutional racism and privilege, attempting to draw the boundary lines between
their experiences and the White women's. "I think that none of the solutions
that usually people tend to use ... [such as] 'Well I can understand what you're
going through,' would be so much easier," Julia, Latina, explains. "I don't
think that anyone would benefit from what I've been through. I don't think
you have to walk in my shoes. I don't want that. I mean I don't need to walk in
their shoes to understand. I think that's the problem that everyone has to understand and sometimes you're not listening."

Instead of listening and responding to Julia's critique of the White
women's need to understand and relate, Katie feels compelled to elaborate
her "knowledge" of Latina culture, perhaps to prove she is different from
the other White women in the room. She speaks at length about her "envy"
of the "sense of family," such "a fertile cultural marker" of Latino culture,
and "just the female ... in the Latino community":

> I know a lot of [Latinas] in high school that had children and ... they did
> well with it, were just great with their kids and it was really ... I don't know, it
> made me see like wow, a 10-year-old girl that has a kid. And then has to
> think about actually supporting herself and be like going out and getting a
> job and that would be like the lack of tolerance for many girls to take that
> road and have a kid and have to deal with it ... it's such a part of your ... like
> experience growing up. The family is like there for you.

Katie's analytic distortions of the "fertile markers" of Latino culture, said
in an attempt to compliment and connect to Julia, brings a controlled, intellectual response. Julia, her face now expressionless, invokes the film *La Vida
Loca* and renders a structural reading of the actions of one of the characters:

> What I saw from the movie is there were a lot of issues about power and pow-
> erlessness ... I don't know, maybe I'm just thinking that because of where I

come from. And because of where I grew up and where I am ... I look at the show of power ... you have like the whole issue of women obtaining power and why do the guys get to decide. Yeah, I have two kids to support. And you have like ... especially in the Latino culture and the women are not in like positions of power traditionally. It says a lot in the movie. Ya know, because young women with children who are in one way or another trying to seek that power that they don't have within their own community, within their own neighborhood and social structure. And then when you talk about pride. It's like I've got pride. She has her little girls; she has a huge ego. It's just like the whole issue of pride. When they're insulting each other, calling each other like a bitch and whore and a puta—it's a whole issue of pride and belonging to something.

Julia is angry and it's at this point that whatever connection there was between the White women and the women of color disintegrates. The conversation becomes a kind of strange and familiar dance: The White women express their embarrassment; and profess their guilt, fear, and agony about "being White." The women of color say little or, if they do speak, they do so in depersonalized ways. Ironically, their silence for much of this group conversation—a sign of their growing anger and frustration—make the White women feel more comfortable, "safe," and "less self-conscious."

VOICE 2: BORDER INVASIONS—THE WHITE WOMEN

The White women began their segregated conversation by expressing their resistance to meeting without the women of color. "It felt that the last time it really started to get comfortable,"[4] Katie said, like things "were just getting good." When we explained that the women of color requested this separation and that they did not share the White women's experience of the group meetings, and in fact that the White women's need for comfort and assurance was appropriating the group space, the White women began to explain and justify their reality. They heard us saying that the women of color didn't want to hear about their struggles with being White and again they reached for similarities. "Being a person of color is something you share," Anna says, directing her comments at Sandy, now the only woman of color in the room. "And we're, us being who we are, we're, being self-conscious about Whiteness is a positive thing ... how do you expect us to just. I mean, like, that's a big thing. We share a commonality of being White and I don't think it should dominate the conversation, but that's not any less.... I feel

---

[4]Comfort for the White women meant feeling "safe to open up," finding a place where it was "not so hard for me to say some stuff," to feel "less-self- conscious about being White," something that felt "really, really self-conscious" about in these conversations. It meant dealing with "the background stuff," getting it out of the way so they could be comfortable.

like you guys don't want to have to talk about that." Again, talking about Whiteness for Anna, Katie, and the others does not mean offering a critique of their privileged social location, but professing their guilt about having this privilege and their frustrations with being boxed into a "blond and blue-eyed" stereotype.

To these White women, Whiteness evokes personal angst, alienation, and struggle whereas color represents homogeneity, unity, support, a unified voice, someone who has your back. "I mean, I'm grasping for someone to support me," Trish explains, "and I don't know any of these people [referring to the other White women in the group] ... and I feel like because they [the women of color] all know each other, there's not sort of ... if I felt closer to the White women ... I mean, it's not knowing each other and having to speak out." In other words, they see no currency and feel no sense of safety or shared reality in their Whiteness; the best they can do is name their isolation and fear and expose their common guilt and sadness about the privilege it affords them.

It's true that the women of color did bond in the first sessions and some of that bonding came from shared appreciation of what it means to be a woman of color in predominantly White contexts, but it's interesting that for the White women to have race in common means to share nothing of value. They believe race gives the women of color power and a sense of intimacy and support that they covet. This projection arises out of a clear desire for this kind of alliance and what it offers. This desire is so real and present for them that they continue to assume that the women of color "all know each other really well," in spite of Sandy's repeated reminders that this is not the case.

The conversation about Whiteness has the potential to become more complicated when these women express their wish to "move beyond White guilt," but instead they return to their feelings: "I'm very, very disillusioned," Trish says. Even when one of them risks a view that "it's a very sort of White concept to need to feel comfortable" or when they begin to consider their upbringing as "limited in imagination in terms of power education" they cannot or will not stay with it. When pushed to elaborate they move to safer ground—they espouse things professors have taught them about race, refer to diversity trainings they've participated in, recite information they've read about "the Harlem Renaissance" or "the media as a separate art form," or return to familiar generalizations like "we all try to find sameness." Ironically, whenever things get dicey or scary, the White women seek comfort in the safety of White, Western, patriarchal binaries that undergird sexism: the separation of feeling and thought, personal and political, Black and White, male and female. Lapsing back into the psychological, they wonder how the group conversation is serving their personal growth—"how does this help me understand?" "It comes back to me," Tessa says, as she struggles with her guilt and her fear of "just saying like humongous things about yourself to total like strangers, basically."

These safe and familiar binaries make it difficult for the White women to appreciate the contradictions in their experiences, the structural nature of their privilege, or the intersection of race and gender in their own lives. Their assertion, in Katie's words, that "I can only do this if I'm in relationship" is the ultimate White middle-class woman's condition—asserting the primacy of closeness and comfort, genuine relationships or real conversation, even as she gets to name the parameters of what makes a relationship genuine or a conversation real. Indeed, the litany of fears the White women express expose the knotted intersection of White privilege and conventions of White femininity: They fear "being close-minded," "thoughtless," "having someone angry at you," "being wrong," "being disliked," "being seen as the bad guy," "causing discomfort," "oppressing others," and "separation."

At the same time that they express such fears, the White women distance themselves from "the submissive nature of White women" and "lame" or "girly" girls. Such derogation echoes their wish to escape the constraints of conventional femininity just as they wish to escape their Whiteness—dominant constructions of both femininity and race are embarrassments, sources of pollution, and something the White women wish to disown, decontaminate from, or at least publicly critique. And yet although they are not, themselves, "girly girls," they seem to fear the directness and unapologetic anger of the women of color.

Interestingly though, when we begin to address anger and White femininity, things break open and threaten to expose the constraints of patriarchy. "I think White women deal with their anger privately," Anna explains. "I don't know how to deal with it." And with this said, the women begin to tell a few of their own stories about being treated badly, lied to, and being "abandoned by everybody": "I was completely under the impression I couldn't talk about [being raped] and I just withdrew because I had no way to deal with it ... I just kept it to myself and I thought it was my fault." They begin to make some connections beyond the personal and to address what might have gone on in the group meetings—that not wanting to be angry or to evoke others' anger "is a White quality ... that's ... holding us back ... We don't want to be angry and we don't want to receive it," and that "what we've been doing is tied to White power, culture, White values ... the White imagination." Even though they do not examine the intersection of race and gender, in this moment they move beyond the purely psychological to explain their guilt, their desire to negate who they are, and their need to feel protected and secure.

Acknowledgment of this fear and their attempts to rationalize it, so grounded in conventional femininity, seems to explain the great lengths the White women go to avoid conflict and their unwillingness to suspend their realities even a little to make room for those of the women of color. It's ironic of course that their wish for and attempts to create connection depends on erasing difference and effacing the women of color. The ultimate fear is of being in the presence of judgment and anger—an anger that threatens to break things open, to expose the truth about privilege and difference and power.

VOICE 3: REDRAWING THE BOUNDARY LINES: THE WOMEN OF COLOR

Because it was the women of color who asked to meet separately, they were filled up when we finally gathered again. The tone of the conversation was open and energetic—a marked contrast to the laborious and controlled discussion with the White women. They had clearly been "frustrated" and "disappointed" in the earlier conversations but now there was a kind of pleasure and humor, as well as an eye-rolling, self-protective critical distance in their interactions with us and one another.

The first thing the women of color wanted to do was talk about the refrain they heard from the White women: "I can't relate." What the White women experienced as an attempt to be sensitive, not to oppress or appropriate the experiences or space of the women of color, the women of color saw as a straightforward example of White privilege. They named the irony—that the White women's assertion of "I can't relate" kept them from any real relationship at all:

> For me what was frustrating was that they kept, you know talking … in great detail about not relating, you know, for a long time. I think a lot of what came out was stuff around being White and female and being afraid of conflict. You know? So they were really afraid to like … relate. [laughing] Like they were afraid to ask questions or even sort of make assumptions about stuff because of the potential of people to get angry. So I think that was part of it.

"I can't relate," they agreed, was a stance they could rarely own. "We can't really say that we can't relate to things because we're so harangued with like certain things," Anita, African American, explains, "where White women can say I can't relate to this because they're used to being White and being around White things. We have to relate to them *and* we have to relate to ourselves.… In order for us to survive we *have* to relate." And although the women of color understood that the "I can't relate" was about the White women's fear, they were impatient. The first two conversations were like too many others they've had "where there's always that fear" and "dancing around words and looking at your expression, trying to figure out if you're going to get upset about what they say."

They also explained that White women would have real conversations one-on-one or when they were in the majority; that "not relating" was a problem only in certain contexts. The White women had plenty to say after the group meetings, something that angered the women of color. As Shana, African American, explains:

> It's funny because after we would leave ... as we walked toward West Dorm, three of them and me, and it's like they had everything to say. All about this and this and that and dadadadada. And I was like why didn't you say that? You know? And it's like, y'know, OK when it's three against one it's a lot easier.... I dunno, maybe there are a lot of things, a lot of sacrifices and a lot of risks that people of color have to make in a White institution, period. You know? And it's like we always have to go into their sphere and have to accommodate ourselves to their standards in order to just survive, and I mean that kind of conversation, they're afraid. Oh no, it's like we've been there. We've been through that frustration and it's like they don't have to do it. Y'know, it's a luxury for them and it's a privilege for them to not have to ... y'know to be able to choose to say or do something like this. And then sit there and be like "oh! oh!" and stay there in their sphere. You know what I mean? Yeah it really is, it's frustrating. It really is.

It is a privilege, the women of color note, to be able to choose when to speak and what is important. Because the White women spoke only of gender and because gender referred to White femininity, the women of color experienced their expressions of reality as raced and felt the White women recoil: "They felt like they were only coming in here to talk about gender," Marianne, Latina, explains. She continues:

> I was frustrated because I think that every time we talk even if we started the discussion, we ended up with the same thing like "I just feel so bad for myself because I can't relate to you." [laughter] It's the same thing the entire time and we always end up on that the same subject that someone will be frustrated and "Oh, I'm almost about to cry because I can't understand" and it was like they wanted someone to feel bad. All the time we discuss them feeling bad because they can't relate.... "This is about me and my feelings and I need to have" ... I don't see how just gender. There's no way you can talk about gender without talking about race.... If I could stay in the bubble where everything would be happy for me, I wouldn't leave either.

The women of color wanted to tackle tough issues and they expected this to lead to disagreement and knowledge. As Julia explains, "I think another issue is that our idea of conflict is different too because I mean we would say this to each other and someone would think it's so mean ... I mean that's not like conflict ... that's just fun."

Because they define conflict and also "comfort" differently than the White women, the women of color entered the film conversations with the assumption, as Marianne, says, that "we were going to be comfortable enough so that even if you were going to say something you were not quite sure of or whatever, regardless we just were gonna say it so there would be discussions." Instead, she adds, "this just turned into another discussion of, ooh, why is it so difficult to talk about White women and race, you know, status.... I just expected it, we're all pretty much in a vulnerable position somehow, so everyone should feel comfortable. Or if not comfortable, at least know that we're all vulnerable here and say what we have to say and have a discussion. And make it comfortable enough for everyone."

Comfort in this sense wasn't about making friends or fully trusting the other people in the group. Rather it was about "learning something that you thought was right and, you know, is wrong." This is not to say that trust wasn't important to the women of color. It just wasn't, based on past experience, what they expected from this group, and it wasn't necessary in order for them to speak their feelings and thoughts.

In one of the most telling moments, the women of color articulated what the conversations with the White women would have sounded like if they went according to their expectations or "hopes": "You wouldn't have to waste time worrying about them ...." Marianne says. The others agreed. Rather than claiming they couldn't relate, they would say things like, "I never thought of it that way" or "Really? Wow, I never knew that" or "Well I used to think that too. I guarantee you that's not it." Or "what's your perspective?" or "Wow, I learned something." What the women of color hoped for was a conversation in which everyone in this constructed liminal space felt like equals, in both their vulnerability and their power to speak, in which disagreements would happen in good spirit, and people wouldn't be silenced. What they experienced was an exercise in frustration in which they were asked to hold White women's fear and were expected to collude in the erasure of White privilege. This group, they said, became another example of how White women assumed all women "come together because of their shared oppression. And then when they're faced with [women of color], and [we] say we want to talk about race and they have to face their privilege—all these women fall apart because they haven't come together." Comparing this group to the student women's group on campus, historically all White, Anita says:

I mean, have they looked at themselves? I mean they stand for women .... I mean it's supposed to be a unity between women, and if they're so concerned with women and oppression they would start there, too. And I'm tired of always seeing them as scared. I think it's not scared anymore. It's like the old thing. They feel comfortable with it. Why should they leave their comfort zone if they don't have to deal with it? They don't have to deal with our issues. And they don't want to talk about our issues.

The women of color said they had no trouble addressing gender, reimagining a space for all women where the conversation could be about, say, "how men overpower women." In fact, whereas the White women found it difficult to articulate the intersection of race and gender, so too did the women of color, albeit in different ways and for different reasons. Perhaps not surprising, given society's racist history, they saw themselves first as people of color. And as the conversations unfolded, gender rarely emerged to complicate their racial identities. Yet, in a moment of insight, Marianne sees the barrier, the reason why "the conversation could have gone in a different direction" but didn't:

> Hey! You know what it is? You know what's really hard about that is because we can't talk about anything because we are women. Once a White woman starts opening her mouth and starts talking you start to feel yourself forgotten. You know what I mean? We were having a conversation in class and the White women were speaking about all the girls this … and throughout that discussion I was like, well there was no mention of anything having to do with race or the complications of ethnicity or different cultures, you know. And it was like whoa, wait a minute! This conversation sounds really White to me, you know … So it's like you start feeling very, very invisible and you feel like you have to stop the conversation and say wait a minute! What about this, what about that, what about this?

"That's where the block is at," Julia agrees. "They'd rather stay neutral because it's easier. It's about being easy." Again the women of color confront privilege head on—"Ain't I a woman?" Anita wanted to know. "Why can't they enter our conversation?" they wonder. What gets in the way? "White women," they conclude, "are ignorant approaching the conversation so they don't know how to hear it the way that we mean it, so we don't say it at all. You know what I mean? We don't want to go there. It's like, it's protection, but it's also like oh god, if I go there this person is gonna think this, this and that. So you don't want to go there." This is why "no one really has real conversations."

As the women return to the discomfort of the White women in the group, it's striking that they are angry, but also more generous with White people's questions and requests for explanation than the White women seem to think they are. If people really risked confronting each other, the conversation wouldn't lead to disconnection, as the White women fear, but as Maritza explains, would go something like this:

> I'll be like, "You know what I mean?" "No, not really, you can go ahead and explain it." I mean sometimes you gotta stop people. That's the problem.

People don't … here on this campus Whites who are so afraid to stop you
when they don't get something because they're so afraid of like breaking the
flow or making you upset, that you have to explain it. It's like sometimes
you're not gonna get everything. You know what I mean?

As those who study the psychology of oppression or the structures of
domination and subordination would predict, the women of color know
more about the White women than the White women know about them (see
Freire, 1970/1992; Miller, 1976). They "get" the impact of White women's
oppression and its relationship with White men in ways the White women
do not:

We don't have like the fear I guess that much as White women because you
know, we go back into our history, it's like White men suck. [laughing]. And
do you see the way the White men look at you, it's like an object and not as like
a female or as a person. And so I mean it's just like, we understand that and
the male/female sort of thing, the male power. But then you know, we don't
have that same fear.

They explain that White women are raised "to please everybody else," to
avoid conflict and not take risks. This knowledge of where White women are
coming from is a source of both frustration and power and sometimes humor. As Marianne says, "I mean their self-perception is they've done a lot of
work, they're read this, they've read that, you know"—and Julia interrupts
"but they still 'can't relate,' so it doesn't matter" [laughter].
    The frustration that "no one really has real conversations" and they are
constantly dealing with people who "think they have the right to always feel
like they can relate" is real for these women. But so is their ability to read
critically the situations they are in and to play with the reactions of White
women to their disagreements and conflicts. In a series of examples, the
women of color develop their critical distance from White femininity and
poke fun at White women's reticence and passivity. Unlike White women,
Maritza insists, "when I interact with White men they see me as nasty or with
a complete attitude and then I just have to break it down for them, that if
someone is gonna be in control, it's gonna be me." Julia describes her arguments with a Latino friend in her class and how freaked out the White
women were "when Jorge and I got into it." People thought we were going
to kill each other … Jorge and I started laughing … "Were playing. It's play.
It's hilarious."
    As they share stories of White women's tentativeness, fear of conflict, and
passivity toward men, it's easy to get caught up in the fun of it all. The reality, however, is more complicated. White men generally do have power, but
not all White men have the same amount or kinds of power. The gender dynamics between men and women of color are much more complicated than

Julia admits; it's not always easy or possible to say "get over it, it's not a problem." Having conflict and real questions "squashed" because majority students and professors are uncomfortable can have a lasting impact. Not all White women are passive or afraid of conflict. For those who are, the fear has real sources and serious consequences. Clearly, it's a limitation to construct White women as a homogeneous group, as Julia does when she claims that "they've been so pampered ... by their parents or whoever has been taking care of them, has always done everything for them.... They can't [confront each other] because that's just not what they know. And they're not willing to know either."

By the end of this conversation the women of color, who initially did not know one another all that well, had bonded through their stories of critique and their experiences with the White women in the larger group. An alliance formed. As Julia, explained, commenting both on a story she had just told and on this moment, "It is amazing when you are in a place, I mean we all get ... that's a kind of power to be a group. You know what it is? It's intoxicating."

VOICE 4: RE-RACE-ING THE BORDER

At this, our conversations both together and apart ended and we were left to consider what happened, to ponder our own idealized expectations, to doubt our facilitation skills, to question our naiveté. What came out of this exercise for these thoughtful young women and did we learn anything useful about the barriers to coalition building across racial lines?

We were both struck by the promising beginning to Chick Flicks and the rather dramatic impasse that developed by the end of the second gathering. Within academe, women of color have taken White women to task for dropping race out of their analysis of the power structure and out of their construction of women (e.g., Collins, 1990; hooks, 1989; Lorde, 1984). Marxist feminists (e.g., Ebert, 1996) have taken White/bourgeois feminism to task for limiting critique and analysis to the psychological realm and for positing issues of identity over structural critiques of class/capitalism and voice over the historical and material underpinnings of oppression.

These critiques resonated whenever the White women brought the conversation back to themselves, their needs and fears, and failed to see the big picture. And they emerged whenever the women of color struggled in vain to convey the intersections of institutional racism and the broader power structure. We found ourselves sitting with the problem, then, and wondering if it was insurmountable. The differences between the women were fundamental—differences in tone (morose vs. light-hearted), in style (tentative vs. assertive), in speech (indirect vs. direct), in analysis (personal/psychological vs. institutional/structural). The women of color and the White women spoke differently about fear, conflict, vulnerability, learning, anger—offering different definitions for each of these concepts.[5]

The primary battle, it seemed to us, was over who had access to reality, who got to name the "problem" of gender, who got to decide what lens brought the social and political world into focus. It becomes impossible to have a conversation about gender—or about anything for that matter—when one party has the unearned privilege to assume their reality exists for everyone. But is it that simple? The White women tried very hard; this conversation really mattered to them; they wanted to be on the right side, "in" on the denigration of sexism and racism, so much so that they willingly negated their Whiteness and separated themselves from conventional views of femininity. The problem was that even here, in this move, there was a form of entitlement—an assumption that they could say or want these things and it would be so—and a familiar disconnect between the personal on the one hand and the structural, historical, and material on the other. The psychological, it seemed to us, was more than a form of analysis for the White women; it was a subject position rendered as "reality" and born of the intersection between racial entitlement and gender oppression.

This construction of reality harbored something fundamental for the White women about living as both racially privileged and subordinate with respect to gender. Learning to offer up feelings and vulnerability in the service of self-protection and creating safe space in frightening circumstances has been a lesson they've learned from earliest childhood. This is, we would argue, the process of internalized oppression—or as Mark Tappan (2002) refers to it, "appropriated oppression."[6] The psychic alienation and tendency to decontaminate from or blame those like oneself (horizontal violence) are common responses to subordination (see Bartkey, 1990; Fanon, 1967; Freire, 1970/1992; see also Brown, 1998). The anxiety and fear induced by conflict, anger, and disconnection, the need to feel safe before speaking or acting, and the need to please and be liked fall more within the realm of middle-class White women's experience of subordination. The women of color became increasingly frustrated with the White women not only because they did not share these responses to oppression, but also because their own response to subordination was more often to act in defiance of this construction of White femininity.

---

[5]Indeed, a good part of each of our subsequent conversations was taken up with translation—the White women were often so indirect and hesitant that Sandy had difficulty understanding what they were trying to say, and Lyn was in the difficult but necessary position of trying to articulate something almost inchoate in its "naturalness."

[6]Tappan writes that the key aspects of internalized oppression—self-deprecation (taking anger and frustration out on oneself) and horizontal violence (taking it out on people like oneself) are not immutable or permanent psychological qualities. They are the result of becoming skilled at, making our own and unwittingly passing on through our relationships those negative and oppressive stories, images, and voices we've experienced in our daily lives.

The White women's tendency to normalize their reality was supported daily in their predominantly White private college where formal and informal education operates to center and reproduce certain identities and realities and to marginalize and efface others.[7] The women of color's stories and direct expression of feelings and thoughts not only marked this Whiteness but the psychology of White femininity. In their sincere struggle to respect differences, to "relate" to the women of color, the White women saw the primary issue as one of connection and voice, and in so doing unwittingly erased the structural and historical underpinnings of their racial privilege and thus effaced the realities of the women of color. It is this erasure that explains the anger and frustration of the women of color at the White women's need for reassurance and affirmation. The White women's dependency on the women of color to understand their fears and affirm their realities "in effect directed the group more toward White securities than toward the struggle against racism" (Pheterson, 1990, p. 39). That these conversations reinscribe rather than disrupt racial privilege and conventions of White femininity would be, we think, a disturbing realization for these White women, who see themselves and want to be seen as brave, compassionate, and antiracist.

Yet before any productive conversation can occur between White women and women of color, White women need to interrogate Whiteness and White privilege. They need also to examine the relationship between gender oppression and racial domination. There is absolutely no question that the White women in this group were both capable of and motivated to do this work. It's our contention that without a much-improved education that can provide students with the critical tools to examine the culture of power (Delpit, 1995; Ebert, 1996; Freire, 1970/1992; McLaren, 2003; Spring, 2001; Tatum, 1997) and its effects on both internalized (appropriated) oppression and internalized (appropriated) domination (see Pheterson, 1990), White students in particular are greatly disadvantaged when it comes to coalition building and antiracist efforts.

Clearly there are limitations to orchestrating liminal spaces, to disrupting social norms and structures, to creating social moments in and out of time. The "recuperative space" we envisioned happened at different mo-

---

[7]As you may recall, all of these young women had taken courses on race, gender, and class differences. But most of these courses identified race as "other," a construction that critically engaged the women of color, who sought out professors and readings as well as student-centered spaces and organizations that would interrogate this view and provide critical analysis that could explain and affirm their identities. In nearly all courses at the college, Whiteness was racially unmarked and as such came upon its universal social standing "naturally." The White women had no need to examine their racial identities because in their experience the "substance of Whiteness is the very behaviors and beliefs that make it appear immaterial" (Kenny, 2000, p. 25). The substance of White femininity was the silence, the culture of avoidance, the desire for connection and sameness, among other things.

ments and for different reasons for the White women and the women of color, as did the experience of communitas. In spite of the unexpected turn of events and the short-lived nature of the project, there were openings and real possibilities for new knowledge in the spaces these women created together and apart. Chick Flicks, more fragmented than we had envisioned, did indeed provide space and opportunity to interrogate and perhaps even alter the usual structures of experience.

As Bernice Johnson Reagon (1983) reminds us, coalitions are not and should not be our homes and we don't have to like each other to work as sisters toward common ends. The White women need to move beyond a ludic feminism in order to consider what it means not to distance themselves from their gendered and racialized identities, but to embody, embrace, and activate them for antiracist purposes. Only then can they be in the presence of the justified anger and reasoned resistance of women of color without taking it personally; only then can they too "just say it" without being immobilized by fear. In so doing they learn to speak in what bell hooks (1994) calls renegade voices and occupy what Bonnie Zimmerman (1991) terms "perverse" or Sandra Harding (1991) refers to as "traitorous" identities—perverse because they choose the margins as a site of radical possibility (hooks, 1990); traitorous because they willfully refuse to do what the culture of the center expects them to do, proclaiming their disloyalty to "civilization" and its racist and (hetero)sexist underpinnings.

DISCUSSION QUESTIONS

1. Why is it that for the White women racism is predominantly a personal or psychological problem, whereas for the women of color, racism is systemic, structural, or institutionalized?

2. What do the authors mean when they say that "before any productive conversation can occur between White women and women of color, White women need to interrogate Whiteness and White privilege?"

3. What does this chapter suggest about coalition building among women?

REFERENCES

Bartkey, S. (1990). *Femininity and domination*. New York: Routledge.

Brown, L. (1998). *Raising their voices: The politics of girls' anger*. Cambridge, MA: Harvard University Press.

Collins, P. H. (1990). *Black feminist thought*. Boston: Beacon Press.

Delpit, L. (1995). *Other people's children: Cultural conflict in the classroom*. New York: The New Press.

Ebert, T. (1996). For a red pedagogy: Feminism, desire, and need. *College English, 58*(7), 795–819.

Fanon, F. (1967). *Black skin, White masks.* New York: Grove Press.

Fine, M. (1997). Witnessing Whiteness. In M. Fine, L. Weis, L. Powell, & L. M. Wong (Eds.), *Off White: Readings on race, power, and society* (pp. 57–65). New York: Routledge.

Fine, M., & McPherson, P. (1992). Over dinner: Feminism and adolescent female bodies. In M. Fine (Ed.), *Disruptive voices* (pp. 175–203). Albany: State University of New York Press.

Freire, P. (1992). *Pedagogy of the oppressed.* New York: Continuum. (Original work published 1970)

Harding, S. (1991). Who knows? Identities and feminist epistemology. In J. Hartman & E. Messer Davidow (Eds.), *(En)gendering knowledge: Feminists in academe* (pp. 100–115). Knoxville: University of Tennessee Press.

hooks, b. (1981). *Ain't I a woman: Black women and feminism.* Boston: South End Press.

hooks, b. (1989). *Talking back: Thinking feminist, thinking Black.* Boston: South End Press.

hooks, b. (1990). *Yearning: Race, gender, and cultural politics.* Boston: South End Press.

hooks, b. (1994). *Teaching to transgress.* New York: Routledge.

Kenny, L. D. (2000). *Daughters of suburbia: Growing up White, middle class, and female.* New Brunswick, NJ: Rutgers University Press.

Lorde, A. (1984). *Sister outsider.* Freedom, CA: Crossing Press.

McLaren, P. (2003). *Life in schools: An introduction to critical pedagogy in the foundations of education* (4th ed.). Boston: Allyn & Bacon.

Miller, J. B. (1976). *Toward a new psychology of women.* Boston: Beacon Press.

Pheterson, G. (1990). Alliances between women: overcoming internalized oppression and internalized domination. In L. Albrecht & R. M. Brewer (Eds.), *Bridges of power: Women's multicultural alliances* (pp. 34–48). Philadelphia: New Society.

Reagon, B. J. (1983). Coalition politics: Turning the century. In B. Smith (Ed.), *Home girls: A Black feminist anthology* (pp. 356–368). New York: Kitchen Table: Women of Color Press.

Spring, J. (2001). *The American school: 1642–2000* (5th ed.). Boston: McGraw-Hill.

Tappan, M. (2002). *"Internalized oppression" as mediated action: Implications for critical pedagogy.* Unpublished manuscript.

Tatum, B. (1997). *Why are all the Black kids sitting together in the cafeteria? And other conversations about race.* New York: Basic Books.

Taylor, J., Gilligan, C., & Sullivan, A. (1995). *Between voice and silence: Women and girls, race and relationship.* Cambridge, MA: Harvard University Press.

Weis, L., & Carbonell-Medina, D. (2000). Learning to speak out in an abstinence based sex education group: Gender and race work in an urban magnet school. *Teachers College Record, 120*(3), 620–250.

Zimmerman, B. (1991). Seeing, reading, knowing: The lesbian appropriation of literature. In J. Hartman & E. Messer-Davidow (Eds.), *(En)gendering knowledge: Feminists in academe* (pp. 85–99). Knoxville: University of Tennessee Press.

Chapter 15

"I Am a Woman Now!": Rewriting Cartographies of Girlhood From the Critical Standpoint of Disability

Nirmala Erevelles
Kagendo Mutua
The University of Alabama

Adolescence marks that confusing and complex space of liminality where one is not quite a child and not quite an adult either. It is in this context of social and psychological flux that gendered identity becomes more clearly (re)constituted. For girls, this process of "girling" (Butler, 1993) brings them into the domain of language and the complex matrix of social relations through the interpellation of gender. However, because adolescence exists in a space of flux, this interpellation into "girlhood" is never final, never fully complete. Rather, this interpellation is itself a temporal process that is (re)constituted via the competing practices of reiteration (Butler, 1993) and destabilization—such that, in the final instance, it is never clear what "ideal girlhood" is really about. It is for this reason that Asher (2002) describes girls as being "in a transitional state of their gender roles" (p. 23)—a space that allows for the possibility of reconfiguring girlhood.

This liminality that marks adolescence therefore provides a space for the articulation of Girl Power—a space where girls have begun to challenge traditional modes of femininity and utilize resources available to them to forge new identities (Adams & Bettis, 2003; Budgeon, 1998). Girl Power marks a shift in the discourses of femininity away from docility, quietness, acquiescence, and passivity, and in support of self-determination, individualism,

253

and sexual subjectivity (Adams & Bettis, 2003). At the same time, Girl Power is still committed to the ideals of traditional femininity. Thus, the discourses associated with Girl Power represent the complex and contradictory interplay of independence, assertiveness, and strength with feminine attractiveness, a demure and deferential attitude, and an adherence to compulsory heteronormativity.

Notwithstanding its oppositional impulse, this articulation of Girl Power can be oppressive when brought to bear on disabled girlhood. In contemporary Girl Power theory, the "disabled girl"[1] is an invisible presence, who struggles to claim recognition at the discursive boundaries of girlhood. To be marked as both disabled and female in an ableist society suggests that you may never really become a "girl" in the manner we have just described. Because as an identity, disability functions as an overdetermined sign, the interpellation of the disabled adolescent into "girlhood" is seldom recognized until "girlhood" forces itself into recognition as dangerous, troubling, and unwanted. This becomes especially significant for adolescent disabled girls (and boys) because it is in this temporal space that physiological transformations (e.g., breasts, menstrual periods, erections, etc.) can no longer sustain dominant constructions of the disabled adult as asexual perpetual child. Perhaps, it is for this very reason that disabled adolescents are often described in strategically nongendered terms—"individuals with disabilities," "children with disabilities," and "adolescents with disabilities," and very rarely as "disabled girls/boys/women/men" or "girls/boys/women/men with disabilities."

Whereas most other liminal identities can be transcended, disability as one marker of liminality appears immutable and all encompassing. Hence, for disabled girls, disability is ever present—explaining all, muting all. Disabled girlhood, therefore, becomes an impossible category within traditional/patriarchal notions of feminism and even within radical feminist constructions of girlhood. It sits uncomfortably at the fringes of third-wave feminist constructions of girlhood and simultaneously disrupts and flirts with patriarchal norms of "girling." Disabled girlhood challenges the heteronormativity that is present even in radical notions of Girl Power, which rest heavily on ableist ideologies of independence, assertiveness, and strength laced with patriarchal notions of beauty and attractiveness. Girl Power, thus defined, leaves neither material nor discursive spaces for a differentially constituted *disabled* girlhood.

---

[1]In this chapter we use the term "disabled girl" in a politically strategic way. In normative publishing practice, it is generally required that one use the term "girl with a disability" so as to emphasize the person first and then the disability. However, within disability studies scholarship, it is argued that "disabled girl" would be more appropriate terminology because within the more politicized understanding of disability as a social and political construct one's disability is to be embraced along with one's identity as gendered.

In this chapter we invoke the theoretical perspective of Disability Studies to explore the social construction of girlhood from the standpoint of Sue Ellen, a girl/young woman with Down syndrome. Critical of ableist discourses, Disability Studies scholars have countered "accepted notions of physical [and mental] disability as an absolute inferior state and a personal misfortune" (Thomson, 1997, p. 6) and have instead retheorized the disabled body as "a site of historical inscription rather than physical deviance ... [repudiating] such cultural master narratives as normalcy, wholeness" (Thomson, 1997, p. 105). Located within the in-between spaces of social identity, the disabled female body therefore becomes the transgressive body—"[the] cultural third term, defined by the original pair of the masculine and feminine figure. Seen as the opposite of the masculine figure, but also imagined as the antithesis of the normal woman, the disabled woman is thus ambiguously positioned both inside and outside the category of woman" (Thomson, 1997, p. 29). This depiction of the disabled feminine subject as transgressive marks the disabled girl as potentially dangerous and disruptive even to radical discourses of girlhood. As a result the disabled girl is constituted as abject (Erevelles, in press) where the abject "designates ... precisely those 'unlivable' and 'uninhabitable' zones of social life which are nevertheless densely populated by those who do not enjoy the status of the subject, but whose living under the sign of the 'unlivable' is required to circumscribe the domain of the subject" (Butler, 1993, p. 3). Clearly, then, definitions of "normative" girlhood are dependent on definitions of "disabled" girlhood to achieve its own legitimacy. But what if disabled girls refuse to be disciplined at the border? What if disabled girls reject their status as abject nonsubjects? What if disabled girls attempt to rewrite the cartographies of girlhood in more empowering ways?

SILENCE AND VOICE:
LEARNING TO LISTEN IN NOISY SPACES

To respond to the preceding questions, we draw on a qualitative case study of a 20-year-old Euro-American girl/young woman with Down syndrome (given the pseudonym of Sue Ellen in this chapter) and her mother Martha. Our interview with Sue Ellen is part of a larger study that explores how disabled girls/women and boys/men with their parents/guardians envision their future life prospects post high school. Like the other students in the study, Sue Ellen attends a school district in the southern United States where she is enrolled in a transitional vocational education program that enables students with disabilities to transition successfully from high school to the adult world. For the purpose of this chapter, we decided to focus on the experiences of Sue Ellen, especially the descriptive details of her unique struggles to claim girlhood/womanhood, notwithstanding the oppressive silences and barriers put forth by an ableist society. Our specific focus on Sue Ellen fits neatly into the research rubric of a qualitative case study that Yin (1994) defines as "an empirical inquiry that investigates a contemporary phenomenon within its real life context, especially when the boundaries between phenomenon and context are not really evident" (p. 13).

Because people with cognitive impairments[2] are regarded as a vulnerable population in the research process, Institutional Review Board (IRB) regulations required that we interview Sue Ellen in the presence of her mother. Originally, we had planned an initial visit with Martha and Sue Ellen to break the ice, provide information on interview procedures, and get both parental consent and student assent to carry on this study. However, at the first meeting, which was held in a private space at Martha's office at an educational institution where she works as a secretary, both Sue Ellen and Martha were eager to begin the interview right away.

The interview protocol we constructed was designed to interview both mother and daughter simultaneously. Although, we prepared separate interview questions for Martha and Sue Ellen, the questions were really mirror questions and therefore our initial thoughts were that both daughter and mother would offer their own perspectives on each question thereby bringing to bear their own unique points of view on each question/issue. The open-ended in-depth interview questions (Taylor & Bogdan, 1984) that were used covered a variety of topics, including perceptions about the utility of transition programs in steering disabled girls toward desired post school/adult outcomes, friends in school and community, leisure/recreation activities in school and community, and plans for the future relating to independent living, community participation, and employment. Through the questions we hoped to get an understanding of the young people's roles, possibilities, and desired life outcomes and ways, if any, in which the factors identified in previous research (Halpern, 1993; Masino & Hodapp, 1996; McNair & Rusch, 1991; Mutua, 2001), including type/severity of disability, sociocultural variables, and gender, mediate those desired outcomes/possibilities.

Through the interview, we followed Sue Ellen's journey through her adolescence and the possibilities her future would hold for her. In particular, the interview foregrounded the contested and controversial issue of sexuality and its implications in the constitution of girlhood, demonstrating how the dominant discourses of femininity are both limited and limiting when viewed from the standpoint of the Disability Rights Movement. As we later

---

[2]In this case we use the term "person with cognitive impairments" because we would like to emphasize the person first rather than the impairment.

discuss in this chapter, we found that even though Sue Ellen was not even aware that there is a Disability Rights Movement, her attempts to redefine her sexual and gendered identity in opposition to ableist discourses echoed the Movement's own struggles for self-definition.

Sue Ellen's speech was not always clearly understood by us, and she often spoke in fragmented sentences that assumed a context that we did not share. That is why initially we were actually pleased that Martha was present during interviews because she was able to provide us with both context and explanation. However, we soon learned that Martha's presence added some complexity to the interview process. When we found it difficult to understand Sue Ellen's speech, Martha would respond for her or would convince her that this was not what she really meant to say, thereby silencing her. Also, in our own enthusiasm to encourage Sue Ellen to speak and/or to clarify what she said, we often offered cues that sometimes had little to do with what she was saying, and therefore unintentionally crowded out her voice.

Additionally, the interview process also brought to bear another ethical dilemma for us. Toward the end of the initial interview, Sue Ellen had grown very quiet when Martha delved into detailed explanations about Sue Ellen's personal life. We instantly recognized that we needed to restructure the interviews whereby first we would interview Sue Ellen with Martha's role being one of only helping with clarifying, reframing, or substantiating questions or responses. We, therefore, conducted a second interview with Martha alone, so that Sue Ellen would not have to sit through a conversation about herself while she was still present.

Clearly, Sue Ellen's responses were not representative of the rich description that is usually touted as good qualitative data. However, we argue that Sue Ellen's monosyllabic responses and sentence fragments were much more voluble than we initially conceived. Furthermore, the interviews demonstrate that it is the silences, the hesitations, the determined yet subtle insistences that speak louder than complete and elegantly put together sentences that are considered critical in good research (Devault, 1990). Having said this, we therefore could not analyze the data collected using traditional qualitative strategies like the constant comparative method (Glaser & Strauss, 1967) and the formulation of thematic codes. On the other hand, each of us carefully reread the interview transcripts several times looking for patterns, repetitions, planned digressions, and our own white noise in an effort to make meaning of what was said and what was left unsaid. Additionally, our data analysis, rather than looking for thematic codes was focused more on foregrounding Sue Ellen's (re)constitution of her selfhood in her own words—an intervention that forced both Martha and ourselves to reconsider our own commitments to the normative discourses of girlhood.

Claiming Voice Notwithstanding:
Disability and the Politics of "Girled" Selfhood

We now turn our attention to Sue Ellen in her final year of high school as a special education student. Like other soon-to-be high school graduates (both disabled and nondisabled), this final year was a critical transitional year at school before she entered into the adult world of responsibility, independence, and work. Like her peers (both disabled and nondisabled), Sue Ellen also viewed this stage in her life with excited trepidation, subtly revolting against her mother's attempts to still hold on to her "little girl." This section is therefore centered on Sue Ellen's attempts to claim both voice and space to articulate her own unique conceptualization of girlhood/womanhood that sometimes disrupted the normative ideals of feminine possibility that were made unavailable to her in traditional discourses of girlhood. Clearly, Sue Ellen may not be consciously aware that she resists and rebels against the restrictive gendered identity that is assigned to her. Rather, it is her subtle but persistent claims to "girled" selfhood in the interview that forces the reader to rethink the limits of normative discourses of femininity, thereby rewriting the cartography of girlhood in alternative ways. Sue Ellen lays claim to several tropes of "femininity"—some normative and some oppositional. Additionally, this section also marks out spaces where Sue Ellen and Martha agreed and disagreed vis-à-vis their collective struggle to redefine girlhood in empowering ways for Sue Ellen.

Like most adolescents close to graduating from high school, Sue Ellen seemed eager to carve out for herself a life of semi-independence. Clearly this entails finding gainful employment, and Sue Ellen was therefore eager to list out for us the various job options that she could pursue in her quest for gainful employment. The job options that Sue Ellen listed were folding, sorting, and ironing clothes; making fast-food staples like pizza, hamburgers, and French fries; mopping floors; and shelving in either a video store, a bookstore, or a grocery store. Clearly most of the jobs that Sue Ellen identified were in the area of domestic labor that has traditionally been women's work. More important, it was the prospect of working that appeared exciting to Sue Ellen. In contrast to the more "progressive" and "contemporary" discourses of "girl power" that define femininity outside the domestic sphere (e.g., tough-ass girls), Sue Ellen took pride in her domestic chores, an option that Martha wholeheartedly endorsed.

Notwithstanding her enthusiasm for entering into independent adulthood, one sensed that Sue Ellen was at the same time aware that independence would require that she leave home and live alone—an idea that at this point in the interview she seemed unprepared to wholly embrace. This hesitancy was manifested in her response whereby she viewed "work" as helping her mother around the house and postponing, at least for now, the actual event of leaving home. Although it may appear that Sue Ellen, unlike her nondisabled peers, was hesitant to fully claim her independence, later developments in the interview offer some clues regarding what Sue Ellen perceived as the appropriate conditions for leaving home. Interestingly, this was one of the only places where mother and daughter concur. In her interview Martha explained her own vision of what Sue Ellen's future would look like:

> But, um, I was wanting her to have a job, something that she did enjoy. Even if it is just a part-time little job, something every day. And her friends ... I am hoping that there is someone [possibly her younger brother] ... who will overlook and oversee some things financially ... [that] she is getting her food.... I just want her to have some type of wings so that she does feel like she's an adult and that she is doing something. Because she seems to be expressing that somewhat now to me and I feel like that is where she wants to move to be like that. She um, she sees that on TV and on the movies and she thinks that's her steps.... She doesn't think she's supposed to live with me forever. But I think she is unsure of what she's going to do, so it might be easier to stay with mommy until she really had everything, where she knew and worked out in her mind. But if she was living in some type of setting, if it was a group home or having some type of roommate or something that helped her. And she got to her job, but she still really needs all of those social things that she enjoys so much to make her happy. Like her dancing, she loves swimming, bowling .... Um, she's got to have that physical outlet 'cause it makes her feel good.

Conscious of both the limitations and possibilities for a disabled girl/woman with cognitive impairments, Martha was nevertheless also very committed to ensuring that her vision for Sue Ellen's future coincides in some degree with Sue Ellen's own conception of her "girled" social life. As a result she has encouraged Sue Ellen to pursue social activities in which girls usually participate. Thus, for example, Sue Ellen's music preferences reflected the tastes of her nondisabled and disabled peer group and included country music (listening to it with her grandmother), Christmas music ("O Holy Night" being her favorite) and teen pop stars/groups like Britney Spears, New Kids on the Block, the Backstreet Boys, and TLC. Like most teenagers she also liked dancing and performed for us a short version of the Macarena during the interview. Her mother also reported that she sometimes took Sue Ellen line dancing where both adults and some younger people attended. Sue Ellen then reported in excitement that she danced with her bus driver, Mr. Casey, whom she described as her "buddy." Loving to party, Sue Ellen mentioned to us, without our prompting, a pool party that she attended in the house of one of her peers, Sam, who also has a cognitive disability. She also reported that she was soon to go to camp with her best friend Sally for the very first time and was excited about the prospect of her first taste of independence on this trip.

But there were limits to Martha's awareness of Sue Ellen's social and personal wants and needs, and this became apparent during the interview when Sue Ellen dropped what her mother perceived as a "bombshell" by claiming that she wanted to marry her boyfriend and have a baby. It all started when her mother playfully reminded Sue Ellen during the interview that she had forgotten to mention one of her friends, Billie Joe, and laughingly admonished her for her shyness. After a slight hesitation, Sue Ellen was more forthcoming about this relationship as is evident in this segment of the interview that we quote in some detail:

Interviewer: Tell us about Billie Joe. Want to tell us about Billie Joe? Who is Billie Joe?

Sue Ellen: Billie Joe. He nice.

Interviewer: Why do you like him?

Sue Ellen: He gonna marry me. [Laughing with a quick darting look at her mother]

Interviewer: He's gonna marry you … [Laughing]. So tell us more about Billie Joe.

Sue Ellen: Billie Joe Smith. We go work together.

Martha: You all work together.

....

Sue Ellen: Washed the tables.

Interviewer: You wash tables together.

Sue Ellen: We eat food.

Martha: Y' all eat together too?

Sue Ellen: Yep.

Martha: They do everything together.

....

Interviewer: How old is Billie Joe? How, how old is he?

Sue Ellen: Twenty-one.

Martha: No he is not. He is 6 months younger than you, so he is 19.

Sue Ellen: 19.

Interviewer: You'd like him to be 21 though.

Sue Ellen: He's older than me.

Martha: So he's not older than you.

Interviewer: Is he cute?

Sue Ellen: Ah, that my boy friend and he's older than me.

Interviewer:	If he's your boyfriend, he has to be older than you?
Sue Ellen:	Yeah.
Interviewer:	He's cute?
Sue Ellen:	Yeah he cute … All the time.

....

Martha:	No, you told me he's funny.
Sue Ellen:	Funny…. At the bowling alley, he makes a silly dance.
Martha:	At the bowling alley he was acting silly.

....

Interviewer:	Are you good in bowling?
Martha:	Yes.
Sue Ellen:	Yes.
Interviewer:	What about Billie Joe? Is Billie Joe good at bowling?
Sue Ellen:	Yes, he just, he can [makes kissing sounds and kisses something in her hand].

....

Martha:	He shares with you and he talks to you like that? [a little incredulously]

....

Interviewer:	Mama's getting nervous here.
Sue Ellen:	Yeah, bowling ball … kiss the ball.
Martha:	He kisses your bowling ball?
SR:	Yep. [We, the interviewers go "ooohhh."]
Martha:	That is silly. [laughing]

....

Interviewer:	So when Billie Joe kisses your bowling ball, you get a strike?
Sue Ellen:	Yeah.
Interviewer:	He's lucky for you?
Sue Ellen:	Yeah. He's been lucky.

....

Sue Ellen:	I like to kiss Billie Joe Smith [muttering under her breath].
Interviewer:	What, I didn't hear you?
Martha:	You just said you like to kiss Billie Joe [a little more incredulously].
Sue Ellen:	Yeah, I get to kiss Billie Joe. Hubba! Hubba! [those are kissing noises along with laughter].

Martha:	[can't understand on the tape but she is shaking her head in disbelief]
Sue Ellen:	Aw! Come on, Ma! Get with it.
Martha:	Alright, alright, I'm not going …
Interviewer:	So what does mama think about you dating? Does mom like you dating Billie Joe?
Sue Ellen:	My mommy afraid. Mommy afraid of it.
Martha:	What? That's nothing. What are you talking about? I'm afraid … of you dating Billie Joe?
Sue Ellen:	No.
Martha:	Of you seeing Billie Joe?
Sue Ellen:	Yeah.
Martha:	Of you having a boyfriend?
Sue Ellen:	I have a boyfriend.
Martha:	Right [to Sue Ellen and then turns to us and says] She knows that OK.
Interviewer:	Why do you think mommy's afraid of you dating Billie Joe?

....

Sue Ellen:	Going to the movies with me … 'Cause he kissing me and in love.
Interviewer:	Oh, OK.
Martha:	Kissing you and love? Yep, yep, that's what I'm afraid about.
Sue Ellen:	He get a ring for me.
Interviewer:	He got a ring for you? [laughing]
Martha:	She knows what you should do.
Interviewer:	… You are only 19 now…. When would you like to get married?
Martha:	Husband and wife.
Interviewer:	Uh huh, but when would, how old do you want to be before you get married?
Sue Ellen:	We'll have a baby [ignoring the question].
Martha:	Yep [very incredulously].
Interviewer:	Oh-oh [laughing].
Martha:	That's the first I heard of that!
Sue Ellen:	My mama had a baby.
Interviewer:	Your mom's married, but your mom's older right. But you're only 19.
Sue Ellen:	But my mama get married to Johnny Brown.
Martha:	That's right.

We quoted this section of the interview in full so that the reader can actually see Sue Ellen's persistence in letting her voice be heard amid the incredulity and interruptions that marked her assertion that she intended to marry Billie Joe and have a baby. It was interesting to note that though Martha tried to play off the relationship as purely platonic, Sue Ellen, on the other hand, was hell-bent on making known to us and her mother her (sexual) desire to kiss Billie Joe, and later on to marry and have children with him. She actually appeared to revel in our shock at her news, adding semiplayful sound effects—"Yeah I get to kiss Billie Joe. Hubba! Hubba!"— much to her mother's shocked disbelief. In response to her mother's claims to the contrary, Sue Ellen playfully quipped, "Aw! Come on Ma, get with it." What was also apparent in this interview segment was that Sue Ellen might have been conscious of the social censure and silence regarding her claims to sexual desire. This became apparent in the ways she sometimes ignored our questions and her mother's insertions, treating them as annoying interruptions that were deflecting attention from what she really wanted us to hear: her assertion of selfhood as also sexual. Aware that Billie Joe, being younger than her would not meet the normative requirement of marrying an "older" man, Sue Ellen insisted that he was older than her so he could qualify as her boyfriend and later (future) husband.

Sue Ellen noted that her own mother had (re)married and had another baby—intimating that she was following in mother's footsteps by claiming her sexual identity that would complete her transformation from girl to woman. This echoed Martha's report regarding Sue Ellen's comment when she told her mother when she turned 18, "I am a woman, now!" In the interview we tried to understand what Sue Ellen meant by this statement:

Interview: I have another question. You told your mama that when you
               turn 18, 'I am now a woman ....' What is different from being
               just a girl; now you're a woman, what's different?

....

Martha: Yeah, what do you mean when you said you're a woman?
               You're not a girl anymore, your not a kid, you're a woman.

Sue Ellen: I'm a woman.

Martha: What does that mean?

Sue Ellen: I not a girl.

Martha: Okay, but why? Why aren't you a girl?

Sue Ellen: I not a boy [laughing].

Martha: She also likes to be funny [talking to us].

Sue Ellen: I had to, Mom!

Martha: I know, but what about ... What makes you a woman?

Sue Ellen: I don't know.

Interviewer: You just know you're a woman, right?

Sue Ellen: Uh huh.

Interviewer: Have you become smarter now? Can you do things on your own? You can …

Sue Ellen: Oh, oh oh, Mommy ooh!! Juliet!

Martha: Mommy oh … Oh, right [laughing]. When she becomes a woman she can become a Juliet and have her Romeo.

Sue Ellen: Oh Mommy. I go with that one.

Martha: She's into love too much. She really likes that. When she becomes a woman.

....

Sue Ellen: Yeah. I got that feeling.

Martha: Oh, she realizes she has feelings of being a woman. This is what she is trying to tell us.

Sue Ellen: I got a lot of feelings.

Aware of our previous reactions to her assertions of her sexuality, Sue Ellen became more cautious in describing to us her experience of liminality in the developmental shift from "girlhood" to "womanhood." Her interaction with her mother mirrored some of that resistance via her "smart alecky" comments—that we also read as subversively political. When her mother admonished her for not taking the question seriously, Sue Ellen said, "I had to, Mom"—perhaps implying that she had to resort to humor to foreground the absurdity of our questions. As a result of our persistent questioning, Sue Ellen interestingly foregrounded sexuality (her "feelings" that are Juliet-like) as the marker of that transformation—a fact that her mother did not realize until this interview. This was representative of Martha's comments that immediately followed this interview segment:

Well she does things a little more mature. It's like all of a sudden, she [Sue Ellen] realizes she's at that [stage]. I didn't know, it just kind of shocked me when it all happened. 'Cause I thought she would not, the physical and the mental that aren't together. But that physical keeps going to where she really started acting like a teenager. She has a brother that is 8 and a sister that's 5. And she talks to them like, you know, she's a big woman and this and that. When she's at home, she's like, "Don't do that, you're going to get in trouble." You know! Those kinds of things. She's taking more of a mature role and … um … I realize she has been having some romantic feelings. And so she is so shady about this. When she turned 18, I see, she thinks that those feelings and all have made her a woman. And I see what she's been trying to tell us.

Martha's recognition of her daughter as a sexual being did not come without some trepidation. Worried that this expression of her sexuality may not be in the best interests of her daughter, Martha initially drew on a discourse of protection when discussing Sue Ellen:

> Like I said before, I just worried about her physical protection and her emotional protection, as far as getting involved with boys. Of course I don't think anything in that area. It's like if someone that is around her that is normal that takes advantage of her. I'm afraid that she's a prime target to be raped, or, and so that could really just, really, really set her back emotionally.... I have not a clue about where to talk to her about sex, and to explain to her, and how even though there can be love that someone can really hurt you with that. I mean, you're right, she totally understands everything you ever talk to her about, but she never vocalizes enough for you to really know what she thinks. 'Cause most of the time I'll always ask her ... "You understand?" ... "Oh yeah!" I mean she's very observant, listens a lot, and pays close attention to things, but she just never has had, like you said enough language and all to have conversations with you to really ...

At the same time, Martha was also critically self-reflective about how her ignorance regarding her daughter's sexuality was not very different from the experiences of mothers of "normal" girls. Thus she claimed:

> This is what I have a hard time with ... from day one with her is to realize how normal she can be in her actions and everything. She didn't want to be talking about her boyfriend and do you think I ever went and told my mother the first time I kissed a boy? Oh no. [laughing]. I mean you think she's going to tell me? Oh no. I'm the mother, I'm thinking wow that was normal, OK. She wasn't suppose to tell me ... but it's just that I feel like she could get hurt easier than I could at her age. 'Cause she, she seems to really want love from a boy. 'Cause see they [her friends] just kept telling me oh they are really fond of each other. That was the only comment I ever got and I am going OK and I never got that she is really fond of him like a boyfriend. And no one ever said those words, and so I didn't have a clue until like I said her grandmother saw them kiss and she told me. ... but, um, and I don't know how his [Billie Joe's] mother feels. In some ways it's like in a way you're thinking ... Well, I just don't want to get into dating issues with them. They just don't want to have those feeling. Uh, they don't need that, but they do.

Recognizing her daughter as a sexual being brought other issues to the fore for Martha when she realized how closed society was about coming to a similar recognition. Thus Martha said:

> I'll tell you, parents, from most of the ones that I have talked to, do not want to discuss that because they don't know ... And they want to say, "Oh no! They don't have those feelings" And they do!... When Sue Ellen said that

she had a boyfriend that was Billie Jo, and that she was kissing him, she [a friend] said, "Oh, well honey ... Believe me they do feel and know exactly what to do whether or not you tell them." ... And I thought, OK so you don't have to tell her how because she'll know but we still need to explain the consequences of that.

Martha believed that Sue Ellen and some of her disabled peer group needed to have access to sex education. However, in a context, where even her own mother was unable to talk to her about sex, Martha found that she was woefully ignorant in this space, given Sue Ellen's cognitive impairment also:

You know, I'm thinking ... she needs to have some sex education. And I don't even know how to begin in a way that she can understand, but not totally freak her out and realize that she does know some of this in the way she feels. 'Cause I can tell she does, physically. And I say part of this probably is because like I say, Sue Ellen doesn't vocalize enough for me to know, what she would understand. I'm not like a teacher, OK, and I don't say she has this IQ and she is functioning on this level, and at this IQ level, they really understand this. You know, and so I don't know how simple to start or how complex. But I think, and maybe I am totally wrong, but I think with her and children that are disabled, is so much more harmful to go through something like that.

The preceding discussion illustrates how her maternal concern for Sue Ellen's future sometimes resulted in the inadvertent imposition of Martha's own values, tastes, and ideas regarding what constituted Sue Ellen's "girled" experiences—a position that we, as interviewers, also were responsible for propagating. Thus, in the final instance, notwithstanding Sue Ellen's own critical stance regarding her sense of "girled" selfhood, the normative discourses of sexuality continue to subscribe to ableist stereotypes that silence her once again.

(RE)THINKING GIRL POWER: (NON)CONVERSATIONS WITH DISABILITY

As our data have suggested, to fully appreciate the complexity of the "nongirling" of disabled girls is to acknowledge the limited "girl" spaces—discursive and material—occupied by girls with disabilities and also the limited "girl" experiences they are encouraged to participate in. Adolescence is a period when young person's concepts of their own sexuality and its expression are socially and culturally defined and articulated. The sociocultural definition of sexuality and the slotting of boys and girls into their gendered identities is made possible through the activities that boys and girls are allowed/encouraged to participate in, including dating, leisure and recreational activities, and sporting activities. These activities function as unique geographies where cartographies of sexuality and gender are inscribed. Disabled girls (and boys), especially those with visibly disabling conditions (i.e., cerebral palsy, Down syndrome) often find themselves excluded from these spaces, and as a result, have to struggle to be recognized as sexual/gendered subjects. On the other hand, disabled girls/boys are cast into gender/sexual passive positions as recipients of assistance and consumers of help—images that radically "impair" their ability to be viewed as possessing the potential for proactive pursuit and achievement of sexual expression, much less pleasure, as their nondisabled peers.

Clearly, Sue Ellen did not buy into these categories. Her calm assertions regarding her sexuality situated her outside the restrictive discourses that dominant culture applies to disabled girlhood. Sue Ellen's disclosures in the interview also enabled her mother, Martha, to rethink her own assumptions regarding her daughter as a sexual being—not a girl any longer but a woman in her own right. And yet this recognition, as mentioned earlier, foregrounds the real fear that parents of disabled girls have to experience—the inadequate information regarding sexuality in a violent and sometimes misogynist world. However, as Martha noted, there is very little sex education available (Christian, Stinson, & Dotson, 2002; McCabe, 1999; Milligan & Neufeldt, 2001) and herein lies the problem. For disabled girls, particularly those coming through a traditional special education program, developing a well-rounded sense of sexuality is not really supported because educational institutions neither viewed her as sexual nor supported sexual activity, thereby actively contributing to the problem that some Disability Studies scholars have dubbed "lack of sex access" (Shuttleworth & Mona, 2002). Although there is a silence in the general population about matters of sex (Fine, 1988; Tolman, 2000), there is still a tacit affirmation of nondisabled girls as sexual beings. On the other hand disabled girls often encounter shock and/or disbelief from the public when expressing their sexuality because ableist discourses constitute them as asexual children (Milligan & Neufeldt, 2001). As the severity of cognitive disability increases, so does the impossibility of recognizing disabled girls as capable of granting informed consent, therefore creating what some have referred to as constructing "prisons of protection" (Koller, 2000) around their sexuality.

Notwithstanding these "prisons of protection," disabled girls like Sue Ellen continue to rebel against these restrictions and persistently claim identities that serve to (re)write the cartographies of girlhood in more radical ways. Based on Sue Ellen's insistent assertions, we have learned that "girl power" is not only called into play via loud assertions of radical/oppositional selfhood (i.e., the bad-ass girls), but also finds a place in the quiet insistence of "girled" identity at the borders of "normality" where notions of "girlhood" are usually challenged. True, Sue Ellen's initial claims to "girl-hood" follow patriarchal rules. But her radicality does not lie in her opposi-tion to those rules but in her insistence that she be recognized as a sexual/gendered subject where her difference as embodied in her disability re-writes the landscape of "normative" girlhood and "girl power."

DISCUSSION QUESTIONS

1. What does liminality mean from the standpoint of disability studies?
2. In what ways does disabled girlhood challenge "normative" con-structions of girlhood?
3. What kinds of critical education interventions will enable girls like Sue Ellen to claim more empowering subjectivities?

REFERENCES

Adams, N., & Bettis, P. (2003). Commanding the room in short skirts: Cheering as the embodiment of ideal girlhood. *Gender & Society, 17*(1), 73–91.

Asher, T. (2002, May–June). Girls, sexuality, and popular culture. *Off Our Backs,* pp. 22–26.

Budgeon, S. (1998). "I'll tell you what I really, really want": Girl power and self-iden-tity in women. In S. A. Inness (Ed.), *Millennium girls: Today's girls around the world* (pp. 115–143). Lanham, MD: Rowman & Littlefield.

Butler, J. (1993). *Bodies that matter: On the discursive limits of "sex."* New York: Routledge.

Christian, L., Stinson, J., & Dotson, L. A. (2002). Staff values regarding the sexual expression of women with developmental disabilities. *Sexuality and Disability, 19*(4), 283–291.

Devault, M. (1990). Talking and listening from women's standpoint: Feminist strate-gies for interviewing and analyzing. *Social Problems, 17*(1), 94–119.

Erevelles, N. (in press). Understanding curriculum as normalizing text: Disability Studies meets curriculum theory. *Journal of Curriculum Studies.*

Fine, M. (1988). Sexuality, schooling and adolescent females: The missing discourse of desire. *Harvard Educational Review, 58,* 29–53.

Glaser, B., & Strauss, A. (1967). *The discovery of grounded theory.* New York: Aldine de Greuyter.

Halpern, A. S. (1993). Quality of life as a conceptual framework for evaluating tran-sition outcomes. *Exceptional Children, 59,* 486–498.

Koller, R. (2000). Sexuality and adolescents with autism. *Sexuality and Disability, 18*(2), 125–135.

Masino, L. L., & Hodapp, R. M. (1996). Parental educational expectations for ado-lescents with disabilities. *Exceptional Children, 62,* 515–523.

McCabe, M. P. (1999). Sexual knowledge, experience and feelings among people with disabilities. *Sexuality and Disability, 17*(2), 157–170.

McNair, J., & Rusch, F. R. (1991). Parent involvement in transition programs. *Mental Retardation, 29*, 93–101.

Milligan, M. S., & NeuFeldt, A. H. (2001). The myth of asexuality: A survey of social and empirical evidence. *Sexuality and Disability, 19*(2), 91–109.

Mutua, N. K. (2001). Importance of parents' expectations and beliefs in the educational participation of children with mental retardation in Kenya. *Education and Training in Mental Retardation and Developmental Disabilities, 36*(2), 148–159.

Shuttleworth, R. P., & Mona, L. (2002). Introduction to the Symposium. *Disability Studies Quarterly, 22*(4), 2–9.

Taylor, S., & Bogdan, R. (1984). *Introduction to qualitative research methods: The search for meanings.* New York: Wiley.

Thomson, R. G. (1997). *Extraordinary bodies: Figuring physical disability in American culture and literature.* New York: Columbia University Press.

Tolman, D. L. (2000). Object lessons: Romance, violation, and female adolescent sexual desire. *Journal of Sex Education and Therapy, 25*(1), 70–80.

Yin, R. K. (1994). *Case study research: Design and methods* (2nd ed.). Thousand Oaks, CA: Sage.

Afterword:
Girlhood, Place, and Pedagogy

Pamela J. Bettis
Washington State University

Natalie G. Adams
University of Alabama

What do the seating arrangements in a Christian high school classroom, the 4 minutes to change class periods and period products, the bedrooms of middle schoolers, and the backseats of a school bus tell us about the role of place in the lives of adolescent girls? How do the words of pregnant teens, Beauty Walk contestants, girls who are labeled sluts, and a sexually aware young woman with Down syndrome help us rethink what and how we teach in schools? What can we learn from the contested identities of Preps, Cheerleaders, Sex Mob members, and fifth-grade leaders? How might the discursive practices surrounding girls who fight, lesbians, and ideal femininity be disrupted so that girls can more deliberately choose healthy and vibrant ways to be?

We ask these questions because we believe that thoughtful fieldwork can help us reconsider how girls become female in our schools. As several authors have pointed out, adults, including teachers and parents, often are the least perceptive about what girls are thinking and living. Shinew and Thomas note that the fifth-grade teachers they interviewed would not have identified the same girl leaders that the girls themselves named. Merten's teachers and parents of middle school girls were supportive of an "expansionist" agenda for these adolescents and seemingly unaware of

271

the continued significance of home in these girls' lives. Finally, both Erevelles and Mutua as well as Sue Ellen's mother are all shocked when Sue Ellen proclaims a sexual identity and articulates her own desire. All of these examples should not be surprising in that what we "see" and know of life in schools as teachers, administrators, teacher educators, and even field researchers emanates from an adult vision and adult understanding of the world.

Thus, the foundation of this concluding chapter is driven by what we have learned from the girls/women we all spent time with, the stories they have told us, and what we have observed. The authors in this text have taken us into the literal and often mundane places that girls and young women inhabit, places that are frequently kid controlled. They have taken us also into discursive spaces where the meanings of ideal girlhood and sexuality are fought over, challenged, and recreated. These various geographies of girlhood, from school lunchrooms to professors' homes to baseball metaphors, become places for important gender work to take place. So what have we learned from all of these explorations? First, we have learned that place must be taken seriously in schooling, and obviously we are not talking about the classrooms of schools; second, that teachers and scholars need to understand the socialization of girls or the "production of girlhood" differently; and third that by taking place seriously and understanding the production of girlhood differently, we can construct a pedagogy that is place and gender based.

WHERE ARE THESE GIRLS/WOMEN?

Recently, there has been a flurry of theoretical activity regarding the role of place in education, or rather its neglect. Ecology, place-based education, eco-feminism, and a critical pedagogy of place (Gruenwald, 2003a, 2003b) are part of a new discourse in education, one that focuses on the important role that local contexts and places take on in all of our lives. The thrust of much of this work in education is an advocacy to reconnect the school curriculum and the students inside the school with their surrounding environment for a deeper, more meaningful connection. Grunewald (2003b) explains that:

> The point of becoming more conscious of places in education is to extend our notions of pedagogy and accountability outward toward places.... Place-conscious education, therefore, aims to work against the isolation of schooling's discourses and practices from the living world outside of the increasingly placeless institution of schooling. (p. 620)

We applaud this discussion. Clearly, the girls and young women in the foregoing studies are all engaged in important identity work, and not in some abstracted manner, but situated in real places. However, we feel that something is missing in this emerging educational discourse. And that something is gender. Places are not neutral; they are gendered as well as raced and classed. McDowell and other feminist geographers note that the hierarchies and divisions of gender are infused in how place and the environment are lived, understood, and used. "This binary division is also deeply implicated in the social production of space, in assumptions about the 'natural' and built environments and in the sets of regulations which influence who should occupy which spaces and who should be excluded" (McDowell, 1999, p. 11). This gender difference plays out in the lives of children and adolescents as well. Katz (as cited in Nespor, 1997) notes, "All studies of children's outdoor play … have found significant differences between girls' and boys' autonomy, the extent of their free range area, and the ways in which they use space" (p. 101).

What we learned from the words and actions of the girls and young women in these studies is that the in-between and supposedly mundane places of everyday life are central to their identity work. Those mundane places are not always part of the "natural environment," and they are not places that adults would often consider significant. But in fact, we have learned about the importance of the bedroom and the backseat of the school bus, both places that girls use to tease out who they are and who they are becoming. Furthermore , most of these sites of identity work are found in kid-controlled places at school, like the lunchroom. As critical scholars, we agree with critical pedagogues' assessment of schools as placeless institutions in that they represent the factory or corporate model of schooling with a focus on standardized testing and curriculum. As well, we want to engage students in curriculum that acknowledges, analyzes, celebrates, and critiques the local environment, both natural and built.

However, as feminist scholars also, ones who listen carefully to girls and young women and who are attuned to their everyday habits of life, we know schools are certainly not placeless. They are full of sites where important identity work takes place. A lesbian participant in Petrovic and Ballard's study explains that football games and the bus rides to and from these games sometimes provided a special place and opportunity in which she could express her feelings for another girl by holding hands under a blanket. For Spicard Prettyman's pregnant teens, the lunchroom becomes an important site for these young women to explore who they were becoming: "We're still teenagers, you know, and so this is like time for us … So lunch is kind of like for that, we get to talk about stuff that like we want, like clothes, and guys and stuff that matters to us. You know, it's about like more who we are, not stuff we have to learn." Vicky's comments speak to the work that most adolescents desire, that of identity. Unfortunately, Vicky notes that this type of work is separate from "stuff we have to learn," which represents the placelessness and lack of relevance that Grunewald, among others, is critiquing. This lunchroom could have been any lunchroom in any name-less school, but its importance is what these young women make it, the meaning they associate with it. It is a space in which these young women could engage in important identity work, among themselves, and away from adults.

Besides literal places, the authors of this text have acknowledged and opened up discursive spaces that are also central to girls' identity work. In Merten's study, girls are concerned with how they decorate their bedrooms as well as where they locate themselves in the enduring sexual baseball met-aphor. Although not a literal place, the baseball metaphor provides a very concrete map for girls to fix their location as a sexual being. One girl com-ments that "If you go to third [base], that is too far for seventh grade." She uses the common image of a baseball field to sort out the complexity of ado-lescent sexuality. It shouldn't be surprising that girls, along with boys, use a male-dominated sport to position themselves sexually because discursive spaces just as literal places are infused with gendered meanings.

In this book, we want to open up the notion of place as discursive as well as physical and emphasize that both are always gendered. Based on what the girls and young women described as important sites for them, we want to challenge those working toward a critical pedagogy of place to acknowl-edge that gender is often central in how individuals understand place and that for many adolescent girls, school is not necessarily "placeless."

HOW DO THESE GIRLS/WOMEN BECOME FEMALE?

As we discussed in our introduction, much of the earlier literature on the construction of gendered identities centered on the role that schools, teach-ers, and administrators played in reproducing dominant ideology about the proper role of girls and women in society. These reproductionist theo-ries of gender position girls as unreflective, passive consumers of the domi-nant-gender regime, thus accepting of their subordinate status in the society. All of the authors of this book point to the important work that di-verse adolescent girls are involved in while negotiating a gendered identity. Far from being passive dupes of a girl-poisoning culture, many of the girls in this book are actively engaged in resisting, challenging, and critiquing dominant ideologies.

Sometimes this resistance occurs with the help of a thoughtful adult as a part of the formal curriculum as in the case of Carla, a teacher in Spicard Prettyman's study who brought a sexist and racist newspaper editorial de-scribing pregnant teens to the girls' attention and used it to create an en-gaged curriculum. In Lalik and Oliver's work, Kim encourages a small group of girls to observe carefully the ritual of the Beauty Walk, survey girls in the school, and interview a select group of girls about this yearly activity. Then armed with data, the girls construct a critique of this Southern ritual and publicly protest the event. Although this was not part of the formal curriculum of the school, these eighth-grade girls certainly benefited from Kim's guidance and project.

However, most of the resistance strategies, as detailed in this book, emerge from within the context of girls' interactions with one another, and not necessarily with the guidance of an adult. For example, although Brown and Grande provided the informal setting and pedagogical strategy for a group of diverse undergraduate women to engage in gender and race identity work, it is the young women themselves, in this case the women of color, who disrupt their professors' plans and request to meet separately from the White women. Certainly, Shameeka's need to be "outspeakin' " as found in Bettis, Jordan and Montgomery's work and Sharon's proclamation of "I fight for rulership, to show I'm somebody" found in Adams' study both resist the dominant notion of ideal girlhood. These girls, along with other members of the Sex Mob, the backseat bad-asses, and Sue Ellen are examples of girls and young women claiming their own identities, which may or may not conform to gender and ability stereotypes.

The girls and young women in this book point to the need to understand the socialization of girls or the "production of girlhood" differently. In the foregoing chapters, we see evidence of how girls are disadvantaged in the school setting. The girls labeled sluts in the Liston and Rahmini-Moore chapter, the lesbians in the Petrovic and Ballard chapter, and the teenage mothers in Spickard Prettyman's work are positioned as less than the ideal female. The race, ethnicity, and social class of some of these girls/young women limited the choices that were available to them. But as Bettis, Jordan, and Montgomery point out in their study, the White middle-class Prep girls were constrained, in some very important ways, more so than those "less privileged" members of the Sex Mob. In fact, it is members of the Sex Mob, girls who are not necessarily considered ideal, who are able and willing to try on and play with various female identities. Thus, reproductionist theories do not address the contradictions of privilege, power, race, social class, and gender—how girls simultaneously embrace and resist facets of normative femininity. As Jones (1993) points out, "the point is that the social order within which femininity is discursively constructed ... is not seemingly consistent; girls—within and between class and ethnic groups—cannot simply be seen as uniformly repressed. It is in the gaps opened by this unevenness that the possibilities for resistance and change can be developed" (p. 4).

The backseat bad-asses certainly are not passive dupes of socialization. From their seats of power, they yell sexist comments to men on the sidewalk and reign supreme over the inhabitants of the school bus. As Jewett points out, the bus provides a liminal space for identity work and these queens of the bus may not reign in the classroom, but for the time that they inhabit the bus, they are "somebody." Shinew makes that very point in her chapter on fifth-grade leaders when she quotes Jones: "A discursive construction of women and girls as powerful, as producing their own subjectivities within and against the 'spaces' provided is useful in offering more possibilities for women and girls to develop and use a wider range of practices" (Jones, 1993, p. 164).

The chapters in this book point to the ways in which girlhood is not a universal construct experienced the same by all girls. As these authors point out, a girl with a disability, girls who identify themselves as lesbian, girls who occupy peer groups with low status, and girls struggling with what it means to be female and Christian experience girlhood differently. Yet, we also recognize the importance of strategically using girlhood as a universal construct for the purposes of social change. For example, as Adams points out, girls who fight and girls who participate in cheerleading seem to be occupying two very different girl worlds; yet, an examination of the discursive practices involved in each reveal that all girls are subjected to contradictory messages about what it means to be a "woman" in today's society—messages that are confusing to girls as they try to sort out what is and isn't appropriate behavior.

We offer a beginning vision of what a curriculum and pedagogy could be for girls in today's world, one in which they are framed as powerful, powerless, confident, demure, strong, nice, pretty, and athletic. As feminists who wear both sensible shoes and dancing slippers, we want schools to be places that are not placeless but are seen by girls as full of possibilities for who they may be and who they may be becoming. "Identifying girls as agents who negotiate school differently suggests that the more fertile a school in terms of opportunities, role models, and recognition of a wide range of female behaviors and achievements, the more apt are girls to flourish" (Research for Action, Inc., 1996, p. 9).

A PEDAGOGICAL MAP FOR GIRL PLACES

Three of the chapters presented in this text provide girls/young women with that "recognition of a wide range of female behaviors and achievements." In fact, in all three cases, thoughtful teachers/researchers guided the students initially in considering how gender as well as race and social class played out in their lives as well as the lives of other students and society at large. Spickard Prettyman's delineation of how an alternative school teacher encouraged her students to critically examine and respond to how pregnant teens were framed in an newspaper editorial is a provocative example of transformative education. Rosary Lilak and Kim Oliver's focus on a curriculum that would engage girls in reconsidering the Southern social ritual of the Beauty Walk in terms of race and privilege demonstrates what can be done outside of the formal classroom as well. Lyn Mikel Brown and Sandy Grande's exploration of undergraduates' understandings of race, sexuality, and gender is further testimony to the power of out of classroom learning and the importance of place. In two of these studies, data is presented that demonstrates that although adults initiated the critical questions that clearly engaged these girls and women, it was the girls/young women themselves who continued to discuss, reflect, and ask new and difficult questions. It is important to note that these discussions took place during lunch and sometimes in the walking home after a group meeting. These are the in-between places of schooling, the informal places, often without adult supervision, in which important pedagogy took place and important identity work as well.

We return to the concept of liminality to help us rethink the purpose of schooling and the construction of a gendered identity. In reflecting on the liminal time period, Turner regretted that he failed to note the playfulness and the possibilities inherent during this time. The liminal time is one in which individuals lose their status distinctions and become a unified group. How might teachers and administrators construct a curriculum and a space that would allow for and even encourage the type of liminal experiences that Turner described? How could a school create a space in which girls could drop peer group hierarchies and normative ways of being female and encourage girls to try on different versions of femininity? What would a curriculum look like in which girls could critique and play with what it means to be a girl/woman in this nation at this time and understand the historical contexts in which femininity is constructed? How might students interrogate how race, social class, heterosexuality, dominant beauty norms, and other means of privileging and disparaging girls/women operate in society at large and, more important, in their own lives?

Ideal femininity is always being rewritten, and adolescent girls and young women are part of that continual revisioning:

> Girl culture is the key to understanding what it means to be a young woman today or in the past. In every historical epoch, girls have formed a unique set of activities and concerns generated by their developmental needs as well as the adult society in which they live. What girls do, how they think, what they write, whisper and dream, all reveal a great deal about them and about us. (Brumberg, 2002, p. 5)

The authors in this book have observed and listened carefully to today's "girl culture." But they have done so with the culture and structure of schools ever-present. Lesbian adolescents dream about leaving town and going to college. A young woman with Down syndrome dreams about being married and having a family. Adolescent girls talk about being nice and being a fighter and being a leader. High school young women consider how they negotiate menstruating at schools. Adult African American women reflect on their adolescent experiences in predominantly White schools. Adult Southern women reflect on what being labeled a slut meant and how that label came about. All of these understandings are part of girl culture, but in this case, girl culture at school. But as Brumberg points out, what girls do and think about tells us much about them as well as much about us, the adults in their lives. Thus, we think back to Vicky's comment, "You know, it's about like more who we are, not stuff we have to learn" to reflect on a pedagogy that takes girls and place seriously.

We ask teachers and teacher educators to create curriculum that honors the concrete places as well discursive spaces that are important to girls and young women. We imagine the curriculum of schools to be full of the kind of identity work that Vicky so desires, that of figuring out "who we are." This focus on adolescent female identity work does not mean that standard curriculum is ignored; it means that the standard curriculum works for and through this adolescent need for understanding identity.

We imagine a health or biology curriculum that delineates female biology and also explores the cultural myths and gendered nature of how menstruation is constructed in the society at large as well as among adolescents. Having girls analyze menstrual-product advertising and how this "natural" biological process is understood in this society as well as in others would provide girls and young women with a different understanding of being female. Furthermore, we ask school administrators to live the place of school by opening lockers, changing books, and using restroom facilities during the 4 minutes to move between two classrooms. Then we ask them to consider the time needed to change menstrual products.

We envision a geography curriculum in which kids map out the important places in school and describe what happens there, not from the adult perspective but from the kid perspective, so that alcoves, bathrooms, and corridors are opened up to all of the social interaction and identity work. Peer group interactions and sexual harassment and fighting and exchanging notes are all activities that hallways offer to adolescents who crave these places in their lives. We imagine a geographical study of place, both natural and built, that starts with the school, encircles the surrounding neighborhoods, and then opens up to the city and town in which the school is located. Girls and boys could describe which places are important to them and why and where they feel welcomed and not. Race, social class, and gender could become part of this discussion of nearby places.

We can see an English curriculum that explores how women and girls who are considered less than ideal, like those found in *The Scarlet Letter* and *The Bluest Eye*, negotiate their denigrated status, and compare their status with girls who are labeled sluts or tomboys or queer or dogs. We want classrooms full of references to the Preps, Cheerleaders, Sex Mob, and fighters, so that power and privilege is openly acknowledged, analyzed, and critiqued. We want race, ethnicity, and social class to always be considered when exploring how gender operates in the society at large as well as in the day-to-day lives of girls and women.

More important, we hope that we all rethink the purpose of schooling and reconnect it to the important discussion of identity. Girls and young women desire to be engaged in identity work, work that allows them the opportunity to articulate who they are and who they want to become. This type of work is done in schools, but on the margins of the classrooms, in the lunchrooms, and crammed into the 4 minutes between classes. It needs to be pulled out of the playgrounds, the backseats of buses, chats on the Internet, and the hallways of schools and made central to the curriculum so that girls may more thoughtfully and critically consider how they are becoming female.

REFERENCES

Brumberg, J. (2002). Introduction. In L. Greenfield, *Girl culture*. San Francisco: Chronicle Books.

Grunewald, D. (2003a). The best of both worlds: A critical pedagogy of place. *Educational Researcher, 32*(4), 3–12.

Grunewald, D. (2003b). Foundations of place: A multidisciplinary framework for place-conscious education. *American Educational Research Journal, 40*(3), 619–654.

Jones, A. (1993). Becoming a 'Girl': Post-structural suggestions for educational research. *Gender and Education, 5*(2), 157–164.

McDowell, D. (1999). *Gender, identity and place: Understanding feminist geographies*. Minneapolis: University of Minnesota Press.

Nespor, J. (1997). *Tangled up in school: Politics, space, bodies, and signs in the educational process*. Mahwah, NJ: Lawrence Erlbaum Associates.

Research for Action. (1996). *Girls in the middle: Working to succeed in school*. Washington, DC: American Association of University Women Educational Foundation.

Author Biographies

Natalie Adams is an associate professor in the College of Education at The University of Alabama. She is the mother of a middle school cheerleader and was sorely reprimanded in fifth grade for beating up a boy. She is the coauthor of *Cheerleader! An American Icon* (2003). Her current research interests focus on high school girls who play sports. Her recent work on adolescent girls was published in *Gender & Society* and *Sociology of Education*.

Rebecca M. Ballard will receive her PhD in instructional leadership and women's studies at The University of Alabama in 2004. Currently she is finishing her dissertation in which she re-presents life histories of six LGBTQ women and their challenges and experiences in higher education in the South. Rebecca is a self-proclaimed "failed Southern lady" as defined by Florence King (1990) and as part of her continuing failure as a Southern lady, she persists on a journey toward being an effective LGBTQ activist. On that path, she is the cofounder of Queer Women on Campus at The University.

Cerri Banks is a 3rd year doctoral student in the Cultural Foundations of Education Program at Syracuse University. She received her Bachelor's degree in Elementary and Special education at Syracuse where she graduated summa cum laude and was selected as a University Scholar. Her research interests center on issues of equity and access in education at all grade levels and the study of popular culture.

Over the last 20 years as a secondary teacher and researcher, **Pam Bettis** has spent a lot of time in middle and high school classrooms, corridors, lunchrooms, and outdoor hangouts, trying to understand how adolescents, particularly girls, make sense of the world and themselves. She is currently an assistant professor in the Cultural Studies and Social Thought in Education program in the College of Education at Washington State University. Fortunately or unfortunately, she was not selected as a cheerleader in high school although she has always been considered nice, and the meaning of niceness is the focus of her current research.

Lyn Mikel Brown is associate professor of education and women's, gender, and sexuality studies at Colby College. She received her EdD from Harvard Graduate School of Education. She is the author of numerous articles and three books on girls' development: *Meeting at the Crossroads: Women's Psychology and Girls' Development* (with Carol Gilligan, 1992, Harvard University Press); *Raising Their Voices: The Politics of Girls' Anger* (1998, Harvard University Press) and, most recently, *Girlfighting: Betrayal and Rejection Among Girls* (2003, New York University Press). She is cocreator of the nonprofit Hardy Girls Healthy Women (www.hardygirlshealthywomen.org).

Stacey Elsasser is an assistant professor of teacher education at The College of Saint Rose in Albany, New York. Believing the best research comes from personal experience, Stacey frequently explores issues of religion, the body, and the intelligence of cats. Despite her research, she still attends church regularly, but only one with a female pastor.

Nirmala Erevelles is an associate professor of social foundations of education at The University of Alabama. Her areas of expertise include the sociology of education, disability studies, feminist theory, postcolonial theory, multicultural education, cultural studies, and qualitative methodologies. Her work is published in several journals including *Educational Theory, Studies in Philosophy and Education, Disability and Society*, and *Journal of Curriculum Studies*. She is currently working on a book tentatively titled *Bodies That Do Not Matter: Disability and the Politics of Difference in Global Contexts*.

Laura Fingerson is an assistant professor of sociology and an affiliated faculty with the Center for Women's Studies and the Urban Studies Program at the University of Wisconsin–Milwaukee. Her research interests are in the sociology of children and adolescents, gender, social psychology, medical sociology, and research methods. She is currently completing a book manuscript, "Ragging: The Body in Adolescent Social Life." Her other projects explore adolescent sexuality, teens' interpretations of their bodies and appearance, and food and health in teens' social lives.

Sandy Grande is an assistant professor in the Education Department at Connecticut College. Her research is profoundly inter- and cross-disciplinary, and has included the integration of critical, feminist, and Marxist theories of education with the concerns of Native American and environmental education. She has written several articles including "Beyond the Ecologically Noble Savage: Deconstructing the White Man's Indian," *Journal of Environmental Ethics*; "Critical Theory and American Indian Identity and Intellectualism," *The International Journal of Qualitative Studies in Education*; and "American Indian Geographies of Identity and Power: At the Crossroads of Indigena and Mestizaje," *Harvard Educational Review*. Her book, *Red Pedagogy: Critical Theory and Native American Geographies of Identity and Power*, is forthcoming from Rowman and Littlefield (2004).

Laura Jewett is a doctoral student at Louisiana State University where she teaches multicultural education. Currently, she is working on an autoethnographic project examining liminality and the curriculum of cultures among Creole of Color people in Southwest Louisiana.

Debra Jordan is a professor and Graduate Coordinator in the leisure studies program at Oklahoma State University. She received her degrees from Slippery Rock State College in Pennsylvania, Western Illinois University, and Indiana University. Deb is an active writer having written more than 30 articles and book chapters, more than 25 technical reports, and three textbooks. Deb's area of expertise is leadership, and she is especially interested in gender issues as they relate to leadership. Deb loves to learn and travel and has had opportunities to do both in such places as Central America, Europe, and Asia. Reading, riding her motorcycle, and playing with her two cats are favorite leisure activities.

Rosary Lalik is an associate professor at Virginia Polytechnic Institute and State University where she serves as Director of Education Programs on the Northern Virginia campus. Literacy Studies is her focus for teaching and research. She is especially interested in the development of critical literacies. Rosary has published her research in numerous journals including *The Journal of Literacy Research, The Reading Teacher, Elementary School Journal*, and *The Journal of Curriculum Studies*. For several years now she has collaborated with Kimberly Oliver on a line of study examining adolescent girls' use of critical reflection as a means for increasing their life chances and general well-being.

Delores D. Liston is an associate professor of curriculum and foundations at Georgia Southern University. Her research and teaching interests focus on the application of philosophical, ethical, and feminist understandings to education. She has served as the President of the Philosophical Studies in Education Special Interest Group of AERA, and President of the South East Philosophy of Education Society. Her publications include articles in *Holis-*

tic Education Review, Journal on Excellence in College Teaching, and Curriculum Inquiry, and two books, *Joy as a Metaphor of Convergence: A Phenomenological and Aesthetic Investigation of Social and Educational Change* (2001) and *Learning to Teach: Critical Approaches to the Field Experience* (1998).

Don E. Merten is a cultural anthropologist teaching at Ball State University. His research has a dual focus. On the one hand, he seeks to understand the lives and experiences of young people. On the other hand, he also seeks to understand the complex cultural processes that enculturate young people into American society. These two foci intersect when examining how youth learn those aspects of American culture that are largely tacit, that is, are seldom openly taught or celebrated, for example, when exploring how girls learn to use meanness to express their power and protect their popularity.

Diane Montgomery is professor of educational psychology at Oklahoma State University where she directs the gifted education programs. She serves on the board of directors for The Association for Gifted, a division of the Council for Exceptional Children, and several editorial boards. Her research interests include creativity, transpersonal development, Native American Indian studies, and wisdom.

Regina E. Moore-Rahimi is a middle school teacher in Savannah-Chatham Public School system in Savannah, Georgia. She received her EdD in Curriculum Studies from Georgia Southern University. Her research interests are in feminist theory and social issues impacting girls' education. She has presented at the 2002 Conference of the Southeastern Philosophical Society and AERA.

Kagendo Mutua is an assistant professor of special education at The University of Alabama. Her research revolves around cross-cultural studies of transition and secondary programming for adolescents with severe/multiple disabilities and their families in Kenya and the United States. Her work is published in several journals, including *Journal of Special Education, International Journal of Disability, Development and Education,* and *Educational Studies.* She has also coedited a volume with Beth Blue Swadener, *Decolonizing Research in Cross-Cultural Contexts: Critical Personal Narratives,* and is a coeditor, with Cynthia Sunal, of a book series: Research in Africa, the Caribbean, and the Middle East.

Kimberly Oliver is an assistant professor at New Mexico State University in the Department of Physical Education, Recreation, and Dance. She teaches courses in foundations and elementary and secondary physical education methods; she also supervises student teachers. Her research focuses on developing curriculum to assist adolescent girls in critically examining forms and processes of bodily enculturation that threaten their health and well-being. She has coauthored a book with Peter Lang Publishing titled *Bodily Knowledge: Learning About Equity and Justice With Adolescent Girls* (Oliver & Lalik, 2000) and has several research articles in journals such as *Teachers College Record*, *The Journal of Curriculum Studies*, and *Journal of Teaching in Physical Education*.

John E. Petrovic is an assistant professor at The University of Alabama teaching in the social and cultural foundations of education. He is interested in the radicalization of liberal democratic thought to promote social justice, especially as concerns LGBT issues in education and language minority education. He teaches courses in philosophy of education, bilingual education and language politics, and multicultural education.

Sandra Spickard Prettyman is an assistant professor at the University of Akron in the Department of Educational Foundations and Leadership. Her research focuses on how schools act as sites for the construction of gendered identities, and the relationship of race, class, gender, and sexuality in the construction of adolescent identities. She is also interested in understanding and interpreting alternative forms of pedagogy, in order to better comprehend and improve the teaching and learning process. She thanks her own teenage children (and her partner) for giving her constant support and encouragement, as well as insight into the adolescent experience.

Dawn M. Shinew is an associate professor of social studies education at Washington State University and a principal investigator on the Collaboration for Teacher Education Accountable to Children With High Needs (CO-TEACH) project, a grant funded through the U.S. Department of Education's Teacher Quality Enhancement program. Her research interests focus on the role of community and education on issues of equity, gender, and power.

Deborah Thomas Jones is a research associate at Washington State University pursuing an interdisciplinary PhD in counseling psychology, sociology, and women's studies. Jones' research interests include intersections of race, class, culture, and sexual orientation.

Subject Index